Human Resource Management in International Firms_____

Human Resource Management in International Firms

Change, Globalization, Innovation

Edited by

Paul Evans
Professor of Organizational Behavior at INSEAD

Yves Doz
Professor of Business Policy at INSEAD

André Laurent
Professor of Organizational Behavior at INSEAD

M
MACMILLAN

1989

First published 1989
Reprinted 1990

Published by
MACMILLAN ACADEMIC AND PROFESSIONAL LTD
Houndmills, Basingstoke, Hampshire RG21 2XS
and London
Companies and representatives
throughout the world

Printed in Great Britain by
Billing and Sons Ltd
Worcester

British Library Cataloguing in Publication Data
Human resource management in international firms.
1. Multinational companies.   2. Personnel management
I. Evans, Paul   II. Doz, Yves L.   III. Laurent, André
658.3
ISBN 0–333–51501–3

Contents

Notes on the Contributors vii

Introduction xi

PART I FRAMING THE CHALLENGES 1

 1 The Economics of Organization
  William G. Ouchi 7

 2 Future Perfect
  Stanley M. Davis 18

PART II MAJOR ORGANIZATIONAL CHANGE 29

 3 Lessons From Practice in Managing Organizational Change
  Alison Farquhar, Paul Evans and Kiran Tawadey 33

 4 Organizational Culture: What it is and How to Change it
  Edgar H. Schein 56

 5 A Cultural View of Organizational Change
  André Laurent 83

PART III MANAGING HUMAN RESOURCES IN THE
    GLOBAL FIRM 95

 6 The Implications of Globalism: New Management Realities
  at Philips
  George van Houten 101

7   Managing Human Resources in the International Firm:
    Lessons from Practice
    Paul Evans, Elizabeth Lank and Alison Farquhar   113

8   The Two Logics Behind Human Resource Management
    Paul Evans and Peter Lorange   144

PART IV   INNOVATION THROUGH HUMAN
           RESOURCES   163

9   Fostering Innovation Through Human Resources: Lessons
    From Practice
    Paul Evans, Alison Farquhar and Oliver Landreth   169

10 Managing Engineers and Scientists: Some New Perspectives
    Thomas J. Allen and Ralph Katz   191

11 Managing Technological Innovation in Large Complex
    Firms: The Contribution of Human Resource Management
    Yves Doz   200

PART V   CONCLUSIONS   217

12 The Dualistic Organization
    Paul Evans and Yves Doz   219

Select Bibliography   243

Index   251

Notes on the Contributors

Thomas J. Allen has been a faculty member with the Management of Technology Group at MIT's Sloan School of Management since 1966. Prior to that, he worked with the Boeing Company in Seattle, Washington. Professor Allen's principal research interests have focused on management of technical professionals.

Stanley M. Davis, author and business advisor, is President of Stanley M. Davis Associates of Boston. He is a principal of the MAC Group, and has been a research faculty and professor at Boston University. His previous appointments were with the Universities of Harvard and Columbia.

Yves Doz is Professor of Business Policy at INSEAD and the Timken Europe Foundation Fellow. He is a graduate of the HEC in Paris and holds a DBA from Harvard University. His research focused on strategy and management of multinational corporations and high-technology industries. Currently his work concentrates on the problems of innovations in the large complex firm, and on collaboration between companies.

Paul Evans is Professor of Organizational Behavior at INSEAD. He has a law degree from Cambridge University, and a PhD in organizational psychology from MIT. His research focused earlier on adult and career development, then on human resource management, and more recently on the organization of complex multinational organizations.

Alison Farquhar is a strategy consultant with Alliance Consulting Group in Cambridge, Massachusetts. She received her MBA from INSEAD in 1985 following two years in international banking. She then spent three years as a Research Associate at INSEAD specializing in mergers and acquisitions.

George van Houten joined Philips in 1956 after completing his studies at Groningen University. After various positions in the research laboratories, Dr van Houten was successively appointed as director of the Center for

Manufacturing Technology, the Center's Manufacturing Director, and Corporate Director for Product and Production Innovation. In 1984 he was appointed as a member of the Board of Management of Philips.

Ralph Katz is Professor of Management in both the College of Business Administration, Northeastern University, and the Management of Technology Department at the Sloan School of Management, MIT. Dr Katz has carried out extensive management research on technology-based innovation with a particular interest in the management of technical professionals and project teams.

Oliver Landreth received his MBA at INSEAD in 1986 after having worked in advertising in New York. After INSEAD he worked in Italy and is presently working for a management consulting company in Paris.

Elizabeth Lank is a manager for human resource development with ICL. She is a recent graduate of the INSEAD MBA program, with a BA from Mount Holyoke College in the USA. A Canadian/American, she spent the first part of her career in Geneva with an American computer firm.

André Laurent is Professor of Organizational Behavior at INSEAD. André Laurent holds a doctorate in psychology from the University of Paris. His previous appointment was with the Institute for Social Research at the University of Michigan. The focus of his current work is on the cultural dimensions of organizational behavior.

Peter Lorange is Wurster Professor of Multinational Management at the Wharton School, University of Pennsylvania. He received his undergraduate education from the Norwegian School of Economics, an MA in Operations Management from Yale, and a DBA from Harvard University. He has written extensively on the subjects of corporate planning, strategic management, strategic alliances and control.

William G. Ouchi is Professor of Management, Anderson Graduate School of Management, UCLA. He is a graduate of Williams College, and he has an MBA from Stanford University and a PhD from the University of Chicago.

Edgar H. Schein is the Sloan Fellows Professor of Management at the MIT School of Management, where he has taught since 1956. He was trained as a social psychologist, and has published many books and articles on organization development, career dynamics, process consultation, organizational culture and leadership. He is a frequent consultant on these topics to multinational corporations.

Kiran Tawadey works with the Ashridge Strategic Management Centre in London. She completed her MPhD in economics and went on to credit analysis with ABN Bank Dubai. Her present project is on the role of corporate mission.

Introduction

This book was conceived in 1981, based on the belief that human resource management would become an important focus of top management attention, particularly in multinational enterprises – more than just the functional interest of personnel management. One could foresee that the corporate challenges would shift from the "whats" of international strategy and structure to the "hows" of implementation, which means people and organization (Evans, 1984).

The business scene was changing. The term "globalization" had just been coined. Innovation and responsiveness were new criteria for effectiveness. We were becoming aware of the need to transform the very cultures of our firms.

The concept of human resource management captured some of the challenges we sensed ahead. At INSEAD, the international school of management, we launched an interdisciplinary *International Human Resource Management Program*, the objective of which was to develop our competencies to face these challenges. We could not achieve this by closeting ourselves in academic ivory towers, and so a series of evolving partnerships with business leaders, multinational corporations, and scholars from other universities were initiated. The results of these partnerships are reported in this book.

A READER'S GUIDE TO THE BOOK

The aim of this book is to assimilate the experience and views of senior executives from leading edge multinational firms, and of management scholars from both sides of the Atlantic, concerning human resource management in international firms. We have tried to blend the lessons-of-practice with what scholars see as the state-of-the-art.

The twelve chapters are divided into five parts. Part I (Chapters 1 and 2) introduces the challenges of human resource management, from the perspectives of the past, the present, and the future. Its introduction also outlines the rationale behind the three themes of the book: change, globalization, and innovation.

Parts II to IV (Chapters 3–11) take up these themes successively. These three sections are structured in a similar way. Each begins with one or two chapters distilling the lessons from the experience of leading multinational firms in Europe, the United States, and Japan. Then, two scholars from the United States and Europe present what they see as the state-of-the-art and the future challenges.

An overriding message emerges from these viewpoints: the complexity of international operations in our competitive and turbulent environment is challenging traditional ways of thinking about management and organization. The final chapter in Part V (Chapter 12) takes up this issue. Here a new way of thinking about management and organization is outlined. This centres on balancing the opposite forces that international enterprises appear to experience – the forces of centralization and decentralization, of individuality and teamwork, of change and stability, of strategic develop-ment and operational performance, of diversity and control, of innovation and commercialization . . . So many such dualities emerge in this book that one starts asking whether this reflects something more fundamental, more paradigmatic, about the ways of managing people and organization that are needed in these complex transnational enterprises. As a product of our seven-year study of human resource and organizational management, this chapter sets theoretical and practical directions for the future.

Few readers of such a book will sit down and digest it page by page. Most will be interested in dipping into a chapter here and a section there. Each part (except for the concluding chapter) has an introduction – a commentary on the theme that is discussed in its chapters, as well as an overview. In this way, we hope that the reader can dip into this book by reviewing the four introductions, and then going on to read particular chapters of interest.

THE PARTNERSHIPS BEHIND THIS BOOK: SOME ACKNOWLEDGEMENTS

As mentioned earlier, this book reflects an INSEAD project, its Inter-national Human Resource Management (HRM) Program, and the partner-ships that this led to. Some of these partnerships are directly apparent in its contributors and text, others are hidden behind the proverbial scenes.

To get such a project off the ground takes funding. This was initially provided by the endowment from a professorial chair at INSEAD, the *Raoul de Vitry d'Avaucourt Chair in Human Resource Management*. The generous sponsors of this chair were the friends and family of the late Raoul de Vitry (chairman of the French Pechiney group), the IBM Corporation, and Kodak–Pathé.

The initial steering group to formulate the direction of our project needed expertise beyond that of our faculty. Among those who contributed that expertise were Warren Bennis (Professor of Management at the University of Southern California), Roger Blanpain (Professor of Industrial Relations at the University of Louvain in Belgium), Len Peach (then director of personnel for IBM in the United Kingdom), and Bill Paul (at the time on sabbatical at INSEAD from Exxon).

Out of that steering group was born the idea of a pan-European executive *Forum*, which was to become the cornerstone partnership in the Program. There was at the time no European vehicle for in-depth exchange on human resource management issues. Bill Paul (who is today responsible for organization development at the Exxon Corporation) developed the concept of this Forum, and meticulously implemented it. Together with Paul Evans, he co-directed INSEAD's HRM Program and became the first director of the Forum in 1982.

The members of this Forum were senior executives from international corporations, people with wide experience in the management of human resources. The visions and insights of its members are reflected throughout this book, particularly in the chapters on the lessons-of-practice. The members of the Forum were:

Sheldon Davis (Digital Equipment Europe)
Olof Ekman (SAS)
Selwyn Gurney (Honeywell Europe)
Kees Krombeen (Philips)
Berth Jönsson (Volvo)
Claude La Peyre (Exxon Chemicals Europe)
Daniele Mosca (Olivetti)
Len Peach (IBM, United Kingdom later UK National Health Service)
René Robin (Kodak–Pathé)
Siegurd Schmidt (Deutsche Bank)
Rolf Skillner (Ericsson)
Paul Smith (Marks & Spencer)
Peter Smith (Marks & Spencer)
Edgar Vincent (ICI)
Joseph Wells (Ciba–Geigy)

An academic symposium was organized at INSEAD in August 1985, in collaboration with Professor Noel Tichy from the University of Michigan and the journal *Human Resource Management*. Its objective was to frame the challenges of international HRM by means of exchange between forty leading scholars and executives from Europe, the United States, and Japan. Its results were published in a special issue of the sponsoring journal.

The Forum members felt that their exchanges merited a wider audience, and four of them became the sponsors of an INSEAD symposium that took place in February 1986. These sponsors were Shel Davis (organizational development advisor at Digital Equipment Europe); Kees Krombeen (director of the corporate staff bureau at Philips); Len Peach (today on secondment from IBM as Chairman of the British National Health Service); and Edgar Vincent (responsible for international personnel at ICI). Shel, Kees, Len, and Edgar became firm supporters of INSEAD's ambitions, investing substantial time and energy even at the difficult phases that are inevitable in any such venture.

This successful 1986 symposium was entitled "The Leading Edge of International Human Resource Management". It was attended by nearly 200 executives, with 25 keynote and panel speakers from prominent corporations and universities. The basic structure of this book parallels that of this conference.

There were three other key players from industry in these INSEAD ventures. The first was Harold Rush, who in 1983 succeeded Bill Paul as director of the Forum and co-chairman of the Human Resource Management Program. The Exxon Corporation permitted this one-year secondment, and Hal is today director of international human resources for Avon Cosmetics.

Hal Rush also tackled a vital task, namely systematically documenting European innovation in the field of human resource management. We knew a fair amount about American and even Japanese practice, yet little about leading edge experimentation in the different countries of Europe. This led to a series of research and teaching cases, reported in this book, based on the experiences of the following companies (the sponsoring executives are mentioned in brackets):

Courtaulds: the use of performance-based reward systems (Geoffrey Burch).

Deutsche Bank: management training and human resource development (Axel Osenberg and Siegurd Schmidt).

ICI: the management of major organizational change (Edgar Vincent).

Marks & Spencer: human resource management in the internationalization of the retailing industry (Paul Smith and Michael Abrahams).

McKinsey Europe: the management of human resources in a growing professional service firm (Brigadier Harry Langstaff).

National Westminster Bank: training and management development in the changing banking sector (Philip Norcross).

Philips: international management development (Kees Krombeen).

Volvo: improving productivity and the quality of working life at the plant (Berth Jönsson).

Further corporate studies were undertaken by Paul Evans, aided by two research associates (Avivah Wittenberg and Alison Farquhar):

Apple Computers Europe: human resource management in a high growth but turbulent business environment (Stefan Winsnes and Michel Perez).

BSN and Evian: human resource planning as a component of business planning, and preparation for the introduction of new manufacturing technology (Henri LeCallier and Pierre Marcou).

Lafarge Coppée: strategic human resource management in a diversified firm, and the development of a corporate charter to increase corporate cohesion (Daniel Destrument, Claude Carrière, and Yves de Clerck).

The second key player was Didier Berthoud, an IBM personnel manager with long experience at IBM France and IBM Europe. IBM permitted his secondment to INSEAD for a twenty-month period in 1984–86, succeeding Hal Rush as director of the Forum and co-chairman of the Program. Didier also directed and realized the 1986 executive symposium mentioned earlier, and his work is behind the scenes in many of its chapters. It was due to his contacts and energies that partnerships with other enterprises were cemented.

The third key individual was Tom Glynn Jones, who recently retired from his role as head of management development at British Petroleum, today working as a consultant on human resource issues with many organizations. Since the early 80s, Tom has in many official and unofficial capacities performed a bridge role between INSEAD's academic interests and those of European industry. As this book was being written, he was to become a key sparring partner in the debate on human resource management and on the future of our own HRM Program.

Many members of INSEAD's faculty have played prominent roles in this project over the years. Apart from the three editors of this book, central individuals have been members of our Organizational Behavior department: Michael Brimm, Manfred Kets de Vries, Susan Schneider, and Linda Brimm. Their experiences and research have influenced many of the chapters of this book, as have those of Jacques Rojot (Industrial Relations), Kasra Ferdows and Arnoud de Meyer (Operations Management), Philippe Haspeslagh and Dominique Heau (Business Policy). Among the many scholars outside INSEAD who have enriched our project have been Noel Tichy (Professor of Organizational Behavior at the University of Michigan), Edgar Schein (Professor of Organization Studies at MIT's Sloan School of Management), Brooke Derr (Professor of Organizational Behavior at the University of Utah), Vlado Pucik (Assistant Professor of International Management at the University of Michigan), and Mitsuyo Hanada (Professor of Management at the Sanno Institute in Japan).

A venture such as the Program underlying this book requires institutional backing. That support and funding came from our two Deans – Heinz Thanheiser and Claude Rameau, and later also from a new Dean, Philippe Naert. Behind this acknowledgement lies a considerable investment of their time and energy in protracted discussions and difficult decisions, but also a shared belief in the vital importance of human resource management for the future of multinational enterprise. Salvatore Teresi and Claude Michaud (respectively director and deputy-director of the European Centre for Continuing Education (CEDEP) on the INSEAD campus), also provided their support for specific projects.

Sally Simmons skillfully helped us in the editing of many of the chapters. And finally, the partnerships behind this book are the daily relationships with many administrators, assistants, and secretaries at INSEAD, whose patient work has brought this project into fruition. Two persons should be singled out: Marianne Ugé and Henriette Robilliard. Since 1983, Marianne has been the secretary responsible for the Human Resource Management Program, and her outstanding skills in conference organization were also behind the success of the 1986 symposium. She has patiently and untiringly supervised most phases in the project and the development of this book, as has Henriette in her superordinate capacity as secretarial coordinator of INSEAD's Organizational Behavior Department.

Fontainebleau   PAUL EVANS

Part I

Framing the Challenges

Introduction to Part I

"Human resource management": twenty years ago, the term didn't exist. It began to gain currency among those who felt that people were just as important as other corporate resources, such as money and materials – probably even more so.

Unlike "marketing" and other post-war management concepts, human resource management isn't part of the popular vocabulary. Ask the layman what it means, and you'll get a bemused expression. Most managers know the term and its acronym HRM, and they'll tell you that it's a fancy label for the personnel department. Perhaps they'll add that it is something that the wave of management bestsellers (Ouchi's *Theory Z*, 1981; Peters and Waterman's *In Search of Excellence*, 1982; Blanchard and Johnson's *The One Minute Manager*, 1982) brought into vogue.

But then wander through the corridors of power in the multinational enterprises that are beginning to dominate the world economic scene. Stop off to talk with the board members, the chief executive, the general managers, as well as with those in the personnel department. And the tune changes. "Human resource management, it's one of our major challenges", is what you will probably hear. The discussion may start with the difficulties of steering the culture of the firm away from bureaucracy and towards profitability. You hear stories of strategic plans that failed because of the lack of the right people. Their quality program, vital to compete with foreign firms invading the home market, is foundering because employees aren't responding. They tell you about their concern for a growing subsidiary in some far-flung region of the world, where the talented general manager is undercutting his success because he doesn't have a nose for people. And about social resistances to information technology and computer-aided manufacturing. The conversation moves on to new product development, where those research guys aren't talking to the marketing people. Moreover, the time it takes to develop a new product from research to its launch in major worldwide markets has to be shortened from twenty years to five years. The obstacles here are that people in different functions and subsidiaries don't know each other, and the firm is gripped by the "not-invented-here" syndrome. They point out that the executive committee spends a quarter of its time discussing key assignments and management development: getting the right people into the right places at the right time. But here they are plagued by difficulties – resistance to mobility, increasing recruitment problems now that the "baby boom" supply of people is drying up, the tendency of local managers to hide their best talent, the problems of reentry into the mother country after expatriation, difficulties in retaining capable people . . . Then they move on to talk about the problems they are experiencing in tightening control over hitherto decentralized subsidiaries. This leads in turn to the headaches of integrating the different culture of a major acquisition, and then to their problems in persuading key people to take positions in a joint venture that has recently been negotiated.

This book is about such problems. These challenges are so vital for the prosperity and even survival of the international firm that they are increasingly occupying the agendas of top executives. While personnel managers have a critical role to play in the management of human resources, the prime responsibility for this task lies with general management. This is an assumption that runs throughout all the chapters of this book. It is worth pointing out that none of its nine academic contributors is a personnel specialist. They are professors of management, international business, corporate strategy, business policy, organizational behavior, and technology management. All, from their different perspectives, have come to the conclusion that human resource management is a critical element of corporate management.

We have structured issues such as the above into three themes – Change, Globalization, and Innovation.

1. The first, that of *major organizational change*, is addressed in Part II. We are currently witnessing a process of cultural transformation in international enterprises. The cultures of these firms were created in the relatively stable, nationally-focused era of post-war growth and prosperity. The 70s changed all that. Competition, internationalization of markets, massive investments requiring a quick payoff through global marketing, the need for careful but rapid decision-making: these and other forces mean that most firms are having to develop more performance-oriented, more international, more responsive cultures. The challenges here are not the "whats" of what-to-do, which are typically well-known. They are the "hows" of managing a change in the deeper culture of the firm.

2. The second theme is taken up in Part III, namely *managing human*

resources in the global firm. Internationalization has brought new problems of managing a worldwide workforce, people with different conceptions of the rights and wrongs of organization. And it has led to new theoretical and practical challenges, like the task of building an organization that is both integrated and locally responsive, escaping from the centralization–decentralization pendulum that has oscillated with increasing frequency in recent decades. The task of developing managers who can provide leadership in the face of ever increasing complexity has itself become a major challenge. Indeed, many scholars go as far as to suggest that the complexity of international organization and of people management is such that the basis for the competitive advantage of the multinational firm has shifted from its material and financial resources to the capabilities of the organization and its people.

3. *Innovation through human resources* is the third theme and the focus of Part IV. The widespread concern for innovation reflects the increasing pace of change, and the term covers more complex issues than that of developing entrepreneurial spirit in big firms. These issues range from introducing computerized methods of production to improving the product development process. Innovation means establishing closer links between centralized research and the marketing people spread throughout the world. It means updating the know-how of scientists and technicians, diffusing the insights in one part of the firm rapidly to others. Indeed, innovation implies developing a more responsive, interdependent, and flexible organizational culture. Contrary to the cliché that only small firms are innovative, large firms with multiple competencies and operations throughout the world have a massive potential competitive edge – that is, if they can realize that potential.

FRAMING THE CHALLENGES OF HUMAN RESOURCE MANAGEMENT

Before we turn to these topics, we want to provide a frame for them by discussing the changing business environment from a human resource perspective. This is the purpose of Part I of this book. The two chapters here have complementary perspectives. Bill Ouchi begins with a survey of the past, while Stan Davis takes us from the present into the future.

William Ouchi is Professor of Management at the University of California at Los Angeles, and author of the best-selling book *Theory Z: How American Management Can Meet the Japanese Challenge* (1981). In Chapter 1, he reviews the evolution of thought about management, taking us back to Adam Smith and the early days of the industrial revolution. He shows how management attention over the centuries has alternated between a focus on the "hard", the rational and quantitative aspect of organization, and the "soft", its human and cultural features. The recent concern for corporate culture is one of those pendulum swings back to the "soft", and attention is already moving on to the "hard". Ouchi advocates bringing together the separate logics of "hard" micro-economics and "soft" organization theory in what he calls "organizational economics", where human resource management is a key element. He illustrates this with an analysis of firms who achieve super-normal rates of return, arguing that these firms are capable of the unnatural act of combining individualism with the capacity for teamwork. This is supported by the evidence of another recent paradox, partnerships between competitors.

The theme of managing tension between opposites is a fitting opening to this book. In subsequent chapters by quite independent contributors, the reader will find these oppositions to be a recurrent concern – that which the concluding chapter in Part V addresses.

Stanley Davis takes us into the future in Chapter 2. Formerly a professor of international management at Columbia, Harvard Business School, and Boston University, he is today a business advisor to multinational corporations. His argument is that we are already far into the post-industrial service economy, although our models and ways of thinking about management and organization are still based on the industrial economy. Drawing upon analogies taken from science and physics, he sets out to outline the new model of management for the new economy, one where people are no longer the constraints of the industrial society but the cornerstone resources of the service economy.

Our typical way of thinking about time in the shape of strategic and business planning is out of tune with the new reality. The world is now moving in real-time, and just-in-time production processes are an example of the new emerging model. Our assumptions about mass are still Newtonian rather than Einsteinian as we focus on managing tangible products rather than intangible information. We limit ourselves by assumptions about physical and geographic space in a world where consumer needs are already tuned to any-place globalization. Davis views the challenge of human resource management as that of bridging the gap between the emerging nature of the economy and the outdated way we manage our enterprises.

Chapter 1

The Economics of Organization

William G. Ouchi

My purpose is to reflect on some of the lessons of the past in the study of human resource management, particularly as it relates to the themes of change and innovation, before turning to present and future concerns in this field. At first, I considered making observations only about the last ten years but find that my own involvement over the period makes objectivity impossible. So I have gone back a little further and would like to offer a very personal historical overview of the various principal developments in the study of human resources that have brought us to our present point. I stress "personal", since another academic would give a quite different, equally legitimate and, to his mind, far superior account.

The central theme which arises from this review is that we are well advised to be modest about the zeal with which we embrace currently popular views of management. The history of scholarship on management is a history of competing views, one a "hard" analytical view which suggests that the problems of management can ultimately be resolved through thoughtful analysis and consistent implementation; the other a "soft" view that management is about people, that people can never be regularized or dominated, and that management is thus inevitably more art than science. The lesson of history, however, is that whichever of these views we embrace at the moment, we are likely next to abandon in favor of the opposite view.

THE ORIGINS OF TODAY'S HUMAN RESOURCE MANAGEMENT

The first and most important date is 1776 with the publication of Adam Smith's *Wealth of Nations*. The Industrial Revolution was well along and new mass manufacturers in Europe had begun to supplant the small craft shops of four, five or six workers. Because of the efficiency of the new large-scale manufacturers, many small companies were threatened with bankruptcy. Many small business men in the towns grouped together in the hope of gaining governmental protection against the new larger, more efficient producers. Adam Smith saw this happening and recognized that as each industry sought protection, it was unwittingly inviting the heavy hand of government into the affairs of the private economy. Such a trend would be difficult ever to reverse.

Smith, in 1776, was aware that no one in government could be wise enough to tell each industry just how to act. The human mind is of limited capacity. In 1986, more than two centuries later, we realize that no individual in any organization can have the breadth of intellect to show each and every subordinate exactly what to do. No foreman in a factory, no manager in a company is wise enough to guide each worker individually. If workers are trained properly and granted some autonomy, they will reach the best possible decisions about how best to do their jobs.

This fundamental principle, established in the eighteenth century, continues to lie at the heart of every contemporary theory of organization. There is a consistent need, in the study of organizations, to recognize the superiority of decentralized decision-making, which is a necessary consequence of the limited mental capacity of each and every one of us.

Most important, *Wealth of Nations* espoused the view that an economy can operate in a fully rational manner, that the price mechanism will lead to socially optimal results, and it has produced a still commonly held faith in the power of markets to bring rationality out of the complex mosaic of human endeavor.

The next significant historical landmark comes in the late nineteenth century with the work of the French philosopher, Emile Durkheim, who is regarded in the United States as the father of modern sociology. He observed that the firm was not merely a rational, hard economic entity, but that it also possessed an organic, ambiguous aspect which defied analytical comprehension. In modern terms this could be described as a company "culture". Durkheim applied this notion to both relationships within a firm and between firms, pointing out that it is the commonly held values and beliefs which bind together both the employees of one company and the various industries of an economy. It is, he suggested, an underlying faith in this long-term commitment to one another which regulates economic activity, rather than an explicit rational calculus as envisioned by Adam Smith.

At the turn of the century, Henry Ford introduced the assembly line into the United States. The resulting work processes involved, for the first time, a complete separation of thinking from doing. The jobs were so distasteful that the Ford Motor Company was required to pay far more than the going wage in order to persuade people to accept such dehumanizing conditions. The justification for such methods came in 1911 with the publication of *Scientific Management* by Frederick Taylor, who provided a rationale for the division of work tasks. In his view, some people in the world have large brains while others have broad shoulders. The former group, typically called industrial engineers, were best employed designing how work should be done, whereas the latter group was more fitted actually to doing it. Taylor thus justified the complete separation of thinking about work and doing work that had been adopted by Ford.

Taylorism is still with us today, in the form of the time and motion study. One of the most famous studies of time and motion was published in the 30s by Roethlisberger and Dickson in a book called *Management and the Worker*. The authors were conducting several Taylorist scientific management studies in an electrical plant. One of these involved a group of workers employed in the dull and repetitive job of soldering telephone switch boards. The specific purpose of the study was to establish the relationship between illumination on the workbench and worker productivity. Since the room was, indeed, poorly lit, they replaced the 50 watt bulbs in use with 100 watt bulbs. Productivity was measured and, sure enough, it had gone up. Productivity seemed to be associated with the degree of lighting, which made sense. To test this theory further, they decided to repeat the experiment with 150 watt bulbs. The same phenomenon was observed and reconfirmed, even when the strength was increased to 200 watts.

However, in line with scientific tradition, Roethlisberger and Dickson knew they should test the theory in reverse before claiming proof. Thus, the 200 watt bulbs were replaced with 150 watt bulbs and productivity was again measured. Illumination was down but productivity had again gone up! Suspecting what we call "noise" in the data, the two repeated the experiment with 100 watt bulbs. To their confusion, the result was a further increase in productivity, and so it went on until the work force was virtually operating in the dark – productivity at an all time high.

At this point, the authors did something totally innovative – for the first time in the history of management studies, they went and talked to the workers. When asked why they were producing at such a high rate under such difficult circumstances, the workers responded that since all these professors and research assistants had been wandering around with executives visiting the factory for the first time and asking questions about their work, their crushingly boring days had become more interesting. As a result their interest was up, their attention was up, and productivity was up.

Today we refer to this as the Hawthorne effect. In my opinion, it has been widely misinterpreted. In the majority of companies several years ago, if not still today, it was commonly believed that when a participative management approach, such as a quality circle, was introduced, it would produce a one-time Hawthorne effect. Productivity would increase due to attention or novelty only to degenerate again as this wore off. This raised the question in people's minds of how to go about constantly introducing innovations which were fun and kept employees at the same peak of excitement.

To my mind this is a fundamental misinterpretation of the study. The correct interpretation, I believe, stems from the point made by Adam Smith but missed by Taylor: there is no person, no matter how wise, who is wise enough to tell each worker just what to do. The involvement of workers in participative management will typically produce a permanent rise in the quality of work-related decisions, as well as a rise in workers' sentiments of involvement.

The work of the 20s did not reach a worldwide audience. In 1947, however, the first translations of Max Weber's work, *The Theory of Social and Economic Organization*, began to appear in English. Weber argued that what really mattered were not the subtleties, not the issues of the Hawthorne effect revealed by the Roethlisberger–Dickson research, but rather the structure of the firm, its girders and beams, the position of its rivets. Weber was a great fan of bureaucracy. The only alternative, in his opinion, was dilettantism. The bureaucratic form, as he defined it, comprised the following elements: an extensive set of job descriptions, each quite specific; a professional training program with which to equip people for each of those job categories; an impersonal and therefore impartial process of testing for qualification and for promotion. If these were in place, he argued, then the system was a bureaucracy and there was no more efficient way to organize.

By the 50s, there was a return to a more organic view and what we now know as the human relations school grew up. Maslow's hierarchy of needs, McGregor's theories X and Y, and Likert's Systems One through Four all contributed to a flowering of the participative approach. For the most part, this did not stem from a belief in the importance of decentralization of decision-making to the worker but more often from social concerns relating to the balance of power. The human relations scholars often argued, for example, that participative management is to be recommended because it is a more democratic, less autocratic mode of management, and thus preferable.

In the mid-60s an important event occurred: the general purpose digital computer became widely available. As a result, every graduate student in the social sciences learned how to use packaged multivariate statistical programs and was able to cram data into a computer without any idea as to how the machine functioned. This led to a fascination among academics with the power of multivariate statistical study as compared with the more traditional case study or observational study.

Unlike their development in Europe, the Social Sciences in the United States were more attached to the physical and natural sciences than to a tradition of philosophy. Behavioural scientists equated themselves with physicists, chemists, or engineers and yearned for a method or technique as precise as those associated with these disciplines. The computer provided just such a possibility. For the next twenty years or so, there was a heavy emphasis on statistics in management research, particularly as seen in the work of Peter Blau, The Aston Group from Birmingham in England, who with Pugh, Hickson, Hinings and others, became perhaps the most well-known group of scholars.

In the early 70s, a Dutchman by the name of Cornelius Lammers brought this infatuation to light. He visited every major graduate school of business in the United States, spoke to the faculties, and then wrote us all a letter which was published in a leading journal. The letter, entitled *Travel Impressions by a Dutch Cousin* (Lammers, 1974), revealed the following: Lammers had interviewed forty or fifty leading scholars in the field of organizational studies and asked them what they considered to be the most active field of research at the time. The answer was "multivariate statistical studies of organizational structure". He then inquired as to what they felt to be the least useful line of research. The answer was "multivariate statistical studies of organizational structure". When he asked what they considered would be the most active area of research in the future, back came the same answer: "multivariate statistical studies of organizational structure". As he so acutely underlines, we had become blinded by multivariate statistical analysis through the tool of the computer, to the extent that any research which could not be expressed in this medium was considered invalid. More recently, some of us have concluded that very little that is of importance or interest relating to organizational life can be studied in this manner.

From this realization has grown the next wave of thought, encapsulated in the concept of corporate culture. A tremendous outpouring of studies ensued sponsoring discussion of cultural issues: those by Ronald Dore, the European Group on Organizational Studies (EGOS), Rosabeth Kanter (*The Change Masters*, 1983) and Peters and Waterman (*In Search of Excellence*, 1982) are among the better known. As I see it, this represents a return to what has always been the mainstream of organizational studies – namely, that which is subtle, complex, ambiguous, and impossible to express in numbers.

The consequence of the twenty-year emphasis on computer-aided statistical studies mentioned above was that the research of management scholars was inaccessible to the uninitiated. No-one but a scholar would be likely to read, let alone understand, such esoteric data. There was an advance in learning over the period, but it was largely inaccessible to the manager. The new wave of thought which developed four or five years ago was significant in that it legitimated the idea that a scholar might write something in a language that a layman could understand. As a result, twenty years of scholarship became accessible, overnight, to the management world. I personally believe that this accounts for the outpouring of works under the label of organizational culture over the last few years.

Today, we can see the development of a very exciting new domain of study on the economics of organization, with its origins in the work of Herbert Simon, Oliver Williamson (*Markets and Hierarchies*, 1975), and the group at the International Institute of Management in West Berlin. Typically, in the past there has been a gap between the field covered by behavioural science research and that covered by economics. The former took topics such as motivation at the microscopic end of its inquiries and went to no higher macro-analytic level than the study of large firms. Economics, on the other hand, ranged from the comparison of economies at a macro level to the structure of industries. But until now, there has never been an overlap between the two. In the last few years a small overlap has at last been created, giving rise to tremendous vitality and a whole new range of work. Amongst other things, this work is bringing about a revolution in American anti-trust legislation and has formed the basis for the major anti-trust defences of the last few years. We shall see an important new ideology emerge in the future as a result.

ALTERNATING "HARD" AND "SOFT"

If we step back from this historical overview for a moment, it becomes clear that the different periods alluded to can be separated into two categories: the "hard" and the "soft". The first term represents the view that organizations can ultimately be wrestled to the ground, understood, analyzed, and rationalized. The second believes that these messy things called organizations can never be fully understood or rationalized; they contain too much ambiguity to be reduced to such terms.

As we move through the schools represented in turn by Adam Smith (hard), Emile Durkheim (soft), Frederick Taylor (hard), Roethlisberger and Dickson (soft), Weber (hard), the human relations school (soft), computer mania (hard), corporate culture (soft) and, lastly, the economics of organization (hard), we recognize a successive alternation between the two categories.

I, therefore, would like to issue a warning and suggest that *what we purvey at the moment is what we have at the moment.* I wish I could believe this to be a developmental sequence towards greater wisdom and know that we are not retracing ground, but I am not sure that that is so. However, I am reasonably sure that these intellectual tensions are inevitable. There is tension in every organization resulting from the need on the one hand for clarity and structure, and on the other hand for flexibility and change. Furthermore, the prevailing view of how best to approach human resource management will continue to fluctuate from time to time, though with what cycle length I cannot say for sure.

BEHIND THE SUPER-NORMAL RATE OF RETURN

The coming together of micro-economics and organization theory observed since 1985 has led me and some colleagues to certain conclusions which I shall now advance. The goal of every organization is to achieve super-normal returns. A "super-normal return" is defined as any rate of return higher than a firm's weighted average cost of capital (WACC). Any basic economics course, however, will inform you that such returns are not possible. In a competitive economy, if a company is seen to be earning super-normal returns, other competitors will enter the market until the original firm's advantage is whittled away and it is again reduced to a normal rate of return – namely, its weighted average cost of capital. Super-normal rates of return are thus impossible over a sustained period.

The trouble is, they happen! Who has not heard of companies which, despite a WACC of 12 or 13%, consistently show a return of 20%, 27%, 28%, and do so with product after product, year after year, and decade after decade. There has been no satisfactory theory to explain this phenomenon.

Faced with such facts, we must conclude that super-normal rates of return can be achieved only if a company is capable of performing "*unnatural acts*". Such a company must be capable of something which cannot readily be imitated. For example, if consistently high return on investment is the direct result of having a genius in software design on the staff, we know that other firms will either lure this human asset away or bid up his wage to the point at which he secures all the super-normal returns for himself, while the firm is reduced to a normal return. The same is true if your scarce resource is a team of people or a physical asset. These, too, can be duplicated or bid away.

If this line of thought is taken to its logical conclusion, we realize that there is only one form of unnatural act which cannot be taken away from a firm: its capacity for teamwork within the organization, from side to side and from top to bottom. This "asset" can be taken away only if the entire company is bought. In such a case, of course, the shareholders would recapture the full value merely in a different form.

We also know that the limits of the human mind render central planning in an economy or a company impossible, as discussed earlier. Individualism is, therefore, necessary within a firm, particularly when it comes to decision-making, initiative, responsibility and innovation. And yet, as Alfred Chandler stated in his history of industrialization, the only form of comparative advantage, fundamentally, is the capacity to manage the interfaces between stages in a multistage process of design, manufacture and delivery (Chandler, 1977). Put more simply: Teamwork. I would suggest that achieving a balance between these two poles, *individualism and teamwork*, is an unnatural act.

It is relatively easy to build an organization in which teamwork is emphasized to the detriment of individual spirit. It is easier still to build a firm in which the reward system fosters individual effort, with teamwork being kept to a minimum. But in the long run neither can succeed. It is, on the contrary, extremely difficult to create a setting in which both a high level of individualism and a high level of teamwork can be simultaneously achieved. It is an unnatural act, but precisely that unnatural act which characterizes all great companies, that is those which consistently earn super-normal returns.

ORGANIZATIONAL FORM

This allows us to understand the new forms of organization that are emerging. These new economic and sociological perspectives have led to a recent consensus among those of us who specialize in the study of large firms. It is now agreed that only three pure forms of corporate structure are possible, with a nearly infinite array of permutations and combinations among them. They can be classified as U-form, H-form and M-form.

The "U" or *Unitary structure* is the best known, so-called because its specialized departments have no meaning by themselves (see Figure 1.1). The organization thus has no meaning except as a unit.

FIGURE 1–1
The U-form Organization

Two principal disadvantages arise from such a structure. First, since the departments are so specialized, whenever a new product launch is envisaged or an internal administrative system change is considered, the process is slowed down by the fact that everyone has to talk with everyone else. Second, whenever clashes arise between department heads, the only person who has complete information and a balanced point of view is the chief executive officer (CEO). If the U-form company reaches a certain size, the

CEO's information processing capabilities overload and the organization suffers. The last few years' research supports this theory and indicates that medium or large sized U-form companies are low profit performers.

If the U-form fails because it is overcentralized, the second type, the *H-form*, is in a sense too decentralized. The true H-form is a holding company which grows through acquisitions and has operating units in totally unrelated businesses. Consequently there are no transfers of intermediate products or services between them and each operating unit's financial results can be precisely measured. In such a company it is typical to find a corporate staff of no more than a dozen people despite a combined operating unit turnover of several billion dollars. This results from the corporate office's sole function of capital allocation. Normally, a global budget is announced each year and bids are solicited from operating units along with estimated rates of return on the investments envisaged. Corporate financial staff evaluate the applications and forecasts with a sceptical eye and allocate capital accordingly.

This organizational structure, like the U-form, has its weaknesses. The disparate nature of the businesses means that there is little capacity for teamwork. Consequently, there can be no common rules for capital allocation. Nor can the operating heads be expected to agree on a system, each one's requirements being so different. The entire task of capital allocation must, therefore, fall to the CEO, the very person least informed about each of the individual businesses. Again, the last few years' research reveals that large H-form companies are low profit performers.

In the long run, it is the "M" or *multidivisional form* of organization which achieves high performance. There is some dispute as to where and when this structure had its origin, but most people would agree that it was brought from Europe to the United States by the Dupont company and then applied in General Motors. Interestingly enough, General Motors transformed itself over the years back into the world's biggest U-form company. Last year, however, it embarked on a process of organizational change in an attempt to return to the M-form.

This third type of organizational structure is simultaneously centralized and decentralized – decentralized in the sense that each divisional general manager is required to act as though he is running his own business, centralized in the sense that the divisions are in related businesses and draw upon common corporate resources such as laboratories, marketing services and/or manufacturing facilities. This centralization gives rise to much joint decision-making, and hence inter-manager teamwork is an essential ingredient. To give an example, a component plant designed to serve three divisions cannot possibly serve each one exactly as each would prefer. It is critical, therefore, that the managers sit down together and talk the issues through until the best overall solution is reached. If they can do this, the M-form works well.

The M-form is thus one of those unnatural acts which, it was suggested, are the secret to achieving consistently super-normal returns. It succeeds when the two elements which have developed historically in organizational study – namely, the hard and the soft, the rational and the ambiguous – are blended together. Teamwork and autonomy: the two must be combined if the firm is to succeed.

PARTNERSHIP BETWEEN COMPETITORS

The implications of this precarious balancing act are far-reaching and have a particular impact on attitudes to competition. If we extend the findings to a logical extreme, we will find joint research and development activities between competing firms. This is already common practice in Japan where I have been studying the major joint research and development projects of the last twenty-five years.

The most striking example there involves the success of the VLSI (very large scale integration) technology research association which took place from 1976 through 1979. Originally, this three tiered structure was composed of five companies, each undertaking its own research in its own laboratories. From there, three companies (Hitachi, Fujitsu, Mitsubishi) formed into the CDL Group and the two others (NEC, Toshiba) into the NTIS Group, each undertaking to carry out some generic process research. The rationale behind the co-operative structure was that the group had to be sufficiently small for control purposes since each depended on the output, and sufficiently compatible to have common technology goals. Thereafter, the two groups came together and formed a joint laboratory of a hundred scientists with the capacity to fabricate and run new processes. The expense of these processes, if borne individually, would have created a considerable cost disadvantage. Of course, the problems of who will possess the intellectual property or patent rights in such a venture are complex. Equally, the issue of anti-trust law can produce complications. The Japanese overcame the difficulties at the time because their semi-conductor industry was in such a poor state.

In 1975, the Americans disparaged the competitive threat of the Japanese in semi-conductors. In 1976, the Japanese embarked on their co-operative project. Let the results speak for themselves. In 1975, the leading volume product in the worldwide semi-conductor industry was the 4K dynamic random access memory chip – the 4K D-RAM – where Japanese manufacturers held 15% of the world merchant market. The next generation product was the 16K D-RAM, in which Japan gained 40% of the world merchant market. The current volume leader is the 64K D-RAM. The Japanese have a 65% market share. The next volume leader will be the 256K D-RAM, a product whose world merchant market is already 85% Japanese held. And as for the future, it is predicted by some in Silicon Valley that the product leader to come, the one megabyte D-RAM will go 100% to Japanese merchant suppliers (although the so-called "captive" suppliers such as IBM will manufacture large quantities of one megabyte D-RAMs for their own internal use in their computer products).

I would suggest that substantial changes are underway in the rest of the world in our attitudes towards teamwork, individualism, and the organization of human effort. In the United States, for example, a new law, the National Cooperative Research Act, was passed in 1984 limiting the civil and criminal anti-trust exposure of joint research and development projects. Since that date some serious joint research and development efforts have come into being. By way of example:

- The Micro-electronics and Computer Technology Corporation (MCC) in Austin, Texas, is a group of twenty-one companies engaged in seven streams of joint research and development.
- The Software Productivity Consortium consists of the eleven major airframe manufacturers in the US who are co-operating to improve the productivity of their software (this constitutes the largest single expense item for aerospace manufacturers).
- The Tailored Clothing Technology Corporation, composed of nearly fifty companies in garment, textile and artificial fibre manufacturing plus two labor unions, is working on sewing robotics in an effort to retain at least some garment manufacture in the States.
- SRC, the Semi-conductor Research Corporation, is made up of the thirty-one major chip manufacturers in America including names such as Texas Instruments, Motorola, IBM, and AT&T, who, despite being direct competitors, know that they must find ways to pool their technology efforts.

These examples do not represent a "normal" state of human affairs. I therefore conclude that only by enforcing rules upon ourselves can we arrive at a state of effective competition. For, beyond the fact that individualism and teamwork must be balanced together, the lesson of history shows us that without teamwork, we cannot have individual competition.

It has always been relatively simple to build an organization which rewards individual achievement but which sacrifices teamwork. It is no more difficult to emphasize harmony at the expense of individual recognition. In the end, neither of these forms of organization can achieve returns of the superior kind. It has always been and will ever be difficult to maintain, within an economy or within a firm, the delicate balance which emphasizes at once both individualism and teamwork. To perform that balancing act through a skillful use of structure, process, rewards, and leadership is, in the end, the central function of the executive.

Chapter 2

Future Perfect

Stanley M. Davis

A New Perspective

- Scientists make discoveries about the universe.
- From these discoveries evolve new technologies.
- Utilizing the new technologies, we build new products, services and businesses.
- Lastly, we shape organizations to run those businesses.

None of these steps can precede the one that goes before and clearly, organizations are the last link in the chain. Newton, for example, made discoveries about the universe. These developed into industrial technologies from which we grew industrial economies, industrially-based corporations and, finally, industrial models of management and organization. Then Einstein and colleagues in his field made new discoveries about the universe. Resultant new technologies are now coming on stream, we are building new businesses, and we do not yet have new models of management and organization. To place ourselves currently, we are moving into new businesses in the new economy. Until they have developed, we are bound to use earlier models of management and organizational forms that, in fact, are no longer appropriate to the new products and services that have emerged.

The indictment is that we use industrial models of management and organization to run post-industrial economies. We would not use farm models to run a factory economy; we ought not to use factory models to run what is fundamentally an office-based economy. Yet we continue to do so.

This chapter, based on my recent book *Future Perfect* (1987), is to present a new approach to managing and organizing in the new economy.

FROM INDUSTRIAL TO SERVICE ECONOMY

If one takes the United States as an example, it was basically an industrial economy from about 1865 until 1945–50, that is to say an eighty-year period. Most people would agree that the corporation that created the most widely used model of management and organization in the industrial economy was General Motors. This model, though, was not created until 1921.

In other words, the United States was already three-quarters of the way through its industrial economy before its major model for management and organization was even created.

In addition, it took a decade to put into place within General Motors and several more decades to spread throughout American industry, by which time, of course, the industrial sector was no longer the dominant one. Thus we see that models of management and organization do not develop until the economy is quite mature. We are now several decades into a new economy, whatever label we choose to give it. The most commonly heard include: the post-industrial economy, the service, information, or office-based economy.

Those people working for industrial companies may say this line of thought is relevant only to the new service businesses and does not apply to them. I argue to the contrary, for even if they do work in the industrial sector of the economy, they are no longer in the industrial sector of an industrial economy. Rather, they are in the industrial sector of a post-industrial, service-based economy. And, just as the agricultural sector was transformed as we moved into an industrial economy, so too the industrial sector will be transformed as we move into this new economy.

Some real examples may serve to underline this mismatch. Only 6% of IBM's employees, some 20,000 people, are involved in industrial manufacturing. Yet IBM is still using the same basic models of management and organization that were developed decades before, in the twilight of the old economy. General Electric, an industrial manufacturing firm, is already 35% into services, Westinghouse is at 50%. How much further will we go, before some new models develop?

If we examine trends in how the overall economy has been divided between the agricultural, industrial, and service sectors in terms of employment and GNP, the growth in services and the decline in industry can be clearly seen (see Figure 2.1).

At present, the overall productivity added to the economy by these different sectors is more or less in balance. If these trends are projected to the year 2001, though, a different picture emerges. The agricultural sector

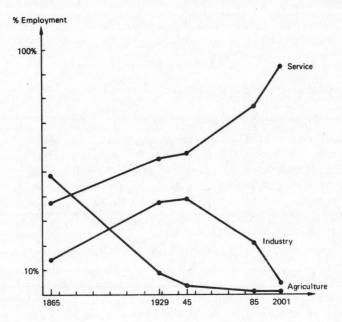

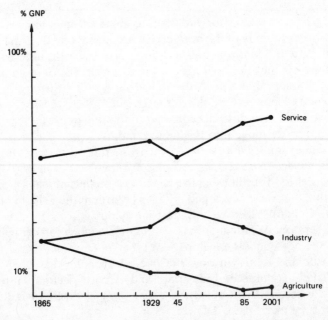

FIGURE 2–1
US Employment and GNP, by Selected Years, for Agricultural, Industrial
and Service Sectors.

remains relatively constant. However, the industrial sector will employ only 5% of the workforce while producing 24% of the gross national product (GNP), whereas the service sector will employ about 93% of workers for about 73% of the GNP. Although employment is shrinking in the industrial sector, it is all too clear that its contribution *per capita*, its value added to the economy, is far higher than in the service sector. There is, therefore, a considerable lag in the capitalization of the office economy, a fact which has serious implications for both employment and the GNP.

Towards a New Model of Management For a New Economy

I am suggesting that in order to understand the future of management and organization, we must look for it in its antecedents – in the new businesses that are developing based on the new technologies that spawned them, and back to the scientific knowledge that arose from understanding basic dimensions of the universe. Let me then presume, therefore, to address some fundamental dimensions of the universe and how they relate to management and organization. Decades ago, science led to new concepts of *time, mass* and *space*, and the implications have not yet been digested in our models of management and organization. One thesis in my book is that in the industrial economy, these were treated as constraints; in the new economy we must come to treat them as resources, and develop models to manage them as such. Let us begin with these basic dimensions.

Time

Although Newton made certain world-shaking discoveries about the universe, it was not until Einstein that we heard of time as being an intrinsic dimension of the universe. One would expect, true to our framework, that management methods would be slow to absorb the implications of this.

It could be said that strategic planning is the business function that makes time most intrinsic to its framework. Its basic orientation is towards the future and it employs the life cycle notion in which time is a fundamental dimension. Strategic planning is, indeed, a relatively modern concept, having been in formal management use for, at most, a few decades. That is to say, it is part of the new economy. The same holds for management information systems, another area in which time is an intrinsic concept and which has come into existence only in the last few decades.

In the agricultural economy, the relevant unit of time was the season; in the industrial economy it was perhaps the working shift, but we have not, as yet, defined the relevant unit of time in the new economy. I would like to take a step towards doing so.

The present approach most used in the business world regarding time works as follows: first, we look out, into the future; then, depending on what we see, we devise a business strategy. The chosen strategy is then implemented by the organization and the performance of the past is measured (see Figure 2.2). This seems to make sense.

Performance	Organization	Business strategy	Environment

Past	TIME	Future

FIGURE 2–2
The Typical Conception of Time in the Business World

Yet it is dangerous to judge the validity of an approach on its popularity and the length of time it has been in use. Remember, it was believed that the earth was flat and the centre of the universe for thousands of years. The validity of this much-used business model is equally questionable.

Its logic says that we have to know *what* we are doing (strategy) before we know *how* to do it (management and organization). If business strategy comes before organization, then that is the same as saying that organization comes after strategy. In other words, organization lags behind by definition, and the best it can do is almost – but never quite – to catch up. So we try to reduce the lag through management training and the like. When this is achieved, however, it is to little avail, for the business strategy will have changed with the latest evaluation of the future, and we are still doomed to play catch-up.

This model, therefore, is fundamentally incomplete. By definition, our models of business strategy exist in the future and by definition, our orientation about management, organization, and culture comes from the past. We are using models from the past, in the present, to get to the future. We can't get there from here.

The objective of industrial models was to reduce this lag-time to a minimum. In fact, the target was zero-down time, since changing the specifications on machinery was extremely expensive. The logical consequence was increasingly high volume, long runs, and standardized products, providing what we call economies of scale.

From the producers' point of view, new technologies such as computer-aided design and manufacturing (CAD/CAM) allow instant setting and resetting of specifications to the extent that set-up time has effectively been reduced to zero. With the lag eliminated, one starts to move in *real-time*. In essence, real-time implies no lag between formulation and implementation, between conceptualization and consumption. Ideas become acts. Until now we have achieved real-time technology but not real-time organizations. What we have are lag-time organizations and this we must change as we move into a world where real-time production is of the essence.

From the consumer's point of view, we come to exactly the same conclusions. Customers want goods and services when they need them – *any-time*. We have to learn to live in a world which is not governed by work shifts, by nine-to-five, by when "the next agent will be available to see you". Banking is no longer ten-to-two pm., it is twenty-four hour and seven-day week banking. Hotels traditionally say that check-out time is eleven a.m. while check-in time is two p.m.: "We need that lag-time of three hours to clean the rooms". What would happen if a hotel chain launched a campaign to reduce the lag-time to two hours by 1990, and in 1992 they launched a campaign that said, "Check in or out any-time you want! We'll bill you (any) time you use these services!"

Mass

Another dimension of the universe that has implications for business and organization is that of mass. When scientists wanted to find out what the universe was made of, they decided that if only they could reduce it to its most basic component part, then they would have found the building block of all reality. They duly applied this reductionist approach down to the level of elementary particles, only to discover that the ultimate concrete reality they had been seeking did not, in fact, exist. Primary reality is intangible, something Eastern philosophy and religion had been telling us all along.

Einstein went further and told us that primary reality was *energy*. Mass is energy divided by a constant, the speed of light squared (transposing his famous formula: $M = E/C^2$). Matter, then, as in our "tangible" products, is no more than energy, slowed down by a constant to a velocity that the mind can comprehend as having some tangible existence and meaning.

Our obsession with tangible products comes from our focus on industrial manufacture and an industrial economy. In the new economy, however, the emphasis is steadily shifting towards one of intangible needs. As a consultant pointed out to the Stanley Tool Company, it is not in the business of manufacturing drills, but in the business of making holes. If a customer buys the product, it is with that end in mind. Using this new perspective, the precise technology used to make these tools becomes secondary. The best technology is simply the latest available for hole making. Already, we have passed from mechanical to electric drills. In all probability, before the century is out, we will be buying laser drills (in "hardware" stores?).

The American economist, Paul Hawken, has expressed such a shift in the economy as an increasing ratio of information to mass. Taking the ratio a step further, I suggest that the value of deliverables (products and services) and also of organizations, can be expressed as an equation:

$$\text{Value of deliverable} = \frac{\text{Information}}{\text{Mass}}$$

Concrete or steel, for example, has a large mass and little information. A computer chip, on the other hand, contains a great deal of information relative to its mass.

Another classic example is dinosaurs! They survived for 160 million years before becoming extinct. They were big, though with a small brain in proportion to their mass. When their environment changed, they could not adapt and thus did not survive. The ratio of their brain to their mass was small, and so they were forced to use almost all of their information processing capacity on internal body maintenance, and therefore had too little to spare for successful negotiation of the external environment. Is this not what happens to the dinosaurs that are companies? They, similarly, spend a disproportionate amount of their information processing capacity on internal management and co-ordination and not enough on negotiating the needs of the external environment. Economies of scale, an industrial concept, create diseconomies of co-ordination in terms of internal management and organization in the new economy.

Space

I would now like to look at space, a third dimension of the universe, and examine what lessons it has for us in terms of management and organization. In the industrial economy, manufacturing takes place in the factory space. When we look at the new economy, however, "manufacturing" is increasingly moving out of the physical space of the producer into the physical space of the consumer. Furthermore, this new consumer is participating more and more in the final assembly if not the design, engineering, and manufacturing of his or her product. The final manufacture of a software application, for example, occurs when the user presses the return button on the computer.

Consumers not only want goods and services whenever they need them, they also want them wherever they are at the time. Banking is a good example. From its days in marble-pillared buildings in town centres it has moved through branch operations, kiosks, automatic machines to wafer-thin credit cards which we carry around with us to use whenever, and almost wherever, we want. We are moving towards *an any-time, any-place world* in which our ability to deliver products and services at any moment at any location better than our competitors constitutes a key advantage.

FROM MECHANICS TO HOLISTICS

Our basis for today's business and management stems from science and technology and, in particular, from Sir Isaac Newton's mechanistic view of the universe. In a mechanism, you look at the parts and the whole equals the sum of the parts. Today, however, we are moving towards a holistic interpretation of the universe, where the whole is present in every one of the parts. Already the holographic technologies are coming on stream and it is now up to us to create holistic concepts of management and organization. As yet this remains a metaphor, distant from our daily reality, but nevertheless very real.

Science has already shown us that the universe operates holistically, not mechanistically. Our genetic structure provides us with a good example. According to the mechanistic model, the whole is equal to the sum of its parts and therefore, we would expect a skin cell to contain all the information about itself, a bone cell to have information only about bone, and a blood cell to know only about blood. This is not the case. Every part, contains not only information about itself, but about every other factor constituting that entire body. Our skin cells contain information about our bones, our hair, our blood and every other part of us. That is, the genetic structure functions holistically.

This approach is just as valid for businesses. If the whole exists in every part, then the entire business must exist in every product, in every service and every employee.

Consumers already have a holistic approach to companies. For if you receive particularly bad service you are unlikely, in the future, to have a favorable overall impression of the company. The lapse is not excused simply as one part of the whole which did not work. Instead, the organization as a whole is condemned. The consumer reacts holistically. Jan Carlzon from SAS, for example, has an insightful expression called "50,000 moments of truth every day". What is a moment of truth? It is each interaction between a customer and an employee. In that moment of truth, the whole company is at stake, not just that one part.

Managers and employees must realize that they cannot work effectively in a business that represents a part without understanding its simultaneous relationship to the whole. Businesses function holistically and we must adjust our theories of management and organization to take account of the fact.

Information, for example, comes in four forms: words, data, images, and sound. For example, words are associated with publishing, data with computing, images with television, and sound with telecommunication. In the past this was a valid categorization of reasonably distinct fields. Today, however, we are witnessing a confluence of these technologies as world demand moves more and more towards a systems orientation. The challenge is to interconnect typewriters, computers, images on screens, and the telephone to create something totally new. Consequently, in the information "industry" it is no longer possible to look at just one part of the whole and survive in business. The secret of success lies in a company's capacity to integrate these areas into total systems and solutions. This is a holistic concept and only now are we beginning to utilise it in our theories of business and management.

MASS-CUSTOMIZATION

Up until this point, the concepts of time, space and mass that I have discussed have been general. In our management of organizations, though, we will have to develop specific theories and specific concepts. I would like to choose *scale* as an example.

In the industrial economy, economies of scale lay at the core of our theories on how businesses work. This has shifted more recently to ideas of *flexible scale* but still remains firmly within the production function. I believe that there is a larger context that we have to understand, and this can be expressed in a paradox.

During the agrarian economy, goods were custom built for individual customers. In the industrial economy, we moved to mass production for undifferentiated mass markets. I believe in our new economy that we will deliver customized goods and services but on a mass basis: we will mass-customize.

This will have far-reaching implications for organizations. At present we are still rooted in the industrial models which are characterized by either/or choices: you either centralize or you decentralize, you either customize or you mass produce. Science already has shown us that this is not necessarily the only approach. At the turn of the century, for example, scientists attempted to define the nature of light. They were perturbed to discover that light was neither a particle nor a wave as hypothesized, but both simultaneously. This discovery led in turn to quantum mechanics, relativity theory and a whole new approach. This is just what we need inside businesses and organizations: models that accept contradictions in a larger synthesis, rather than trying to eliminate them.

What, then, does mass-customization imply? For an automobile purchase it means being able to specify a customized model which is also mass produced and mass delivered. This concept provides an explanation for the success of Cabbage Patch dolls which despite not being very attractive *per se*, sold in phenomenal numbers. The dolls were mass produced and mass delivered, but computer technology made each one different. This *mass* production of *unique* articles was further enhanced by the marketing ploy of providing adoption papers for the new owners. Thus every customer received a unique product without any sacrifices having been made in economies of scale.

The same mass-customizing applies to markets as well as to products. The small fragmented markets of the agrarian economy led to the undifferentiated mass markets of the early industrial economy. Then mass markets segmented. Then niches were found. The ultimate logic leads to the mass-customization of markets. The same thing is happening today in international business, with the "global markets" of multinational enterprises analogous to previous mass markets. We have to shift to a global business, but soon we will start identifying global segments and, by 2001, global niches and even mass-customization on a global basis.

IMPLICATIONS FOR HUMAN RESOURCE POLICIES

The above trends will also be witnessed in organizations and their human resource policies. We are going to be shifting, for example, from hierarchies to networks. Electronic information systems enable all parts of the whole organization to communicate directly with each other, where the hierarchy would not otherwise permit it. What the hierarchy proscribes, the network facilitates: each part in simultaneous contact with all other parts and with the company as a whole. The organization can be centralized and decentralized simultaneously: the decentralizing mechanism in the structure, and the co-ordinating mechanism in the systems. Soon, we will have to learn how to manage networks of people as effectively as we manage hierarchies of people.

Other systems will have to make similar adaptations towards increased flexibility. Benefits systems, for example, used to be totally standardized, with only small firms having the flexibility to tailor to individual preferences. Nowadays, though, we are beginning to customize to the needs of the individual; for example, recognizing that the young employee is more interested in a salary rise and a car loan, whereas the older worker is more drawn by health care benefits and insurance. "Cafeteria benefits" demonstrates a move towards mass-customization in the management of human resources, a trend that is likely to continue.

Most fundamentally, perhaps, must be a shift in the accounting of human resources. In the industrial economy, human resources were treated as physical laborers and our accounting systems dealt with them as liabilities, as fixed and variable costs. Such an approach is no longer appropriate in the new economy. We must develop accounting systems that treat human resources as mental laborers, who are treated as capital assets. Financial accounting has distinguished between sales, assets, and earnings for a long time; human accounting will have to learn how to do the same. What matters is not just a body count relative to sales, or the number of PCs per employee, but rather the asset value and earnings contribution of human resources.

THE NEW WORLD

In sum, we are moving into an any-time, any-place world of intangible products and services, and in which mass-customization will become the norm. Our task is to create organizations that can meet these criteria. Our management cultures have their roots in an industrial heritage. What we must now develop are real-time cultures appropriate to our new economic world. It is a world in which a company's ability to outperform its competition depends on its ability to develop models and methods of management and organization that are appropriate to the new economy. Those that continue to use our industrial models and methods will fall further and further behind.

Part II

Major Organizational Change

Introduction to Part II

Although change is the very nature of life for individuals, organizations and societies, the nature of its challenges themselves change over time. "Change" is defined in different ways at different periods in history.

Two decades ago, many firms were concerned with organizational improvement and development. The literature on Organizational Development (OD) was booming. The message was that organizational change should and could be actively planned. The emphasis of the times was on planning, also reflected in a wider concern for strategic planning.

More recently fierce international competition, globalization of markets, and fast-spreading technological innovation have radically transformed the scene of organizational change. There is growing cynicism about planning. And in many cases the development and improvement of existing resources is not sufficient to ensure survival. Large corporations are going through massive rationalization of their operations, restructuring of their assets, major strategic reorientation, turnarounds, mergers, acquisitions. They are entering joint-ventures and a variety of business partnerships on a scale never before imaginable. To survive, many firms are having to learn how both to co-operate and to compete with other organizational and national cultures, and how to transform their own cultures.

Today's concern is with *major organizational change*, transformational change, and the emerging question is how to build the capacity for *evolutionary, adaptive change* into the culture of the firm. These issues are the focus of Part II of the book. Chapter 3 reviews the experience of a number of corporations, building on the testimonies of key actors from ICI, SAS, Marks & Spencer, Olivetti, Volvo, The World Bank, IBM, SKF, ICL, the Schneider group, Xerox, and others. The framework distilled from their experience does not lead to any simple or painfree recipes, but the chapter presents a rich array of "hows" and views on problematic questions.

Is crisis a prerequisite for major change? Can strategic reorientation take place without a major crisis? Can one induce such change by "selling" a future crisis? How do organizations monitor an evolutionary process of change? The reported cases illustrate a spectrum of attitudes around such issues.

Turnaround management is a particular emphasis in this discussion, and these firms are at different stages in the process: the trigger stage, the destruction stage, the first wave of rebuilding, and the often unanticipated second wave. How do transformational leaders show the way? What stages can be observed in the turnaround process? How do companies build a new culture? Can they avoid excessive dependence on their leader? Is middle management just left behind?

Invariably the transformation process implies some form of cultural change. This becomes the topic of the next two chapters written by academics. They provide the reader with conceptual maps in order to understand and master the complexity of change processes in organizations.

In Chapter 4, *Edgar Schein*, Professor of Organization Studies at MIT and an authority on organizational culture, deals with two important questions: what is organizational culture, and how do we change it?

After sweeping away some of the current oversimplifications about corporate culture, Schein invites the reader to look at culture as a learned phenomenon. Much of the behavior and values in an organization reflect successful solutions to problems of external adaptation and internal integration, solutions that were often invented or discovered by people long in the past and now forgotten. These solutions have gradually become assumptions that are taken for granted. The essence of an organization's culture is the pattern of such learned and underlying assumptions.

If one also bears in mind that the concept of culture was originally developed by anthropologists to describe the *least* changeable elements of a society, then one obtains a challenging but realistic basis for building a theory of how to change culture.

Schein meets this challenge by offering an evolutionary theory of culture change. The ease with which one can bring about such change varies with the stage of development of an organization (organizational infancy, mid-life, and maturity). Since the cultural assumptions of the mature organization are stronger and more hidden than one in its infancy, these stages call for different types of change mechanisms. Eleven such mechanisms are richly described, ranging from natural evolution to planned change, from technological seduction to coercive persuasion and turnaround. Since culture serves different functions at these various stages, the message is clear: you have to understand your organizational culture if you ever want to change it.

In Chapter 5, *André Laurent*, Professor of Organizational Behavior at INSEAD, brings together the three concepts of culture, organization, and change to propose a cultural view of organizational change. Throughout the chapter, cultural assumptions about organizational change are successively probed at the individual, organizational, and societal levels of analysis.

In order to understand organizational change, Laurent argues that our own assumptions about organizations and their change require some systematic questioning. For instance, do we think in terms of linear shift or in terms of spiral transformation? Is there, indeed, evidence that modern organizations resist change as opposed to embracing it? Is the rigidity of traditional organization a property of its organizational form, or the result of some rigid pictures we have in our minds? Can our minds be managed or only inspired? Here we are reminded that organizations are social inventions, and that they can change only if people change the way they think about them. Looking at organizations as cultures and at organizational change as cultural change provides a different way of thinking about transforming our institutions.

Finally, Laurent argues on the basis of comparative research that strategies for organizational change should take into account the broader social culture, and particularly the national context. Different change strategies will be needed in different cultural environments.

After reading Part II of this book, it will be up to the reader to decide whether "*plus ça change, plus c'est la même chose*", or whether "*plus ça change, moins c'est la même chose*". These represent other deeply-rooted assumptions about change that affect the nature of change itself.

Chapter 3

Lessons From Practice in Managing Organizational Change

Alison Farquhar, Paul Evans and Kiran Tawadey

The fact that we live in an era of change has developed into a truism during the last ten years. Increasingly since the late 70s, not a day goes by without feature stories in the business press of major reorganizations, massive layoffs, and strategic reorientations.

A truism this may be, but we have not yet digested the implications of it. Many of today's management challenges centre not on the "whats" of what to do but on the "hows" of how to accomplish change. Managing change is difficult enough at a small group or departmental level – how much more complex it is when it comes to managing major organizational change, or strategic and structural reorientation.

In this chapter[1] we look at the experiences of some major corporations which have either had change forced upon them or have set in motion a process of major change. We have structured the chapter around the stages in such change – the trigger, leadership, and destruction stages, and the first and second waves of rebuilding. But we also take a look at firms which are seeking tools to build the capacity for change into their cultures.

THE TRIGGER FOR CHANGE

What triggers an organization to change? Some studies suggest that successful companies reorganize every two to four years. However, the cynics argue that although pressures for change may build up over years, if not decades, it takes a crisis to spur major change. Crisis acts as a trigger, often leading to a new leadership and political structure, and the beginnings of substantive change.

Whereas major change that is rapid and sweeping appears to require the imperative of crisis (in the form, for example, of unacceptable anxiety or financial pressure), it would seem that a great deal of less dramatic change can be brought about without such a pressing catalyst. Strategic organizational change takes different forms, ranging from radical "revolutionary" or "turnaround" change to what we might label "evolutionary" change.

SAS, the Scandinavian airline company which experienced a turnaround in the early 80s, would tend to go along with the change through crisis theory. In the words of its entrepreneurial president Jan Carlzon:

> Probably, before meaningful changes can be effected, it is necessary that the market dramatically reveals that the old, well-proven formulas are no longer valid. The shipyards continued to build supertankers long after the market had plummeted. The LKAB mines in northern Sweden continued to produce expensive and phosphor rich ores long after demand had tapered off. Facit continued to manufacture mechanical products long after the electronic revolution.
>
> To carry out measures of adequate scope, market forces must make their necessity plain for all to see.

Large organizations, in particular those which have enjoyed decades of success, tend to become complacent about their competences. They fail to perceive the need for change until confronted with necessity in the form of a crisis. ICI is a case in point. The growing vocal support for change from various parties in the organization in the twenty years prior to the economic crunch of 1979–81 led to little but the reports of working parties and incremental improvements. Then suddenly ICI was faced with overcapacity in Europe, comparatively high inflation in the UK, and a strong pound. These were heavy blows to a corporation which exported 40% of its national production, and the resulting crisis provided the necessary imperative for action. A new chief executive officer (CEO), John Harvey Jones, was appointed, the top management structure was overhauled, and ICI began its successful strategic move from bulk to specialized chemicals.

International Computers Limited, ICL, of Great Britain, faced an even more pressing crisis at the same period. In May 1981, the financial situation was such that Her Majesty's Government exercised its powers under a loan guarantee agreement and nominated three new directors to turn the company around. Bankruptcy had been knocking at the door.

SKF, the Swedish ball bearing company, shares a belief that people and companies will not change unless they feel threatened. In their own case this occurred when competition strengthened just as market growth took an unexpected dive. These pressures led to a total restructuring of manufacturing activities, a 40% reduction in manpower, and a new business orientation designed to balance manufacturing and market needs.

Sometimes the "crisis" may be hidden by inadequate accounting systems, autonomous companies, long production and marketing cycles, or poor communication and control structures. Didier Pineau-Valencienne relates the situation he found in 1981 when he took over as president of the French Schneider group of companies, with diverse businesses in electrical and electromechanical sectors (Merlin Gerin and Jeumont–Schneider), in general contracting (Spie–Batignolles), in steel and nuclear energy (Creusot–Loire), and in other markets:

> I realized we were making overall losses from this mixed bag of businesses but I was unaware to what extent. Today I know that the total consolidated loss from 1978 to 1983 was 8 billion francs, set against assets of 3 billion. There can be no clearer definition of bankruptcy!

> Yet the group was not bankrupt. At the time we thought we were making money in most of the major sectors. We were unaware of our losses with Creusot–Loire because of the long production cycle and plant building time involved in the nuclear industry. Its nuclear interests and involvement in armaments were so top-secret that its management, aided by the French public administration, refused us access to the accounts of our own firm!

> This situation had been allowed to develop for several reasons. First, there was a lack of rigor in strategic choices because the group was decentralized to such an extent that the various corporations were practically autonomous. Second, we were unaware of the cash drain in many sectors because investments made by the holding company or by the companies themselves were not sufficiently controlled, leaving losses unrecognized and consequently not depreciated on time. Furthermore, the situation was exacerbated by an extremely poor internal communications system.

The appointment of a new leader like Pineau-Valencienne, and the crisis alarm bells that he rings, may be the trigger of change that is visible to the outsider. However, Andrew Pettigrew argues that crisis is often the *end* of the process that triggers major change, not its beginning. Based on his longitudinal study of change at ICI (Pettigrew, 1983), he shows that individuals within ICI had been arguing for reorganization and a strategic shift from bulk to speciality chemicals, often putting their careers on the line, for more than twenty years before its 1979 crisis. Decades of discussion, of task force analyses, and of incremental steps may not have brought about the dramatic shift, but they served to sensitize the organization so that it could move fast when the crisis trigger came.

We tend to think of strategic change as starting with a new strategy, which is implemented with a new organization and a new culture. But Pettigrew argues that this is only the visible half of the strategic change process, as Figure 3.1 shows. The process often starts long before with the birth of the new culture in the shape of a vocal minority who challenge the system. This minority builds coalitions and establishes credibility through successful though incremental change. Then the crisis acts as a trigger which catapults

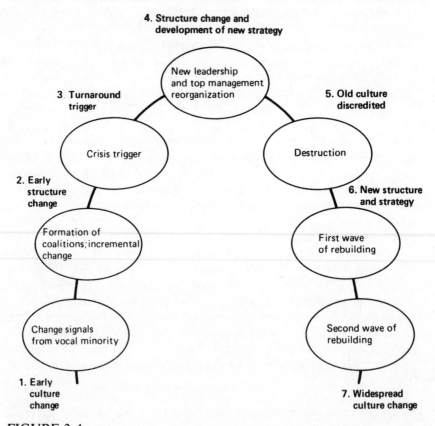

FIGURE 3–1
Typical Stages in the process of Major Organizational Change and Strategic Reorientation

this coalition into power. They reorganize the company, and only then does the firm commit itself to the massive investment that the development of a new strategy entails.

Not all companies see crisis as a prerequisite for major organizational change. The World Bank, for example, believes that a trigger of another kind may be sufficient. This could range from the aspirations of top management, through anxiety about an uncertain future, to a downturn in results. The World Bank thus actively monitors organizational morale in the hopes of detecting future crisis in its early and most treatable phase. In their words, "It is better to take the temperature at regular intervals, rather than waiting till you have a fever". Peat, Marwick, Mitchell, the international audit and consulting firm, departs still further from the "crisis before change" theory in their commitment to change *without* crisis. In their eyes, change should not be a reaction to a particular set of circumstances which can no longer be ignored, but rather a capability built into the fabric of the company. With an inherent capacity for adaptation, an organization should never be reduced to the limited choices which a crisis inevitably imposes.

Reorientation without Crisis

Xerox is a large multinational corporation which, although now facing tougher competition than ever before, has not been confronted with overt crisis. Nevertheless, it has a positive policy of managing change. The vice-president for personnel and organization describes how the corporation's environment changed over the years and the impact this had on its photocopying operations:

> In the 60s, we had the only plain paper copiers in the market, and the sales people sat there by their phones and took orders. In the late 60s, competition started to come in from IBM, and then in the 70s with Kodak. But this was what I call "friendly competition" in that it fed on features and services but not so much on price. But when the Japanese started to come after us, in full force, in the late 70s, they introduced quality products at a much lower price. They are extremely cost-effective competitors.

> One of the challenges we had is that our infrastructure and all our policies and practices were built on the financial structure of a monopoly. At one time we virtually had the whole market, though this decreased dramatically with these competitors. Our financial performance suffered. We needed to improve products, we needed to improve our market share. Specifically, the problem we identified was that lack of adherence to quality principles inside and outside the company was costing at least $1 billion.

In 1981, the top managers of the corporation decided on a program of action. It was to be based on employee involvement and competitive bench marking, and was called "business effectiveness". In 1983 this activity evolved into a total quality control process and the name was changed to "leadership through quality".

Xerox had no doubts as to the importance of consistency from the top when embarking on such a program. Equally vital was the process of communicating its meaning to the entire organization and gaining the commitment of every member. Only in 1985, once all senior managers had been trained and people knew what "leadership through quality" was all about, was it slowly integrated into day-to-day business operations. A senior executive describes the process of bringing everyone on board:

> What you need are rules of the game or a symbol to rally around and to release people's energy. It's not important what type of symbol you have as long as there is something with which to identify your effort. We have what is known as "The Green Book".

> In addition to the very top management actually defining what leadership through quality was all about, endorsing it and signing up to it, we then communicated throughout the entire organization what we meant by leadership through quality, how we were going to implement the strategy and how we were going to expand employee involvement. We also defined what competitive bench marking meant in every area of the business, whether it concerned salary and wages in human resources, or in distribution: who was the best in the business and how we were going to match them. We took literally all our employees through an orientation session to explain to them what this was all about.

Other symbols signalling top management commitment to the program consisted of the formation of a quality office at corporate headquarters and the appointment of a high potential operating executive as vice president of quality.

The project was further reinforced by training programs which focused on employee involvement, techniques for problem identification and solution, and the specification of customer requirements. Reward systems were adapted to recognize accomplishments in line with the program goals, principally through powerful non-economic awards. To improve management effectiveness throughout the process, a simple bi-annual survey was designed which subordinates had to complete on their bosses, with a subsequent group discussion of the results. This was implemented without exception from chairman downwards.

It was a well thought-out reorientation strategy, sold to the organization by a committed management team and reinforced by appropriate human resource systems. Inevitably, a great deal of corporate time and energy was involved, which led some employees to wonder whether "leadership through quality" wasn't getting in the way of pressing operational issues. The chairman's response to this was unequivocal: "It's not getting in the way, it *is* the way". Reinforcement of this kind and from this level was consistent throughout the program.

What, then, were the results? Xerox measures itself against three objectives: customer satisfaction, return on assets (ROA), and market share. ROA has risen three points since commencement of the program; customer satisfaction has also improved and the stock has gone up by over 150%. Worldwide staff have contributed cost-saving ideas resulting in millions of dollars of added profit.

But this success story should not mislead us into thinking that evolutionary change is either painless or easy to bring about. Xerox, like many large organizations with a long history of success, faced real problems in breaking down resistance to change. In many organizations the culture may be so strong that clear leadership from the top is insufficient to bring about new modes of thinking and behavior. At best, change without crisis is a lengthy and incremental procedure.

Selling the Crisis

Between crisis theory and the ideal of evolutionary change, there is an intermediate view whereby the art of change management is that of "selling the crisis" before it actually begins to bite into the bottom line. Small crises, interpreted by management as signals of what is to come, are used as symbols to pull the alarm bells, thereby mobilizing the energies of change and legitimizing the tough decisions that any major change program entails.

Marks and Spencer is a company in the midst of such a process. The confidence that derives from a century of success and its status as a model in the retailing industry is a major barrier to change within the company. The failure of an early attempt at international diversification was the catalyst that alerted top management (and in particular a new chairman) to the dangers of a changing home market.

The story goes as follows.[2] When Britain entered the Common Market in the early 70s, Marks & Spencer felt that they should capitalize on the event. After all, a high proportion of the customers at their flagship London store were French, Belgian, American, and Arab visitors, who raved about the virtues of M&S wares. However, the operating results of the foreign operations turned out to be disappointing, essentially resulting from a too literal application abroad of the formula that had been so successful in Britain. For example, less than 2% of the French population had ever heard of Marks & Spencer, and tackling this absence of identity was difficult for a firm that did not believe in advertising or marketing. Shopping bags in the first French store were the British bags, a Union Jack with the slogan "Buy British and keep British jobs". Since British stores were always on choice locations in local high streets, similar downtown properties were acquired for the operations in Canada – and only after more than a hundred such premises had been equipped did Marks & Spencer realize the downtown "high street" was dying in North America, with retailing having moved to large suburban shopping malls.

It was overtly a failure, though it hardly dented the bottom line of an otherwise successful firm. But it was a failure which mobilized the firm into making changes in recognition of shifts in the vital home market. British consumers, now more affluent, were beginning to turn from Marks & Spencer towards fashion wares, even for such staples as underwear and sweaters. Specialized chains of boutiques were beginning to eat away at M&S's traditional market share. Meanwhile, invigorated competitors in other wares like quality foods were beginning to imitate and improve upon the M&S formula. Nevertheless, the resistance to change and adaptation within the company was enormous. Employees were unconscious of any malaise because profits continued to increase; even industry observers reinforced the views of employees that "M&S has faced obstacles before and has always delivered the bottom line – they will certainly do it again". Trends like these changes in the home market become clear only with hindsight.

The new chairman, Lord Rayner, who took over Marks & Spencer in 1984, was the first non-family person to hold the powerful top role. Although he had come up through the ranks, as is the tradition at M&S, he had had more exposure to the outside world through secondments to top level government posts. Lord Rayner set in motion a series of changes that are likely to modify the culture of the firm over the next decade from a simple retailing company to a complex, international business. In contrast to the paternalism of his predecessors, Rayner encouraged bottom-up initiatives, and his "Why not?" became the byword of a new era. New business concepts that were anathema to the firm in the past were tried out – advertising, stores-within-stores, credit cards, joint-venture partnerships. Changes occurred at a deeper level too. Store managers were given profit-and-loss responsibility instead of the more traditional responsibility for sales alone, which led them to discover quickly what management as opposed to merchandising is all about. This in turn seems likely to lead to a restructuring of relationships between central buying departments and store manage-ment. Managers were sent on study trips to other enterprises and to business schools to broaden their minds and perspectives, while £2 million were invested in a selection centre to screen a new generation of more analytically-oriented graduate recruits, who would be "fast-tracked" into store manager positions and beyond.

Monitoring

Recognizing the dangers of "change inertia", many companies are keen to develop procedures to fight against it, to lower the trigger threshold. Complementing the vital accounting and control systems are procedures that focus on bottom-up feedback. Opinion and attitude surveys are frequently used to monitor the views of employees, and management-by-walking-around is advocated. Feedback helps mobilize resistant middle managers who, when faced with concrete figures on subordinate attitudes, are more or less obliged to adapt their ways.

As mentioned earlier, the World Bank likes to take the organizational temperature on a regular basis *before* a fever develops. This it does through an institution-wide survey which polls general attitudes toward the organization as well as opinions about work on a broad spectrum of issues, including environment, administration, management, and leadership. Questions are also asked on work satisfaction, reward systems, stress level, career development, and the impact of work on outside life. Another survey focuses on department managers and the way they handle systems, procedures, information, and feedback. The only people to receive the anonymous results are the manager concerned and his or her direct boss. To preserve anonymity and provide unbiased results, the results are computed only for departments with seven or more members.

What came strongly out of the first survey was a general concern among employees with career development and stress. As a result, corrective steps were taken. Stress was principally dealt with on an individual manager basis, but the issue of career development was addressed at an institutional level. For the purpose of future planning, a statistical study was undertaken of growing and declining disciplines; and a Centre for Career Information and Development was opened on the grounds that people need to know more about themselves if they are to define, with the company, a suitable career path to follow.

Xerox also adopted a monitoring system as part of its program to reconstruct the infrastructure of the company:

> There was a time in the 60s, and indeed through the early 70s, when everybody in the company flew first class. And if you had a problem that you could solve by hiring people, or spending money, then you did not have a problem. We have had a difficult time getting attitude changes from many of our top managers, because of the fact that for almost twenty years we had that kind of infrastructure.

In an effort to mobilize change energy they have designed a survey which all subordinates fill out on their bosses twice a year. The questionnaire is simple and asks the employee to rate his or her manager on a variety of points, for example, how the manager keeps the person informed on the state of the overall business, whether the boss removes barriers to getting jobs done, and if the manager gives both positive and negative feedback when deserved. The results are computer summarized for anonymity's sake, and given to the boss who discusses them with his or her subordinates on a group basis. This process is carried out at every level of the corporation and has played an effective role in discouraging management complacency.

A word of caution, however, is given by those companies who employ attitude surveys on a regular basis. Such surveys inevitably give rise to expectations, particularly in areas where dissatisfaction is widespread. Consequently, companies must take care not to gloss over problematic issues. If these are revealed but let unaddressed, dissatisfaction tends to be aggravated and it would have been safer not to have sounded opinion in the first place.

THE TRANSFORMATIONAL LEADER

As the environment becomes more volatile, an increasing number of companies, even those who were labeled as "excellent" in the early 80s, have found themselves on the brink of disaster. It also seems as if an increasing number of turnaround leaders are waiting to step in and guide them back from the edge. Turnaround change has become associated with transformational or charismatic leadership. Some of the figures involved are already household names. Lee Iacocca, Jan Carlzon, Carlo de Benedetti, John Harvey Jones – all these men have captured the imagination of business and non-business communities alike. And research, indeed, suggests that strategic reorientation is rarely successful unless a leader who stands for the change moves into a position of power (Doz and Prahalad, 1987).

It is difficult to generalize about what constitutes a transformational leader. As the director of personnel at SAS says:

Successful leadership is the function of a very specific need. I don't think that we have one way of meeting needs but different needs for different types of leadership. A good leader is the one who can meet the specific needs of the circumstances.

In other words, the right person at the right time. For some corporations, the transformational leader will come from within the firm, someone who has perhaps challenged the system for years, and whose time has now come. Others choose to solicit outside help to guide the company back to health, believing that nothing but new blood will do.

Showing the Way

However, companies which have emerged from crisis tend to agree on certain aspects of leadership which contributed to their success. If management is "doing things right" then we could distinguish leadership as "doing the right things". Put another way, the executive team's purpose is to manage while the leader is there to show the way. For this reason, good leadership must define clear objectives and communicate them through simple messages to enable management to move corporate energy in the right direction.

SKF believes that providing clear information is a prerequisite for gaining support for change. It does not, however, limit itself to communicating facts about a situation. It holds that "you have to be extremely clear on why you analyze things the way you do. You have to explain the desired state and *how to get there*. Then you have to be very, very clear on what you expect people to do".

Olivetti considers that clear messages have been a central part of their successful strategic change: "The new leader of the company [Carlo de Benedetti], after having formed a new management team, decided on a way to bring the internal climate back to business basics by sending out over a period of time a few very clear messages". In a period of radical change, a leader can minimize employee insecurity by keeping communication simple and sharing his or her perception of the situation with everyone concerned with the company.

This was the way in which Jan Carlzon presented his vision of the transformed company to SAS employees, communicating through some now well-known slogans: "Our assets are our passengers, not our aircraft"; "Our goal is to become the businessman's airline"; "It's more important to get a hundred small things right than one big thing right". SAS has specific views about the role of leadership:

> Top management must recognise that most employees are individuals who want to do their best for the company if they know what the overall aims are. Thus, management must be supportive, inspirational, and adjusted to the individual it manages. This does not mean that management abdicates responsibility, but rather that it sets up goals and guidelines and delegates operational responsibility in an extremely strong and clear manner.

> If a company's personnel are to embrace a new philosophy, it is necessary that a philosophy exists. This requires a visionary management which can describe company goals so they are understood and supported by the employees. Goals and strategies must be so clear that all employees can help, based on their own abilities, motivation, and knowledge – but within

the framework set by the management. This is easy to say but very difficult to carry out in practice.

The airline company also considers that an essential part of leadership is to ensure coherence between the diverse elements with which the leader is faced: "A leader has to have some ideas about why, what, when, how and who. He cannot have all the answers but he has to have some ideas on the crucial issues. Only then he can maintain coherence between all activities. And without coherence you won't handle the situation".

The Leader as a Visible Role Model

Another aspect of the transformational leader which seems to span the majority of turnaround cases is his or her visibility and consequent status as a role model.

It is doubtful whether John Harvey Jones, ICI's flamboyant turnaround agent, would have risen to the top of this large and complex British organization if it had not fallen into crisis. As chairman, he was certainly visible. His connections with the media occasionally left the public relations department in despair, but through those appearances he sent messages about his visions and commitments back into the company. He was often heard repeating the same phrases: "change", "the management of change", "linking our innovation to the market", "telling it how it is", "my pride in ICI", "I want the contribution of other people", "people are free to choose whether they work in ICI or not", "do as I do, not as I say". The last message, one of his favorites, particularly cast him as a role model. It encouraged risk-taking. His decision to cut out a level from the corporate board was a direct indication that he expected all other executives to examine their structures, and rationalize them in a similar way.

Olivetti is another company which stresses the importance of leader visibility: "In order for the company to be aggressive, it must have its power concentrated in the hands of a small number of people. Moreover, we believe that there is only one person capable of making the final decision at each point of our organization, and it must always be clear to everyone exactly who that person is". However, the director of personnel is quick to point out not only the fundamental importance of leadership but also its limitations:

We believe that three things are needed to compete in the modern market: strategic direction and guidance, competence as a product of teamwork, and foremost of all, decisions. In a turbulent environment with complex markets, a charismatic leader cannot easily see to all three points on his own. Rapid decisions he can, of course, cope with but he cannot single handedly provide strategic guidance or have the appropriate competence. A management team without an effective leader can provide competence, and sometimes strategic guidance, but rarely fast decision making.

We have experienced that a management team without a leader, or with a leader who has limited power, even if composed of members of great worth and individual personality, leans more to a search for equilibrium within the team than to making real choices and decisions. In our opinion, a company which wishes to survive must produce choices and decisions faster than the competitors.

Planning the Process of Change

The imperatives of moving fast should not blind the leader to the need to plan the change process. One of the issues here is assessing the preconditions for effective change. ICL undertook such an assessment through a survey to test "organizational health". Several useful points emerged which had a direct influence on the company's change program. First, it became clear that there was far greater resistance to change than previously supposed. And if managers anticipate little resistance, they will fail to develop the necessary mechanisms to help people through the predictable phases of shock, retreat, acknowledgement and adaptation. In addition, it became clear that employees identified themselves with their immediate group or project team, rather than with the ICL corporation as a whole. So local reorganization was unlikely to be perceived and accepted as part of a strategy to save the division or corporation as a whole. This survey also revealed that change would never be easy as long as people were treated as passive victims, uninvolved in the process of reconstruction and without responsibility for its success. The only way forward for the company was to involve the innovative capacities of people at all levels, and not merely that of a few strategists at the top. It would not only be technical staff who would have to change their behavior. If the reorientation was to be successful, a totally different style of behavior was also required from managers.

THE DESTRUCTION STAGE

There are various stages in the process of strategic organizational change following the trigger, though the phases may vary according to the nature of the reorientation. In the case of major turnaround, the reconstruction process of building a new culture cannot be undertaken until a certain amount of "destruction" has taken place – rather in the sense that a dentist enlarges a hole before repairing it.

The old culture often needs to be discredited, if not destroyed.

"Unfrozen" is the term employed by behavioral scientists, who have advocated methods such as survey feedback and confrontation to assist employees to understand the problems and to question the status quo. Yet often the survival imperatives are such that raw power is needed.

This is a difficult stage in the turnaround process – there is a need to run the "old business" at the same time as one destroys it, to retain the credibility of clients, and to maximize cash flow as best one can.

Fire, Hire, and Then Build the New Culture

Olivetti has an unequivocal conception of the phases necessary in a major change program. They can neatly be summarized as : FIRE, HIRE, and BUILD THE NEW CULTURE. The company believes that major organizational change requires changes in the behavior of every individual employee; it cannot be attained simply through a top-down effort. Consequently, where it was thought that behavior could not be changed, the axe fell, though obviously much of the pressure for such wide-scale firing was also prompted by financial considerations. Olivetti had set itself a target margin and this was unattainable without a leaner organization. Olivetti's director of personnel comments:

> In the first 3 years, the problem was the margin. We had to recover the margin at the bottom. So the tough job we had was to fire about 20,000 people in Italy and abroad. And at the same time, we had to hire some 8,000 new people to change the basic technology of the company.

> Now I guess that the company is quite different. We are in fact building up a new company. There is no continuity of culture between the old Olivetti and the new one. That is because we had to hire a lot of management executives from outside, meaning a new management team with a completely different culture.

Robb Wilmot, who joined ICL as managing director with the company on the verge of bankruptcy in 1980, adopted a similar approach of "shoot first, ask questions later". Entire development programs were scrapped and headcount drastically reduced. At this stage of the crisis raw power of this type was needed.

Taking over as president of the Schneider group, Didier Pineau-Valencienne discovered that the corporation was losing money, though he did not know exactly where. An audit carried out by consultants quickly revealed these loss-making sectors, leading to rapid action:

> The best investment in payback terms and the most urgent task facing us was to find and stem the hemorrhage. We therefore approached the

government to discuss our proposed plans for restructuring the group. Due to the elections that year, this took longer than anticipated. Nevertheless, within a year we were practically out of shipyards, completely out of machine tools, and we had sold or stopped all diversifications.

Eighteen months after my arrival, we had finished this strategic rationalization program. We were ready to turn our attention to the most difficult company, Creusot–Loire, in spite of the strong resistances inside that company. Our first task was to change management. We duly fired the chairman and top level managers, which proved to be no easy task in political terms. I have often noticed in other turnaround attempts that the agent of change has a tendency to retain the chairman or managing director, firing those who are immediately below them. In general, I believe that one prevents far more chaos if one fires the number one and holds onto his management team. On this occasion, though, we were obliged to do both. I took over the chairmanship of Creusot–Loire and hired a new management team from outside the group.

These are necessary if brutal processes, and effective leadership cannot shrink from the hatchet job. Rapidity, decisiveness, and tough if sweeping decision-making should be the hallmarks of the destruction stage. If the new management takes a series of small axe blows, each followed by a breather, then its credibility will soon be destroyed. There is a natural temptation to prolong the agonies of layoffs and forced transfers, and to start rebuilding at the same time. Yet the pain and uncertainties of destruction hamper the process of rebuilding the new organization and its culture, a lesson that Exxon drew from its experience in cutting back its corporate headquarters from 2,000 to 200 staff.

BUILDING THE NEW CULTURE

Destruction leads to reconstruction, as the experience of ICL illustrates. Once the firing phase was over at ICL, new problems came to the fore, leading to a major project to build a new culture. Consultants involved in the turnaround explain:

The dilemma facing Robb Wilmot was that while the complexity of the strategic problem required him to exploit the collective wisdom of the company, the administrative infrastructure for doing so didn't exist. Lines of communication had been disrupted in the reorganization, the vision had no supporting context of shared culture, and most managers had been too busy scrambling up the beach to try to imagine what lay over the horizon.

There was a need to shift focus, to reduce organizational trauma, and to rebuild teams. In fact, a new culture in which people would seize change opportunities rather than resisting them had to be established. In recognition of these facts, ICL embarked on an ambitious project known as *Management of Change* which based itself on the premise that 'people change, we don't change people'.

Wilmot's vision was to move out of supplying computer "boxes" into the business of supplying specialized, high value-added systems for specific markets. Whereas his pure power-based leadership had been appropriate to solve the financial crisis, the new problem was of such complexity that one leader would not have the necessary skills and energy.

Wilmot made the conscious move of stepping back from operational decision-making, thereby forcing the organization to develop its own capabilities. The vacuum he created by this action was filled only when two important steps were taken to aid the management learning process. The first was structural, consisting of the formation of decentralized "business centres" as a replacement for the old functional organization. These centres were to operate semi-autonomously, with global responsibility for each of the company's chosen "vertical" markets.

The second step, with the help of London Business School academics, was the development of an innovative education program for the company's top two hundred executives. The goal was to create a shared corporate vision together with the competences to implement it. The course was tailored to ICL's needs, and attended by nearly all senior managers over an eighteen-month period. One of the academics involved stresses that "the job of the general manager should have as much to do with organization as with strategy. Most managers still think that organization design should be a staff function". This basic philosophy was emphasized repeatedly during the course.

In order to increase momentum and help top executives filter messages down through the organization, three lower tiers of training were instigated at the same time, aimed at all 2,000 of ICL's managers. These courses were designed to shake up management attitudes about the competitive threats for the future in the international electronics industry. They indicated how a strategically competent organization should operate in a turbulent, unpredictable environment. Attention was especially drawn to the importance of integrating strategy, planning, and organization.

As a more applied back-up to these broad, culture building courses, strategic and marketing techniques were taught to all levels of management along with "skill learning" programs whose subjects ranged from sales techniques to motivational issues.

This "Stage Four" Program, as it is known, won widespread acclaim both in and outside the company. Its benefits reached far beyond financial returns, the most significant being the creation of cohesion in terms of a common managerial language, and in the way managers from different functions and countries began to deal with strategic and organizational issues (see also Chapter 7).

One result of this intensive eduction program has been an increased level of expectations concerning the organization's performance capabilities. Many senior managers are keen for momentum to be maintained through follow-up courses. ICL's next executive chairman (prior to its merger with STC), Peter Bonfield, was all too aware of the dangers of complacency: "You have got to reinforce these things about every six months – otherwise, expectations are frustrated and the effect disappears".

Following Through

A real danger in the process of organizational change is the failure to carry it through sufficiently far. Companies may be tempted to relax when the immediate crisis recedes while they still have not addressed the deeper organizational problems which generated the crisis. The companies which have managed lasting turnarounds recognize this danger.

SKF, faced with dramatically increased competition in conditions of reduced market growth, was forced into a major change of which one of the first steps was to reduce the workforce from 75,000 to 45,000. After this painful process, it was tempting to relax. Yet as one of their executives says, you have to remind yourself that "going back or half way is the easy way out", and ICL's change consultants point out that the awareness of this risk spurred the Management of Change program described above:

> There was a danger that as the crisis ebbed, and the effectiveness of raw leadership dwindled, the company would slowly drift back to the anarchic situation that had existed in 1980.

> This situation was complicated by two further dangers. One, that the company would undertake a massive change in strategy that couldn't be supported by the administrative capabilities of the organization and didn't actually arise out of a careful process of strategic analysis. Such strategies would lack credibility and realism. The opposite danger was that if strategy development remained stalled, if in fact new patterns of resource allocation did not emerge, managers would begin to question the logic of recent organizational changes (business centres, more people changes, time spent in planning activities, etcetera).

The middle stages of the change process are fraught with problems which must be resolved if initial efforts are not to be wasted. Olivetti is very aware of the risk of losing momentum:

> It is very easy to go half way and then to fall back, and one of the challenges we have is to stay the course. At one time we had 117,000 employees. Now we are down to 100,000 and I am sometimes concerned that we did not go far enough. Because the market place started accepting some of our products, and our financial performance improved rapidly, it was easy to say 'Well, maybe we don't have to push as hard as we were pushing'. This is one of our challenges right now, and for this reason the CEO has to be behind the program and drive it personally.

Some organizations face the problem of *too much change* in their subsidiaries with inadequate follow-through, owing to their practice of rotating able general managers every two to three years. These managers initiate major change but do not stay in their posts long enough to ensure effective implementation. Their successors initiate different changes to ensure their personal visibility. This "zig-zag management" is discussed further in Chapter 12.

Strong Leaders Need Strong Teams

If it is generally accepted that turnaround situations need new or charismatic leaders to drive them, are companies condemned to lose momentum when these people retire or move on? And if these leaders are appropriate at a time of crisis, are their skills still appropriate when the danger has passed and priorities have changed?

In theory, post-crisis dependence on the change leader would seem a likely danger. In practice this does not appear to cause undue problems as long as the leader is aware of his or her dependence on a strong and cohesive management team. SAS stresses that Jan Carlzon has previously turned around two other companies which are more profitable today than when he left them. He does not seem to move on until he is sure the company can stand on its own feet. Such a track record is reassuring.

Olivetti equally believes that it is not dependent on its change leader, Carlo de Benedetti. He is now involved only in major strategic choices and the company is basically run by a professional management team.

ICI also denies any dependence on the leader who has guided the company through a major change program. A senior executive explains why:

> We have such a very good management team that knows where it is going that ICI does not depend upon John Harvey Jones to improve its performance. Furthermore, he has not created dependency through the

way he runs ICI. He is not saying to us 'You are dependent on me', he is saying 'I am responsible for releasing your talents and your energy and your contributions'. We have benefited greatly from his catalytic force which was needed at the time. He was elected by his colleagues because he was the right person at that time.

You can't forget that the other seven directors on the ICI Board are big, competent, effective blokes. They're not living in the shadow of their chief executive. When the election comes round, we are likely to have a man elected who has similar approach to John, but I don't think the organization depends on him. The complexity and magnitude of ICI make the proposition that JHJ could be running the whole thing himself a parody.

Harvey Jones constantly sought to encourage management consensus. He asked the executive team to act as drivers of strategic change, rather than as advocates of specific businesses as in the past. Then he asked them, in reaching their judgments on the performance and behaviors of business executives, to act as a team. Managers from specific businesses no longer had friends at court, as in the old days; they faced the whole executive team. This has developed cohesion at the top of ICI's organization.

THE SECOND WAVE OF REBUILDING

While there may be no experience of dependence on the charismatic leader, there is a vital need for continuity of message and reinforcement during the construction of a new organizational culture – perhaps for as long as a decade or more. As the ICI executive observed, Harvey Jones's successor turned out to have some similar attributes. And AT&T perhaps acted smartly in insisting that one of the conditions for their merger with Olivetti was that Carlo de Benedetti commit himself to remain as CEO for a ten-year period.

The process of building the new culture, exemplified in the ICL story, is itself only one step in a chain of actions. The next step involves anchoring these changes in new systems and procedures – from financial control systems to selection, appraisal and reward practices. But nevertheless, the underlying problem seems to lie with middle management. It has been noted that middle management, in particular, has a tendency to resist questioning the status quo. Unless there are massive replacements of such managers, overt behaviors may seem to change, while deeper attitudes change more slowly, if ever.

SAS believed that fresh management was essential for building the new culture:

It is customary to bring in a new management when changes in the market necessitate a large scale reorientation in a company. This is the right approach. Changing a company's culture and structure requires such a thorough revision of the mode of thinking of key personnel that a new management is essential.

Indeed, it is frequently difficult for existing management to review an earlier market situation and radically question, reorient or reject everything that was done during the period. New managements are thus often appointed when market demands on a company undergo substantial changes. New brooms sweep clean.
A fresh management improves the prerequisites for formulating new demands, new goals, new management philosophy and new strategies to achieve these goals, as well as for drawing up a new organization encompassing resultant changes in staffing, systems, and so forth.

For them, this policy was highly successful. Accompanied by massive training, the organization responded rapidly to Jan Carlzon's call; change went fast at the top (with a new management team) and at the lower levels (flight and ground staff), restoring SAS to profitability. This aspect of reorganisation is now known as the "first wave". But the so-called "second-wave" is directed toward middle management. Here progress has been much slower. SAS is finding that it comes only step-by-small-step through replacing managers with a new breed of person. For example, a key position is the station manager responsible for operations at each airport. Station managers were hitherto promoted up the line on the basis of their technical experience and competence. Today, SAS is developing managers for such posts through cross-functional transfers; even though the individual may have less airport experience, they believe that this key job requires proven managerial skills.
As is discussed in Chapters 7 and 8, it is through the slow process of management development that the new culture gradually becomes rooted. Volvo is a good example of one of the earliest European turnaround experiences. Pehr Gyllenhammar began a process of culture change in the late 60s – the public symbols became the humanized and high technology auto plant at Kalmar, and the diversification of Volvo into energy and food products. But the process of cultural change has been slow, as one of Gyllenhammar's right-hand men put it:

If Pehr Gyllenhammar had quit or retired even in the late 70s, Volvo's culture would have quickly slid back to where it was in the 60s. It is only now that he could retire if he wished to, fifteen years after those changes were set in motion. For it has taken that time for a new generation of middle managers to come up in the new Volvo into positions of responsibility. The only Volvo that they have known is the new Volvo, and so the changes have been institutionalized.

THE STRESS OF CONSTANT CHANGE

Many business leaders and academic scholars argue that we have already moved into an era of constant change, the society described dramatically in Alvin Toffler's *Future Shock*, 1971. To many people, the idea of change constitutes a very real threat, and it is worth emphasizing again that this threat is most perceived by middle management. Constant change implies constant threat and gives rise to inhumane levels of stress. How far is this really the case?

SAS considers that whereas stress may be necessary to initiate the change process, something else must be put in its place to continue it. The director of personnel describes his perception of the matter:

I don't believe that people are afraid of change, they are afraid of *being* changed. That's a big difference. The human being that really feels that he or she can control change is not afraid but is afraid of being changed by anybody else forcing their prerequisites on him. That's why I believe so much in information, because if you are informed (or even better, if you yourself have noticed that the prerequisites are changing), then you know why things will happen and you will prepare yourself.

Olivetti seeks constant change through a new interpretation of uncertainty, as Carlo de Benedetti says:

To fight instability does not mean to eliminate it. This would be impossible and would among other things take the legitimacy out of our role as entrepreneurs and managers. Fighting it means governing it, controlling it, transforming it into an opportunity. In short, this suggests a new philosophy for our company: to interpret instability positively. The answer to continuous change is continuous culture.

That is to say, the company continually reinforces its change culture through a few very clear messages, both verbal and symbolic. Momentum is ensured by an objective evaluation system and rewards which recompense innovative, change-oriented behavior.

Companies today are experimenting with such new mechanisms to build change into the fabric of the organization. Performance appraisal is an important element of IBM's human resource management system. A new question in the appraisal review is, "What have you done since the last review to *change* your job?" The intention behind this is to signal that performance which meets the negotiated objectives and the job description is today only sufficient to guarantee a cost-of-living increase in salary. Merit increases and promotional opportunities go to those who proceed beyond that, those who widen, innovate, and change their jobs.

The same is true at Apple Computer, a highly productive firm with 1986 turnover of more than $2 billion coming from 4,500 employees. At Apple Europe, achieving the objectives is only a base-line for adequate performance. One of the principles behind their human resource system is that whenever one places an individual in a position, the job will inevitably begin to change since people will do best what they like doing, not what the job description says. Consequently, there are no job descriptions and change is built into the organization's culture (Evans and Farquhar, 1986).

However, the natural consequence of this flexibility is that people expand their jobs into overlapping territories and that important problems fall through the cracks. So Apple have invented a new mechanism which they call the *Activity Review*. Whenever a boss or subordinate feels that the organization is getting out of control, he or she has the right to blow the whistle and request such a review. At the review meeting, the job boundaries and objectives are renegotiated, and work moves on. As the personnel director for Apple Europe says:

> People are constantly expanding and changing their jobs, that's simply Apple style. We go through some sort of reorganization once every year or so, but this usually reflects what is already happening, not what should happen. New recruits to Apple sometimes find it all a bit stressful. But they quickly adapt, or else they leave. After a couple of years at Apple, people start getting itchy if a year goes by and they feel that there haven't been some major changes.

Companies like Olivetti and Apple may be discovering new formulas for success in a changing environment. Certainly, at Olivetti the new attitudes seem ingrained in the company, but it has not allowed itself to sit back and relax. The director of personnel explains why it can never afford to do so:

> If I look behind me and compare today's situation with that of seven years ago, I find not only different results but also a different company. I am therefore convinced that the change is deeply rooted, structural and solid. There is an awareness that in order to survive and grow, other continuous and equally deep changes both of leadership and of company culture will become necessary. We are living in a world in which obsolescence is one step behind us. Our task, our mission and our motivation lie in never allowing ourselves to be caught up.

Notes

1. This chapter was written by Alison Farquhar (Research Associate at INSEAD), Paul Evans (Professor of Organizational Behavior at INSEAD), and Kiran Tawadey (Research Assistant). It is based in particular on the experiences of the following persons: Didier Pineau-Valencienne, president of the Schneider group; Len Peach, formerly personnel director for IBM (UK); Edgar Vincent, group personnel manager at ICI; Ray Fields, management development manager at ICL; Paul Smith and Michael Abrahams, respectively personnel manager and management development manager at Marks & Spencer; Daniele Mosca, director of personnel at Olivetti; Olof Ekman, director of personnel at SAS; Bengt-Olof Hanssen, personnel manager at SKF; Berth Jönsson, vice president for human resources at Volvo; Charles Kramer, head of human resource planning at the World Bank; Douglas Reid, vice-president for personnel and organization at Xerox; and Stefan Winsnes, formerly director of human resources at Apple Computer Europe.
2. See Evans and Wittenberg (1986), a case study description of Marks & Spencer's history and recent evolution, for a more detailed description.

Organizational Culture: What it is and How to Change it

Edgar H. Schein[1]

A few years ago the concept of corporate or organizational culture was hardly mentioned by anyone but a few social scientists. Today it is one of the hottest topics around because, it is alleged, a better understanding of how to build the "right" kind of culture or a "strong" culture will solve some of our productivity problems. Several recent books, most notably the Peters and Waterman (1982) report on the McKinsey study of excellent American companies, emphasize that "strong cultures" are a necessary ingredient of excellence. So the hunt is on to find strong cultures, and thereby fix our problem.

The dilemma is that we don't know exactly what we are hunting for. And it is not at all clear that we would know what to do with the catch if we found it. All kinds of definitions of organizational culture can be found, and all kinds of models are advocated for creating, managing, changing or even circumventing culture, just in case culture turns out to be an unfriendly animal.

Even if we learn how to decipher organizational culture, it is not at all clear whether full knowledge of one's own culture is always helpful. Sometimes self-insight is a source of anxiety and discouragement, and sometimes self-insight destroys the mystique of what we have. On the other hand, lack of insight into one's own culture leaves one vulnerable to forces of evolution and change which one does not understand and may have difficulty controlling.

One can see this clearly in the introduction of new technologies and processes such as the information, control, and decision support systems that the computer has made possible. Such systems have the effect of forcing managers and employees to confront aspects of their culture which they had never thought about before. For example, the introduction of electronic mail makes managers confront the question of how they prefer to relate to each other and what assumptions they hold about decision-making. In one organization I know of, managers came to realize that they depended on face-to-face contact and frequent meetings. Instead of changing their style, they chose to hold on to this way of working and, instead, subverted the electronic mail system.

In another organization, the introduction of personal computers on all executive desks made it possible for senior managers to be fully informed about all aspects of their organization, a power which they used to question lower levels about any deviations they noticed. This produced so much resentment, hiding of information, and even falsifying of information, that the system had to be modified to introduce time delays into the information flow. Senior management saw data one day later than lower levels to allow them to investigate and find out why things were off.

The whole system of trust, delegation, management by objectives, development of subordinates, and getting decisions made close to the point of action, can be unwittingly undermined by the attempt to introduce some of the new information technologies and practices. If we do not have insight into such consequences, we may threaten our organizations in ways that are neither desirable nor effective in the long run.

Insight into cultural matters also clearly affects the creation and implementation of strategy. Not only does culture limit the strategic options which are conceivable to an organization, but clearly one cannot implement strategies if they run against powerful cultural assumptions. One sees this most clearly in the transition from an engineering-based to a marketing-based organization. Not only is it difficult for the ex-engineer to conceive of marketing in the way that the professional marketer perceives this function, but the implementation of a marketing strategy may be undermined by the kind of people who are in the sales force, the incentive systems used by the company, the issues that executives pay attention to, and so on.

Yet the economic situation of the organization may reveal a need to change some crucial elements of the strategy, and these changes may require that some of the cultural assumptions that have been operating and have become dysfunctional in the current environment be changed. So we need to develop both insight into what those cultural assumptions are, and a theory of how to change culture without forgetting the reality that culture as a concept was originally developed by anthropologists to describe those elements of a society that were, in a sense, the *least* changeable elements. Cultural assumptions are the things that survive through successive generations; so a theory of how to change culture must start with realistic assumptions about how culture is learned and what functions it serves for human organizations.

How then shall we proceed to make sense of this area and to develop some useful insights for the management of organizations? I would like to approach these issues by reviewing a model of corporate culture that emphasizes how culture is learned. If we are to influence the dynamics of culture change, we must first have a clear model of culture origins.

A DYNAMIC EVOLUTIONARY MODEL OF ORGANIZATIONAL CULTURE

The simplest way to think about the culture of any group or social unit is to think of it as the sum total of the collective or shared learning of that unit as it develops its capacity to survive in its external environment and to manage its own internal affairs. Culture is the solutions to external and internal problems that have worked consistently for a group and are, therefore, taught to new members as the correct way to perceive, think about, and feel in relation to those problems.

EXTERNAL ADAPTATION ISSUES (PROBLEMS)
Cultural elements derive from consensus on:

1. CORE MISSION, MANIFEST AND LATENT FUNCTIONS, PRIMARY TASK
2. GOALS DERIVED FROM MISSION
3. MEANS TO BE USED TO ACHIEVE GOALS
4. CRITERIA FOR MEASURING RESULTS
5. REMEDIAL OR REPAIR STRATEGIES

INTERNAL INTEGRATION ISSUES (PROBLEMS)
Cultural elements derive from consensus on:

1. COMMON LANGUAGE AND CONCEPTUAL SYSTEM – TIME AND SPACE CONCEPTS
2. GROUP BOUNDARIES, CRITERIA FOR INCLUSION
3. STRATIFICATION: CRITERIA FOR ALLOCATION OF INFLUENCE, POWER, AND AUTHORITY
4. PEER RELATIONSHIPS: CRITERIA FOR INTIMACY, FRIENDSHIP, LOVE
5. ALLOCATION OF REWARDS AND PUNISHMENTS
6. RELIGION AND IDEOLOGY: HOW TO MANAGE THE UNMANAGEABLE

BASIC UNDERLYING ASSUMPTIONS
The essence of the culture will be the PATTERN of underlying assumptions dealing with the following core areas:

1. MAN'S RELATIONSHIP TO NATURE: ORGANIZATION TO ENVIRONMENT
2. THE NATURE OF REALITY AND TRUTH
3. THE NATURE OF HUMAN NATURE
4. THE NATURE OF HUMAN ACTIVITY
5. THE NATURE OF HUMAN RELATIONSHIPS

Different basic assumptions evolve to deal with the external and internal issues. Their inter-relationships and patterning makes up the cultural paradigm for a given group.

FIGURE 4–1
The Content Areas of Organizational Culture

The kinds of problems that any group faces are shown in Figure 4.1. Think of a company that has just been formed or a new organization based on a merger. This new social unit must develop, if it is to survive in its external environment:

1. a sense of its own *mission or primary task*, some reason for existing (Beckhard and Harris, 1977); from this core mission is typically evolved the following:
2. some *concrete goals*;
3. some *means for accomplishing* these goals, by which I mean the organizational structures and decision processes that are developed;
4. some means of *monitoring progress*, the information and control systems that are utilized; and
5. some means of *repairing structures and processes* if they are not acccomplishing the goals.

In order to function at all, however, the group must have:

1. a *common language and conceptual categories*;
2. some way of *defining its boundaries and criteria for membership*, which is typically embodied in the recruitment, selection, socialization, training, and development systems of the organization;
3. some way of *allocating authority, power, status, property*, and other resources;
4. some norms of how to handle *interpersonal relationships and intimacy*, what is often embodied in the terms style or climate of the organization;
5. some criteria for the dispensing of *rewards and punishments*; and
6. some way of coping with *unmanageable, unpredictable, and stressful events*. This last area is usually dealt with by developing ideologies, religions, superstitions, magical thinking and the like.

Note that organizational culture embodies the solution to a wide range of problems. We must never make the mistake of assuming that when we have described one aspect of a given organization that is very salient, such as how people are managed, that we have then described the whole culture. Such a total description should deal with each of the external and internal issues that have been identified.

I have also observed in those organizations that I know well, that they are to some degree integrated by even more basic assumptions that deal with the broad human issues shown at the bottom of Figure 4.1. It is probably the human need for parsimony and consistency that drives us to these higher order concepts, dealing with fundamental matters of organization–environment relations, the nature of human nature, the nature of human activity and relationships, and, most important, the nature of reality and truth, embodying very fundamental conceptual categories about time, space, and the nature of things.

I call these ASSUMPTIONS rather than VALUES because they tend to be out of awareness, taken for granted, and basically viewed as automatically true and non-negotiable. Values are debatable and discussible; basic assumptions are not. We are up against a basic assumption when our observations or questions are treated as dumb, crazy, or too absurd to be dealt with, as when someone questions whether the world is round, whether it is necessary to make a profit, why one should not schedule more than one person at a time for an appointment, and so on.

Once a group has had enough of a history to develop a set of basic assumptions about itself, we can think of the culture as existing at three levels, as shown in Figure 4.2. At the most superficial level we have *artifacts*, the visible behavioral manifestations of underlying assumptions. They are easy to see, but hard to decipher. If I see that every office has an open door, that people wander into each other's offices and argue a lot, what does that mean? The artifactual visible and hearable environment can provide clues but rarely does it provide answers.

LEVELS OF CULTURE

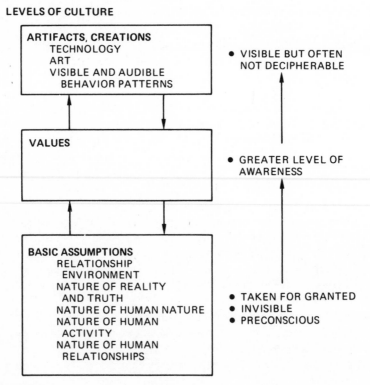

FIGURE 4–2
The Levels of Culture and their Interaction

The next level has more credibility. If I ask people questions about why they do what they do, I will elicit *values* and begin to understand the reasons behind some of the behavior. I may learn that doors are open because the president of the company ordered them to be open; he believes that everyone should always be accessible. I may learn that people chat with each other because communication is highly valued, and that they argue a lot because one is supposed to get agreement on decisions before acting. I may also learn that middle managers are quite frustrated because decision-making is taking too long, but if they try to become more efficient and disciplined, "something" in the environment that they cannot identify "resists".

When I have a good deal of information of this sort I can begin to see why the organization works the way it does, but I have not yet really confronted the essence of the culture at all. The values I have encountered are themselves *manifestations* of the culture, but not what we could think of as the driving force or *essence* of the culture.

I believe that what really drives or creates the values and overt responses is the learned underlying assumptions. As a group or organization solves its collective problems it always develops some world view, some cognitive map, some hypotheses about reality and, if it has success in solving those problems, that world view comes to be seen as correct and valid. It changes from a hypothesis or a view to an assumption and, if it continues to work, it gradually drops out of awareness altogether. It comes to be taken for granted.

Because of the human need for consistency and order, the basic assumptions gradually come to be co-ordinated into a pattern, assuming that the group has a long enough life for this process to happen. So what I really mean by culture, is the PATTERN of underlying ASSUMPTIONS which are implicit, taken for granted, and unconscious, unless they are deliberately surfaced by some process of inquiry.

For example, if I continue to probe in the above company, I will discover that the deep reason why it has open office landscapes, open doors and frequent meetings is the shared assumption that truth can be determined only by some process of testing ideas on each other. This assumption about truth is combined with the assumption that anyone can have ideas but no one is smart enough to assess his or her own ideas, not even the boss, hence mutual testing is the only way to determine truth, even if that takes time and energy.

If one then wonders how people can stand constant confrontation, debate, and mutual conflict around ideas, one discovers that a further assumption held in this organization is that "we are a family who will take care of each other as humans even if we fight over task issues". We will see that people are not punished for being "wrong", and that no-one loses their job or status unless they begin to run off by themselves or start to suppress information or color the truth. Because the company was founded by engineers who were developing brand new technologies it operates on the theory that anyone can be right about a given issue so it is essential for people to speak up even if that means insubordination.

By contrast, in another company that has many locked offices and few meetings, the basic paradigm involves the assumptions that a job is considered to be a manager's personal turf, not to be interfered with unless there is clear evidence of failure, and then only the boss has a right to intrude with suggestions and corrective measures. Whereas in the first organization there is information overload and frustration over slow decision-making because too many people can get into the act, in the second organization there is frustration over the inability to get innovative information from one part of the organization to another. The suggestion that there should be a system of lateral communication simply never gets off the ground because it is assumed that one will threaten and insult the manager if one offers information when none has been asked for.

In this organization there are also co-ordinated assumptions that make up a kind of organizational paradigm. Authority, seniority, and a scientific research background are assumed to be the source of wisdom and truth largely because the success of this company has been based upon its scientific discoveries. It is assumed that employees will be loyal and good soldiers, so that whereas in the first company one expects insubordination, in this second company insubordination would be thought of as a "sin". This company also views itself as a family and is very careful to take care of its people, which shows up in generous benefits and a policy of giving people a maximum chance to show their competence. As a result one finds managers and employees working very hard to be expert and really on top of their job.

Assumptions can grow up about the nature of a successful product, what the market place and customers are like, which functions in the company really are the most important ones, what is the best form of organization, how people should be motivated and managed based on Theory X or Theory Y assumptions, whether or not individuals or groups are the ultimate unit of the organization, and so on for each area shown in Figure 4.1. It is the interlocking of these assumptions into a basic paradigm which is the deep and most important layer of organizational culture.

How is Culture Learned?

There are basically two learning mechanisms which interact:

1. Anxiety and pain reduction: the *social trauma* model
2. Positive reward and reinforcement: the *success* model.

Picture a new group created by a founder. Such a group will encounter from the beginning the basic anxiety which comes from uncertainty as to whether or not the group will survive and be productive, and whether the members will be able to work with each other. Cognitive and social uncertainty is traumatic, leading group members to seek ways of perceiving, thinking, and feeling that they can share and that make life more predictable. The founder may have his own preferred ways of solving these problems which get embedded in the group, but only as the group shares in the solutions and sees that they work can we think of cultural learning (Schein, 1983; 1985).

In addition to these initial traumas, every new group will face crises of survival in its early history. As members share the perception of the crisis and develop ways for dealing with it, they learn to overcome the immediate pain, and also learn ways of avoiding such pain in the future. When a situation arises that is similar to a prior crisis, it will arouse anxiety and cause the group to do what it did before in order to reduce the anxiety. It will avoid as much as possible reliving the actual pain if it can be avoided by ritualistic ways of thinking, feeling, and behaving.

For example, if a young company faces extinction because of a product failure, learns that it has underengineered the product, and survives by careful redesign of the product, it may well learn that to avoid such trauma in the future it should engineer products more carefully in the first place, even though that is more costly. Whatever works in "saving" the organization becomes learned as the way to avoid future trauma. Members of the organization begin to think of careful engineering as "the way we do things around here", and teach new incoming engineers that "that is the way we *should* design *all* products", based on the now unconscious assumption that this is the way to win in the marketplace.

The problem with this learning mechanism is that once we have learned to do something to avoid a painful situation, we continue to avoid it, thus preventing ourselves from testing whether or not the danger still exists. The company that now carefully engineers everything cannot find out whether or not customers now would or would not accept a less well engineered and less costly product. Trauma-based learning is hard to undo, because it prevents us from testing for changes in our environment. Cultural assumptions learned by this means can then be thought of as *defense mechanisms* which the group has invented to cope with anxiety and potential trauma.

The second major learning mechanism is positive reinforcement. We repeat what works, and give up what doesn't. If the young company starts with some founder beliefs that the way to succeed is to provide customers with good service, or to treat their employees as their major resource, or to always have the low price product, or whatever, and action based on that belief succeeds in the market place, than the group learns to repeat whatever worked and gradually accepts it as a shared view of how the world really is, thereby creating a piece of its culture.

But this learning mechanism is different from traumatic avoidance learning in that it produces responses which continually test the environment. If the environment is consistent in producing success and then changes so that previously successful responses no longer work, the group will find out about it quickly, and the responses will be re-examined and changed. On the other hand, this learning mechanism can also produce behavior very resistant to change if the environment is inconsistent, producing success at one time and failure at another time. Unpredictable intermittent reinforcement leads to very stable learning, just as trauma does.

Learning theorists also note, by the way, that avoidance learning is so stable because not only does the ritualized avoidance response avoid the pain, but the actual reduction of the anxiety is itself very rewarding. Some organizational ways of thinking about problems thus produce the immediate comfort of anxiety reduction, even though those ways of thinking may be dysfunctional in terms of adaptation to a rapidly changing environment. And if those ways of thinking have become deeply held, taken-for-granted, basic assumptions about the nature of the world, it is no small task to contemplate how they might change or be changed.

Once we have adopted a learning model of culture, the question of whether every organisation has a culture can be answered in terms of whether or not it has had an opportunity for such collective social learning to occur. For example, if there has been low turnover of people, especially in key positions of influence, and a history of intense experiences with each other, a collective, shared way of thinking can be developed very quickly, as was often observed in wartime military units. One could thus postulate that the strength, clarity, and degree of integration of organizational culture or sub-culture is directly proportional to the stability of the membership of the group, the length of time the group has been together and the intensity of the collective learning which has taken place during that history.

If one adopts such a view of how organizational culture is learned, one cannot simply *create* a strong culture by executive action. Such a culture can evolve only through shared history and a consistent pattern of leadership over a long period of time.

This approach also deals with the problems of what is a sub-culture. Any group within an organization has the potential of developing its own culture if it has stable membership and a history of joint problem solving. We would thus expect to find within a given organization a variety of functional, geographic, rank level, project team, and other cultures which, from the point of view of the total organization can be thought of validly as "sub-cultures" just as the total corporate culture, if there is one, can be thought of as a "sub-culture" *vis-à-vis* the larger society in which the company operates.

SELF-INSIGHT AND CULTURE CHANGE

Given this model of organizational culture, what can we say about the pros and the cons of obtaining insight into this deep level, and how does this relate to organizational culture change? The answer depends on the circumstances in which the organization finds itself, as Figure 4.3 illustrates. I am hypothesizing that the culture issue is different at different stages of development of an organization (Davis, 1982). I am also hypothesizing that the kind of change which is possible depends upon the degree to which the organization is unfrozen and ready to change, either because of some externally induced crisis, or some internal forces toward change (Schein, 1980; 1985).

Figure 4.3 shows three major developmental periods that can be identified in private organizations, and for each period hypothesizes what the major culture issues are, how much self-insight is crucial, and what change mechanisms are likely to be operating.

Birth, Growth, Founder Domination and Succession

I am lumping together here a whole host of sub-stages and processes and am ignoring, for the moment, that this stage can last anywhere from a few years to a few decades. At this stage the organizational culture serves the critical function of holding the organization together while it grows and matures. It is the glue that permits rapid growth and the influx of many newcomers. One might expect to see strong socialization processes that become almost control mechanisms, and one might observe strong defensiveness around the organizational culture, because members recognize how critical the culture is as a force toward integration.

In this stage one can see the culture as a distinctive competence, and as a source of identity and strength. Assumptions about distinctive competence can involve the organization's products, processes, structure, or even relationships. For example, I know of a young and rapidly growing company in the lawn service business that has chosen their employees rather than their customers or stockholders as their primary stakeholders. All their truck drivers, secretaries, and maintenance people fully understand the economics of the business on the theory that if the employees feel totally committed and professional, they will see to it that customers are found and are well treated. The continued success of the business hinges on the ability to maintain such identification with the core mission on the part of a rapidly growing work force.

Self-insight is critical in that it is important for members to recognize what their source of strength really is, but the process of achieving that insight is not easy because one wants to look only at the positive and desirable qualities of the culture at this stage. A company may have gotten where it is by ruthless competition in the market place and ruthless internal weeding out of incompetence, but it does not necessarily want to accept that self-image as being its distinctive competence and source of strength.

During the period when the founder or the founder's family is still

Growth Stage	Function of Culture/Issue
I. **Birth and early growth** Founder domination, possible family domination	1. Culture is a distinctive compe- tence and source of identity 2. Culture is the "glue" that holds organization together 3. Organization strives toward more integration and clarity 4. Heavy emphasis on socialization as evidence of commitment
Succession phase	1. Culture becomes battleground between conservatives and liberals 2. Potential successors are judged on whether they will preserve or change cultural elements

Change mechanisms
1. Natural evolution
2. Self-guided evolution through organizational therapy
3. Managed evolution through hybrids
4. Managed "revolution" through outsiders

II. **Organizational mid-life** 1. Expansion of products/ markets 2. Vertical integration 3. Geographical expansion 4. Acquisitions, mergers	1. Cultural integration declines as new sub-cultures are spawned 2. Loss of key goals, values, and assumptions creates crisis of identity 3. Opportunity to manage direc- tion of cultural change is provided

Change mechanisms
5. Planned change and organization development
6. Technological seduction
7. Change through scandal, explosion of myths
8 Incrementalism

III. **Organizational maturity** 1. Maturity or decline of markets 2. Increasing internal stability and/or stagnation 3. Lack of motivation to change	1. Culture becomes a constraint on innovation 2. Culture preserves the glories of the past, hence is valued as a source of self-esteem, defense
Transformation option	1. Culture change is necessary and inevitable, but not all elements of culture can or must change 2. Essential elements of culture must be identified, preserved 3. Culture change can be managed or simply allowed to evolve
Destruction option 1. Bankruptcy and organiza- tion 2. Takeover and reorganization 3 Merger and assimilation	1. Culture changes at fundamental paradigm levels 2. Culture changes through massive replacement of key people

Change mechanisms
9. Coercive persuasion
10. Turnaround
11. Reorganization, destruction, rebirth

FIGURE 4–3
Growth States, Functions of Culture and Mechanisms of Change

dominant in the organization, one may expect little culture change but a great deal of effort to clarify, integrate, maintain, and evolve the culture, primarily because it is identified with the founder. Culture change becomes an issue under only two conditions:

1. the company runs into economic difficulties forcing leaders to *re-evaluate their culture*; or
2. succession from the founder to professional managers forces assessment of *what kind of successor to pick*.

How, then, does culture change happen in this stage? I believe one can identify four mechanisms:

1. *Natural* evolution, survival of the fittest.
2. *Self-guided* evolution through organizational therapy.
3. *Managed* evolution through *selection of hybrids*.
4. *Managed* evolution through introduction of *key outsiders*.

Mechanism 1: Natural evolution

If the organization is not under too much external stress and if the founder or founding family are around for a long time, the culture simply evolves in terms of what works best over the years. Such evolution involves two basic processes (Sahlins and Service, 1960; Steward, 1977; McKelvey, 1982):

General evolution toward the next historical stage of development occurs through diversification, increasing differentiation and higher levels of integration, growing complexity and creative syntheses into new and higher-level organizational forms. Thus mid-life organizations are likely to have many divisions, to be multinational in their focus, and to have a much more complex governance structure between the headquarters and the various functional and other units.

The elements of the culture that operate as fundamental defense mechanisms are likely to be retained and even strengthened over the years if the company has been successful, but alongside the basic assumptions that are retained there will grow up a number of sub-cultures around the geographic, functional, and divisional organizations because each of them will have its own history and set of emotional experiences. This sub-culture formation can be thought of as a parallel evolutionary process.

Specific evolution, then, can be thought of as the adaptation of each of the major sub-units of a larger organization to its particular external environments, reflecting its own occupational and cultural origins. Thus in a high technology company the R&D unit will develop a highly refined sub-culture, while in a consumer good company, the product management marketing units will develop cultures emphasizing marketing skills. This process, labeled "differentiation" by Lawrence and Lorsch (1967), will cause the different units to develop different and potentially conflicting assumptions about the nature of truth, time, space, human relations, and so on, increasing the problem of integration for the total organization. As we will see in the next section, it is this evolutionary process that makes culture management a very different issue in the mid-life organization.

Mechanism 2: Self-guided evolution through organizational therapy

If one thinks of culture as being in part a defense mechanism to avoid uncertainty and anxiety, then one should be able to help the organization to assess for itself the strengths and weaknesses of its culture, and modify it if that is necessary for survival and effective functioning. Therapy that operates through creating self-insight permits cognitive redefinition to occur, and thereby can produce dramatic changes. Outsiders are necessary for this process to unfreeze the organization, provide psychological safety, help to analyze the present defensive nature of the culture, reflect back to key people in the organization how the culture seems to be operating, and help the process of cognitive redefinition (Schein and Bennis, 1965; Schein, 1969; 1980; 1985).

When this process works, usually because the client is highly motivated to change, dramatic shifts in assumptions can take place. I know of one company that could not make a crucial transition because of a history of defining marketing in very limited merchandising terms and, hence, seeing little value in the function. This assumption (that marketing cannot really help) led to hiring poor marketers and losing the good ones which the company had. Only when key executives had real *personal* insight into how they defined marketing, and cognitively redefined the funtion in their own mind, were they able to adopt the assumption that marketing could help, change the hiring policy, and give marketing-oriented managers more real power.

Much of the field of planned change and organization development operates on the therapeutic and self-insight model. The assumption has to be made that the system is unfrozen – that there is motivation to change and readiness for self-insight, however much pain that might entail. Organizations sometimes have to get into real trouble, however, before they recognize their need for help, and then they often do not seek the right kind of help. Sadly, organizations are no different in this regard from individuals.

Mechanism 3: Managed evolution through hybrids

The above processes highlight evolution through the enhancement of the culture that exists. If the unfreezing pressures are more disconfirming, implying that some of the present cultural assumptions *must* change in some way if survival is to be ensured, how can a young company manage such change without losing its identity? One process is to selectively fill key leadership positions with "hybrids", that is insiders who have grown up in the culture and are accepted as legitimate culture carriers, but whose personal assumptions are somewhat different from the old assumptions and in the direction of where the organization needs to go. Such managers often elicit negative reactions in the sense of "we don't like what he is doing to us", but "he is one of us and therefore must be followed".

For this mechanism to work, some of the most senior leaders of the company must have insight into what is missing, which implies that they must have the ability to get somewhat outside their own culture. Such an ability to be in the culture and simultaneously assess it clearly is, in fact, one of the unique and most difficult aspects of organizational leadership. Once the leaders recognize the need, they can then select for key jobs those members of the old culture who best represent the new assumptions that they want to enhance.

For example, a highly decentralized company that grew on the assumptions of extreme autonomy, delegation, and participation down to the lowest levels of the organization found itself with rapid growth going "out of control", in the sense of losing the ability to co-ordinate and formulate a coherent strategy that could be efficiently implemented in short periods of time. The leaders know that bringing outsiders into key management positions would be rejected, so they gradually filled several of the division management positions with managers who had grown up in manufacturing where more discipline and less local autonomy had been the prevailing assumption all along.

Whether or not to evolve through hybrids or through the selective introduction of outsiders becomes a critical choice point when the founder or founding family begins to relinquish ownership and control. The management of the succession process then becomes *de facto* also a culture management process in that it provides opportunities to bias the evolutionary trend.

Dyer (1984) has examined this change mechanism in several organizations and found the following change cycle to be prototypical of successful change:

1. The organization develops a *sense of crisis* because of declining performance or some kind of failure in the marketplace and concludes that it needs some new leadership embodying some new assumptions.
2. Simultaneously there is a *weakening of those mechanisms that have maintained the old assumptions* in the sense that behaviors and values that have supported old assumptions are no longer seen as workable or defensible.

3. *New managers with new assumptions* are brought in from the outside in key positions to deal with the crisis and are given a good deal of power.
4. *Conflict develops* between the old leaders and the new leaders, but the new ones are allowed to assert some of their new ideas and methods.
5. The *economic situation improves or the crisis is somewhat removed*, and it is perceived that the new leaders were responsible for the improvement (if they are not given credit, their assumptions will not take hold even if the crisis goes away).
5. The new assumptions are now reinforced by new values and new mechanisms and are thus *stabilized*.

Old timers may feel that they don't like the new approach but they can't argue with the fact that the new leaders and the new assumptions "saved" the company. If the crisis is not resolved or if the new leaders are not given credit for resolving it, they will be forced out and the old assumptions will reassert themselves – a fairly common situation in the first and second generation companies.

What will weaken the supports for the old assumptions? One of the most common mechanisms here is change in ownership from tight founder and/or family control to public ownership, or the sale of the company to another company. The power of the founder to enforce his own assumptions is then substantially reduced even though rituals, traditions, and formal mechanisms reflecting the old cultural assumptions are still in place.

Organizational "Mid-life"

When the founding family is no longer in an ownership or dominant position by virtue of occupying key jobs, or if after a number of generations the organization has grown in size to the point where the sheer number of non-family managers overweighs the family members, we are talking about "mid-life". From a cultural perspective, the organization is now facing a very different situation. It is established and must maintain itself through some kind of continued growth and renewal process. It now must decide whether to pursue such growth through further geographical expansion, development of new products, opening up of new markets, vertical integration to improve its cost and resource position, mergers and acquisitions, divisionalization, or spinoffs. The past history of the organization's growth and development is not necessarily a good guide to what will succeed in the future because the environment may have changed and, more important, internal changes may have altered its unique strengths and weaknesses.

Of equal importance in this stage is the fact that some powerful sub-cultures will have developed in the different units of the organization, based either on common occupation, function, geography, market or product. The sub-groups within the organization will have built up their own history and experience and will, therefore, to varying degrees differ in emphasis from the dominant culture. If the organisation has been decentralized throughout its history, there may even be *only* sub-cultures and very little in the way of a common culture.

Whereas culture was a necessary glue in the growth period, the most important elements of the culture have now become institutionalized or embedded in the structure and major processes of the organization; hence, consciousness of the culture and the deliberate attempt to build, integrate, or conserve the culture have become less important. The culture that the organization has acquired during its early years now comes to be taken for granted. The only elements that are likely to be conscious are the credos, dominant values, company slogans, written charters, and other public pronouncements of what the company wants to be and claims to stand for, its espoused values and theories (Argyris and Schön, 1978). At this stage it is difficult to decipher the culture and make people aware of it because it is so embedded in routines. It may even be counterproductive to make people aware of the culture unless there is some crisis or problem to be solved. Managers view culture discussions as boring and irrelevant, especially if the company is large and well established. On the other hand, geographical expansions, mergers and acquisitions, and introductions of new technologies require a careful self-assessment to determine whether the cultures to be integrated or merged are, in fact, compatible.

Also at this stage, there may be strong forces toward cultural diffusion, toward loss of integration, because of the powerful sub-cultures that will have developed and because a highly integrated culture is difficult to maintain in a large, differentiated, geographically dispersed organization. Furthermore, it is not clear that all the cultural units of an organization must be uniform and integrated. Several conglomerates I have worked with have spent a good deal of time wrestling with the question of whether to attempt to preserve or, in some cases, build a common culture. Are the costs associated with such an effort worth it? Is there even a danger that one will impose assumptions on a sub-unit that might not fit its situation at all? On the other hand, if sub-units are all allowed to develop their own cultures, what is the competitive advantage of being a single organization? At this stage it is less clear what functions are served by the total culture, and the problem of managing cultural change is therefore more complex and diverse.

Unfreezing forces at this stage can come either from the outside or from the inside, as in the first stage:

1. The entire organization or parts of it may experience economic

difficulty or in some other way fail to achieve key goals because the *environment has changed in a significant manner*.

2. The organization may develop *destructive internal power struggles* among sub-cultures. In functionally organized companies, one often sees real intergroup struggles between functions such as sales, manufacturing, engineering, marketing, and research and development because each of these groups develops a strong sub-culture based on its occupational background and adaptation to a specific environment (Lawrence and Lorsch, 1967).

In the first stage, integration *per se* and clear identity were crucial; hence, power struggles among individuals and even groups would be unacceptable until a clear cultural identity was forged. In organizational mid-life the culture may be able to accommodate, even expect, individual clashes, because it may be built on assumptions of individual competitiveness. Only when the integrity of the total culture is called into question by competing sub-cultures is there a potential cultural problem.

Managing the change process once the organization is unfrozen is more complicated at this stage, because the organization is not likely to be conscious of its culture, as it was in the first stage. It knows only its own slogans and myths. Key managers now need a deeper level of insight into the content of their culture and into the cultural process that is probably going on, possibly requiring some therapeutic interventions as a precursor to other kinds of change.

All of the mechanisms previously described are applicable at this stage, especially the use of hybrids and the introduction of outsiders. The fact that the organization now has sub-cultures permits another kind of hybridization, in that the key leadership positions can be systematically given to those managers that come from a sub-culture that is viewed to be the most adaptive. In other words, leaders at this stage have the opportunity to really "manage" culture change by selective placement of people, and they will not elicit the degree of resistance to outsiders that would have been evident in the growth stage. But in addition to the mechanisms already described, I see several others that pertain particularly to this stage.

Mechanism 5: Planned change and organization development

Much of the work of organization development practitioners deals with the knitting together of diverse and warring sub-cultures, helping the dominant coalition or the managerial client system figure out how to integrate constructively the multiple agendas of different groups (Beckhard and Harris, 1977). The various conflicts that develop require the creation of interventions that permit mutual insight and the development of commitment to superordinate company goals. Such commitment always seems to involve insight into one's own assumptions and into the assumptions of other groups with whom one feels in conflict. Organizational development efforts therefore almost always start with therapeutic interventions designed to increase self-insight but then continue into various kinds of managed change programs where the outside consultant may play various roles to facilitate the process. Culture change is not usually a goal *per se*, but culture change is usually inevitable if the source of the difficulty is conflict among subcultures within the organization.

Mechanism 6: Technological seduction

At one extreme, this category includes the diffusion of technological innovation and various forms of acculturation where new technologies have subtly changed entire cultures. At the other extreme, it includes the deliberate, managed introduction of specific technologies for the sake of seducing organization members into new behavior, which will, in turn, require them to reexamine their present culture and possibly adopt new values, beliefs, and assumptions.

Many companies have introduced programs of leadership training built around models such as the Blake Managerial Grid (Blake and Mouton, 1964), in order to provide all layers of management with a common vocabulary and common concepts. The assumption underlying this strategy is that a new common language in a given cultural area, such as "how one relates to subordinates", will gradually force organization members to adopt a common frame of reference that will eventually lead to common assumptions. It is doubtful that such a strategy is sufficient to produce real culture change. But the program does reduce initial diversity by creating a common vocabulary and conceptual scheme for addressing the problems of how to deal with people. As the organization builds up a further history and resolves crises, it can then gradually develop new underlying assumptions.

The current practice of introducing personal computers to several layers of management and the mandatory attendance at training courses may be intended to serve a similar unifying function. Senior management sees too much diversity in the assumptions governing management decisions and brings this issue into the open by introducing a technology that forces decision-making premises and styles into consciousness. Some managers also see in the technology the opportunity to impose the assumptions that underlie the new technology itself, such as the importance of precision, measurement, quantification, model building, and so on, in which case we may be talking more about coercive persuasion following the seduction process, but in many cases the seduction is designed simply to surface the cultural diversity so that it can be addressed.

Another example of technological seduction was provided by a manager who noted that the volume of written memos in his organization had become unmanageable and had led to the assumption that one did not really have to deal with any memos. Because managers learned to ignore memos, additional mechanisms for communication were established and the system became overloaded, with devastating effects on the exchange of information. The manager convinced the company to install an electronic mail system as an experiment, without in any way tying the experiment to his diagnosis of the information overload. Once it was installed, it provided managers with a ready alternative to the overloaded phone and memo system. Managers began to use it initially as a way of ensuring that their messages got through, so only important messages were entered into the system. Because there were fewer messages, they were responded to, so that the use of the system was reinforced. The written memo system and the use of phones to communicate gradually atrophied, so the total information load was in the end sharply reduced and new assumptions around what one can and should communicate began to be learned and embedded. This manager is convinced that if he had attacked the information overload problem directly, merely cosmetic changes would have been made, and the underlying assumption that no one really cared what was in the memos would not have been addressed.

Technological seduction can be coercive as well. A manager took over a transportation company that had grown up with a royal charter one hundred years earlier and had developed strong traditions around its blue trucks with the royal coat of arms painted on their sides.[2] The company was losing money because it was not aggressively seeking new concepts of how to sell transportation. After observing the company for a few months, the new chief executive officer abruptly and without giving reasons ordered that the entire fleet of trucks be painted solid white.

Needless to say, there was consternation: delegations urging the president to reconsider, protestations about loss of identity, predictions of total economic disaster, and other forms of resistance. All of these were patiently listened to, but the president simply reiterated that he wanted it done, and soon. He eroded the resistance by making the request non-negotiable.

After the trucks were painted white, the drivers suddenly noticed that people were curious about what they had done and inquired what they would now put on the trucks in the way of new logos. This got the employees at all levels thinking about what business they were in and initiated the market-oriented focus that the president had been trying to establish. Rightly or wrongly, he assumed that he could not get his focus just by requesting it. He had to seduce the employees into a situation where they had no choice.

We should, of course, recognize that many people resist new technologies because they correctly sense that their cultural assumptions are being challenged and threatened. Technological changes not only disrupt behavioral patterns but force one to look at and possibly change underlying assumptions.

Mechanism 7: Change through scandal, explosion of myths

As a company matures, it develops a positive ideology and a set of myths about how it operates, what Argyris and Schön (1978) have labeled "espoused theories"; at the same time, it continues to operate by other assumptions, which they label "theories-in-use" and which more accurately reflect what actually goes on. For example, an organization's espoused theory may be that it takes individual needs into consideration when making geographical moves. Yet its theory-in-use – that anyone who refuses an assignment is taken off the promotional track – virtually negates the espoused theory. An organization's espoused theory that it used rational decision-making techniques based on market research in introducing new products may be superseded by its actual indulgence of the biases and pet projects of a certain key manager.

It is where such incongruities exist between espoused and in-use theories that this change mechanism applies most clearly. Nothing changes until the consequences of the theory-in-use create a public and visible scandal that cannot be hidden, avoided, or denied. For example, in the company that prided itself on taking individual feelings into account in overseas moves, a senior executive, who had been posted to a position he did not want, committed suicide. He left a note that was revealed to the newspapers, and the note made clear that he felt the company had forced him to take the undesirable assignment. This event suddenly exposed an element of the culture in such a way that it could not be denied or rationalized away. The company immediately instituted a new set of procedures built on the espoused theory and was able to abandon the theory-in-use because its negative consequences were now visible. In the case of the domination of the decision-making process by a key manager, what eventually happened is that one of the products he had insisted on failed in such a dramatic way that a reconstruction of why it had been introduced had to be made public. The manager's role in the process was revealed by unhappy subordinates and was labeled as scandalous, he was moved out of his job, and a more formal process of product introduction was immediately mandated.

Recent examples of a more dramatic nature can be contemplated. Though I do not have precise data, there is a strong presumption that major assumptions changed in the chemical industry as a result of the Bhopal disaster, in the space industry as a result of the explosion of the Challenger space shuttle, in the nuclear industry as a result of the Chernobyl disaster, and in the pharmaceutical industry as a result of the Tylenol capsule poisoning. It is in mid-life and mature industries that the risks are greatest that the publicly avowed cultural assumptions will be out of line with the actual assumptions that are operating.

In these cases external events precipitated the change, but one can also imagine situations where insiders "engineer" scandals in order to induce some of the changes they want by leaking information to the right place at the right time. Such leaks are often defined as "whistle blowing", in the sense of exposing internal inconsistencies. Since whistle blowing has the potential for precipitating a crisis that may force some cultural assumptions to be re-examined, one can see why people are cautious about it and why the organization often punishes the whistle blower.

Mechanism 8: Incrementalism

Certain kinds of changes can be produced best if one patiently but consistently uses every opportunity to influence the organization in a certain direction. Incrementalism means that in every decision area under the discretion of a manager, the decision is consistently biased toward a new set of assumptions, but individually each decision is a small change. One version of this concept was introduced by Quinn (1978) to describe what he saw as the actual process by which strategy is implemented in organizations. Leaders do not create massive changes even though they have a clear concept of where they eventually want to end up. Instead, they look for opportunities to make small changes, constantly test how these changes worked out, and concentrate on using fortuitous events to move the system in a desired direction.

Such a process changes parts of the culture slowly over a long period of time, especially if one set of such incremental decisions is the replacement of people in key positions by people with different assumptions. Executive selection and staffing processes are, in this sense, powerful processes of cultural change, but they are also very slow. But even without controlling staffing and selection, one can gradually produce change by coercing behavior changes that create dissonance and, over a period of time, put people into the position of realizing that they are no longer acting according to their prior assumptions. If the new behavior has been successful and becomes embedded, it may be easier to change the assumptions to fit the behavior than to undo the behavior to fit one's original assumptions, as dissonance research has shown (Festinger, 1957; Cooper and Croyle, 1984). This process may happen silently and without conscious awareness, so that one day the organization's members find that things are really different but they don't quite know when it all happened.

Tichy (1983) has noted that organizations can get into great difficulty if they do not notice small but consistent changes in the environment. He likens this process to the "boiled frog phenomenon", in which the frog who is sitting in the cooking pot does not notice his own demise if the increase in water temperature are small enough. It is well known in the psychology of perception that one can change someone's "level of adaptation" by increasing or decreasing stimuli at below the "JND" or "just noticeable difference" level. Thus, if we want someone to adapt to a very brightly lit room, one way of doing it is to increase the brightness so gradually that the person does not notice the increments. In the same way, a culture can change so slowly that one does not notice the changes for a long time.

Another metaphor, "turning the ship around", implies something different about incrementalism. It implies that even when the leadership knows where it wants to go and is open about it, it takes time and energy to get large numbers of people to hold different basic assumptions about something fundamental. There is a massiveness about large organizations because of the sheer numbers of people involved. There is an inertia that must be overcome to change direction. Similarly, the metaphor "Rome wasn't built in a day" reminds us that, even when there is consensus on a sense of direction, it takes a lot of effort to turn concepts into behavioral realities and to embed them into all the daily routines. Experienced change managers thus talk in terms of five to ten years for any substantial change projects.

In summary, organizational mid-life is the period when managers have the most choice of whether, and how, to manage cultural issues, and therefore need to be most aware of how to diagnose where the organization is and where it is going. If organizations face increasingly turbulent environments, one might well advocate not strong cultures, but flexible cultures, where flexibility hinges on cultural diversity rather than uniformity and on looseness in the application of cultural assumptions.

Organizational Maturity and/or Stagnation and Decline

The next and last stage to be considered is perhaps the most important from the point of view of culture change, because some organizations find that over a longer period of time significant segments of their culture become dysfunctional in a dynamic competitive environment. This stage is reached when the organization is no longer able to grow because it has saturated its markets or become obsolete in its products. It is not necessarily correlated with age, size, or number of managerial generations, but rather reflects the interaction between the organization's outputs and the environmental opportunities and constraints.

Age does not matter, however, if culture change is required. If a company has had a long history of success with certain assumptions about itself and the environment, it is unlikely to want to challenge or re-examine those assumptions. Even if the assumptions are brought to consciousness, the members of the company want to hold on to them because they justify the past and are the source of their pride and self-esteem (Sofer, 1961).

Such assumptions now operate as filters that make it difficult for key managers to understand alternative strategies for survival and renewal (Donaldson and Lorsch, 1983). Outside consultants can be brought in and clear alternatives can be identified; but no matter how clear and persuasive the consultant tries to be, some alternatives will not even be understood if they do not fit the old culture, and some alternatives will be resisted even if understood. They could not be implemented down the line in the organization because people simply would not comprehend or accept what the new strategy might require (Davis, 1984).

In such a situation, the basic choices are between more rapid transformation of parts of the culture to permit the organization to become adaptive once again through some kind of "turnaround", or to destroy the group and its culture through a process of total reorganization via a merger, acquisition, or bankruptcy proceedings. In either case strong new change managers are needed to implement the process, and part of the implementation is to unfreeze the organization before change is even possible. Such unfreezing often results from essentially coercive forces.

Mechanism 9: Coercive persuasion

The concept of coercive persuasion was originally derived from my studies of prisoners of war who had undergone major belief and attitude changes during their three to five years or more of captivity during and after the Korean war (Schein, 1961). The key to understanding some of the dramatic changes that the captives underwent was to realize that if one has no exit option, one is subject to strong unfreezing forces which, sooner or later, will motivate one to find new information that will permit cognitive redefinition to occur. Prisoners at first vehemently denied their guilt, thought it was ridiculous to be accused of espionage and sabotage, offered to make false confessions which, however, only produced more severe punishment, and in other ways attempted to cope, but did not question their own assumption base.

After months or years of harassment, interrogation, physical punishment, pressure from cellmates, indoctrination, and the threat that they would be in prison forever unless they saw the light and made an honest confession, prisoners would begin to search for an answer. They would find it when they began to realize that such terms as "guilt", "crime", "espionage", and "sabotage" have different meanings in different cultures and political systems. They were able to make sincere confessions of guilt when they understood that their postcards home could conceivably provide economic intelligence information to a recipient who wanted to use the information in this manner, and that crimes in the captor system were measured not by actual harm done but by potential harm. Guilt was established once one was arrested because the government did not make mistakes. Once concepts such as "guilt" and "crime" had been cognitively redefined, the prisoner was on the way to solving his problem.

What does all this have to do with culture change? Situations where elements of the old culture are dysfunctional but strongly adhered to are comparable to what the captor was up against with prisoners who asserted their innocence. The key to producing change in that situation is first to prevent exit and then to escalate the disconfirming forces while providing psychological safety. This is difficult to execute, but precisely what effective turnaround managers do. By using the right incentives, they make sure that the people whom they wish to retain in the organization find it difficult to leave. By consistently challenging the old assumptions, as in the case of the manager who insisted on painting the trucks white, they make it difficult for people to sustain the old assumptions. By consistently being supportive and rewarding any evidence of movement in the direction of new assumptions, they provide some psychological safety. If psychological safety is sufficient, members of the group can begin to examine and possibly give up some of their cognitive defenses.

Mechanism 10: Turnaround

Turnaround as a "mechanism" is really more a description of a combination of mechanisms, fashioned into a single program by a talented change manager or team of change agents. In turnaround situations I have observed or heard about, what strikes me is that all the mechanisms previously described may be used in the total change process. The first condition for change, as always, is that the organizational culture must be unfrozen. Either because of external realities that threaten organizational survival or because of new insights and plans on the part of the board of directors or the dominant management coalition, the organization must come to recognize that some of its past ways of thinking, feeling, and doing things are indeed obsolete. If necessary, the change manager uses coercive persuasion to produce the unfreezing. Once the organization is unfrozen, change is possible if there is:

1. a *turnaround manager* or team, with:
2. a clear sense of where the organization *needs to go*,
3. a model of *how to change culture* to get there, and
4. the power to *implement the model*.

If any of these is lacking, the process will fail.

The key both to unfreezing and to managing change is to create enough psychological safety to permit group members to bear the anxieties that come with re-examining and changing parts of their culture (Schein, 1980). The turnaround management system must have the necessary insight and skill to manage all the above mechanisms without arousing defensive resistance. For example, if major replacement of people in critical positions is involved, that process must be managed in such a way that it is seen as necessary and carried out according to some of the deeper cultural assumptions that may need to be preserved.

Turnarounds usually require the involvement of all organization members, so that the dysfunctional elements of the old culture become clearly visible to everyone. The process of developing new assumptions is then a process of cognitive redefinition through teaching, coaching, changing the structure and processes where necessary, consistently paying attention to and rewarding evidence of learning the new ways, creating new slogans, stories, myths, and rituals, and in other ways coercing people into at least new behavior. All the other mechanisms described earlier may come into play, but it is the willingness to coerce that is the key to turnarounds.

It should be noted that there are two fundamentally different leadership models that can be used in the turnaround situation. In the first model, the turnaround manager has a clear vision of where he wants the organization to end up, specifies the means by which it is to get there, and consistently rewards efforts in the right direction. This model works well when the future direction can be clearly spelled out. If the organization is in deep trouble, cannot continue in its traditional manner, but the new direction is not entirely clear, the turnaround managers use a second model.

The second model involves a fuzzy vision, forcefully and clearly stated. The leader says "the present is intolerable, we must do better, and we must get better by such and such a time". This message is presented frequently and with high emotional intensity, causing many layers of the organization to begin to try to invent solutions that will satisfy the leader. The leader carefully analyzes the solutions proposed and then selects out those he considers to be the most likely to succeed. Once he sees what is possible he then reinforces strongly those new directions.

The leadership literature is unanimous in its emphasis on the need for leaders to have "vision", but it probably makes a great deal of difference whether we are talking about precise solutions that the leader articulates (the rare case), or fuzzy solutions that the leader articulates with emphasis, forcing the organization to respond innovatively (probably the more common case). The second model would work especially well for leaders who come into the turnaround situation from the outside and have to work with insiders who know the nuts and bolts of the business far better than they do.

Mechanism 11: Reorganization and rebirth

Little is known or understood about this process, so little will be said about it here. Suffice it to say that if one destroys physically the group that is the carrier of a given culture, by definition that culture is destroyed and whatever new group begins to function begins to build its own new culture. This process is traumatic and therefore not typically used as a deliberate strategy, but it may be relevant if economic survival is at stake.

CONCLUSION

This chapter has described various mechanisms that change agents and managers use to change culture. As was noted, different functions are served by culture at different organizational stages, and the change issues are therefore different at those stages. In the formative stage of an organization, the culture tends to be a positive growth force, which needs to be elaborated, developed, and articulated. In organizational mid-life the culture becomes diverse. Deciding what elements need change or preservation becomes one of the tougher strategic issues that managers face at this time. In the maturity and decline situation, the culture often becomes partly dysfunctional and must change in some areas, creating more drastic problems for managers.

In each case the change process must be understood as involving some unfreezing forces, consisting of disconfirming information and the creation of psychological safety, and some mechanisms to permit cognitive redefinition as a way of developing new assumptions. Though not much was said about it, the change process must also provide the opportunity for refreezing, which occurs when new cultural elements solve problems or reduce anxieties.

I would like to conclude my analysis by drawing attention to five mistakes that need to be avoided in thinking about organizational culture. I will put them in the form of "do nots":

1. Do not *oversimplify culture*; it goes beyond slogans, behavior patterns, and values, to basic assumptions.
2. Do not forget *how culture is learned*; if traumatic avoidance learning is involved, remember that people will resist change.
3. Do not *limit your thinking* about areas of culture content; it goes beyond human relations into fundamental concepts of reality, truth, social structure and organization design, how decisions are made, and so on.
4. Do not assume that *culture change is simple*; it involves at least the eleven mechanisms outlined above, and probably many more.
5. Do not assume that more culture or stronger culture is better; it depends on the stage of evolution of the company and its current state of adaptiveness. Instead of seeking that elusive, possibly non-existent, and possibly dangerous thing – a strong culture – try to understand and seek the strength of the culture *you already have in your organization*.

Keep your insight level high and face culture as a potentially friendly animal that can be tamed and made to work for you if you really understand it.

Notes

1. This chapter is based on a talk originally delivered to the Convocation of Sloan Fellows (MIT, October 14 1983). Most of its material was later incorporated in the book *Organizational Culture and Leadership* (1985). It has been specially revised and updated for this volume.
2. This example was provided by Geoffrey Lewis of the University of Melbourne.

*Chapter 5*_____

A Cultural View of
Organizational Change

André Laurent

The management of organizational change can hardly exceed our capacity to conceive it. This capacity is often constrained by our premises, assumptions, and conceptions about the nature of organizations and the nature of change. Major or strategic organizational change requires a transformation of the actors' view of the organization.

This chapter will argue that our understanding of organizational change can benefit from a systematic probing of our assumptions and beliefs about the nature of organizations and the nature of their change. This probing process will be conducted at three interrelated levels of analysis: individual, organizational and societal.

The first part of this chapter will examine a number of basic assumptions that individuals may hold about organizational change and will attempt to assess their validity in terms of the evolution of modern organizations.

Looking at change from the perspective of the actors' assumptions and belief systems and approaching organizations as social constructions will lead us to a cultural view of organizations and their change. In the second part, we will try to assess the consequences and the limits of this image of organizations as cultures, and of conceiving organizational change as cultural change.

This inquiry would be incomplete without paying careful consideration to the wider cultural context of organizations. The third part will thus broaden the picture to the societal level by providing a comparative and research-based cross-cultural perspective on organizational change.[1]

ASSUMPTIONS ABOUT ORGANIZATIONAL CHANGE

To a great extent, the dynamics of organizations reflect what is conceived by individuals as being probable, possible, feasible, and desirable. The process of change is no exception. Organizations are social inventions (Greenfield, 1973). "Organizational change" refers to the ongoing nature of that invention process which is embodied in the actors' assumptions.

The complexity of any organization makes it extremely difficult to recognize the assumptions that have guided its development: the validity of such assumptions cannot be tested empirically. One can only speculate on the logical consequences of alternative sets of assumptions about organizational change. Such speculation is important as a way of exposing implicit assumptions to open inquiry and of broadening the spectrum of options that the architect of change may envision.

Organizational Shift Versus Organizational Transformation

Considered as part of a process of evolution, the understanding of organizational change requires a dual perspective: where we come from, and where we are going. It requires the skills of the historian and the skills of the visionary. A great deal of confusion about organizational change may originate from our mental inability to grasp the process of change in its totality, from our obsessive concern for its expected outcomes rather than its precedents. Indeed, managing organizational change has little to do with shifting from state A to state B; it has more to do with transforming state A into state B, which is very different. A process of transformation requires equal attention to be given to understanding the past, assessing the present, and envisioning the future.

Our linear conception of time in the western world needs to be enriched by the eastern circular conception (Hall, 1983). A spiral is a more accurate imagery of change than a straight line. Spirals remind us of the historical nature of evolution where previous states are progressively transformed into new states. Straight lines may feed the illusion that the past can be left behind, encouraging a "*fuite en avant*" pathology.[2] This is reinforced by the instrumental "doing" orientation of many western cultures, where individuals and groups tend to be defined mostly on the basis of their actions and achievements.

While this orientation may provide impetus and movement, it needs to be balanced by the insight of many eastern cultures, which exhibit more of a "being" orientation where individuals and groups are defined predominantly in terms of affiliative relations. An effective conception of organizational change as a transformation process therefore calls for a dual consideration of the instrumental and social nature of organizations.

Resistance to Change Versus Change Capability

A great deal of organizational literature has been devoted to the issue of resistance to change. Yet the evidence of today's world indicates that organizations *can* change and do change rather drastically over time, as a result of outside pressures, inside initiatives, or both. Dramatic turnarounds abound, as do mergers, acquisitions, and the like. Change is all over the place as organizations move from a state of success to a state of failure, or as they move from mediocrity to excellence. In spite of their supposed resistance to change, the evidence seems to be that organizations have in fact a tremendous capacity for change, a point which has not been sufficiently stressed.

One could reasonably argue that organizations have a much greater capacity for change than smaller organisms like the individuals who populate them, or larger entities like the societies and cultures that constitute their environment. In some schematic way, the relative change capability of individuals, organizations and societies could be sketched according to the diagram in Figure 5.1.

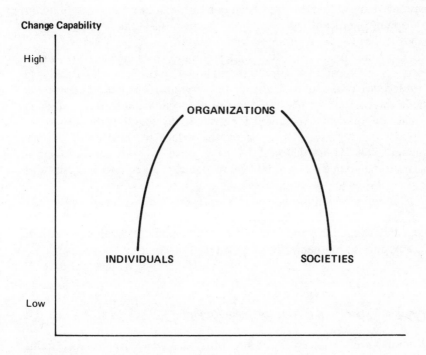

FIGURE 5–1
Change Capabilities at Different Levels of Analysis

Relationships between structural entities may be more amenable to change than structural entities themselves. From this point of view, it may be useful to consider both the individual and society as fairly stable structural entities, whereas organizations can be viewed as temporary systems of relationship and transaction between individuals and their environment. If personality confers stability to the individual and culture confers stability to society, social organizations represent more of a *"lieu de passage"* – crossroads or transaction fields, temporary arrangements which result from choices and initiatives. Organizations are the privileged places where change can occur most drastically. They can also be conceived as the most significant levers of both individual and societal change. They mediate important changes such as technological change.

As they are populated by individuals and embedded in societies, organizations are given individual attributes (we talk about the "personality" or "identity" of an organization) and societal attributes (we now talk about the "culture" of an organization). Even though such concepts may help our understanding, they also contribute a certain confusion. For instance, we may be led to attribute to organizations some of the properties of resistance to change of both individuals and societies.

We may be led to overlook the fact that the accumulation of small but consistent changes in individual behavior throughout an organization can bring about significant organizational change, resulting in major turn-arounds if the process is properly orchestrated.

On the other hand, we often underestimate the impact of the wider context on organizations, notably the national cultures in which they are embedded. We often fail to recognize that organizations tend to reproduce in their internal structures and functioning significant features of their national environments, mediated for instance by the educational system (Brossard and Maurice, 1976) or by the values of their founders and dominant elites (Hofstede, 1985). Furthermore, when organizations become multinational, they are unable to recognize their cultural diversity and to exploit this as an asset – a tremendous loss of opportunity.

Our tendency to reify organizations leads to rigid pictures of what they are, so that we tend to underestimate their change capabilities. Resistance to change may stem more from our way of thinking about organizations than from any objective organizational property.

Traditional Versus New Forms of Organization

Our minds are prisoners of many other traps when thinking about organizations and change in organizations. Significant traps are created by assumptions about the design of organizational structures and systems. The cost of such unquestioned assumptions is that we use obsolete forms of organization that cannot meet the changing requirements of new tasks, new technologies, new people, new environments. Organizational forms remain surprisingly unchanged in spite of such changing requirements.

In spite of the well-known dysfunctions of organizational hierarchies, only limited imagination and effort are being invested in the design of alternative organizational forms that deviate from the traditional pyramid. A majority of managers have negative perceptions of notions such as "boss" and "subordinate". They often substitute alternative labels like "associate", "colleague", and "co-worker", which they perceive as more socially desirable. Yet the same people enrich traditional folklore everyday by acting out, often unconsciously, fixed conceptions of upward and downward relationships that reflect the power differential between the parties in a formal hierarchy of authority (Bartolomé and Laurent, 1986). The cognitive maps of managers regarding their upward relations differ so much from those governing their downward relations that it is difficult to imagine that the same individuals can shift from the role of boss to that of subordinate and vice-versa without losing their sense of personal integrity. These models are based on outdated assumptions about organizational relationships; we end up with the ineffective organizational forms that we deserve.

Most managers remain unquestioningly and emotionally attached to the classical management principle of unity of command in the face of evidence that multiplicity of command may be more effective in a number of situations. The limiting assumption that one cannot have two or more direct bosses is so deeply anchored that it often undermines the effective functioning of matrix-type organizational arrangements (Laurent, 1981). The same mental attachment to traditional hierarchy may prevent multi-national corporations from considering structural evolution toward alternative designs – such as a heterarchy of strategic centers throughout the world that might be more effective than the traditional mother–daughter conception of headquarter–subsidiary relationship (Hedlund, 1986).

Management Versus Leadership of Organizational Change

Organizations exist where they were born in the first place, that is in the minds of people. For organizations to change, people have to change their minds about them, requiring a collective change of mind in the social fabric of the enterprise. However, this cannot occur without the lever of leadership.

Examples abound of carefully planned organizational changes that have failed in spite of systematic management. Management may be an excellent tool to maintain stability, to ensure survival and keep things going. But management is not sufficient to transform or revitalize an organization. Minds cannot be managed. They can only be inspired.

The literature on organizational change and development has created the impression that change can be managed with the help of a few techniques – almost without inspiration. However, the observation of major change in organizations has invariably indicated the presence of some timely hero at the top. This has helped both theoreticians and practitioners to realize that an over-emphasis on management had resulted in underestimating the importance of leadership. Unfortunately, the available literature on leadership was not the most inspiring body of knowledge as this field had been sterilized by a positivist behavioral approach. Salvation came from anthropology. If organizational change implies a collective change of mind that needs to be inspired by spirited leaders, then a conception of organizations as cultures could be helpful: a vision of organizational change as cultural change, and a definition of leadership as managed culture change (see Chapter 4 in this volume).

ORGANIZATIONS AS CULTURES AND ORGANIZATIONAL CHANGE AS CULTURAL CHANGE

Numerous books have appeared in the last few years that have adopted a cultural perspective on organizations (Ouchi, 1981; Pascale and Athos, 1981; Deal and Kennedy, 1982; Peters and Waterman, 1982; Davis, 1984; Frost et al., 1985; Kilmann et al., 1985; Sathé, 1985; Schein, 1985). Many academic journals have devoted special issues to the topic.

One of the benefits of this movement is an invitation to look at organizations in holistic terms, as totalities and as symbolic systems of meaning. The cultural perspective can be seen as a revitalization of systems theory, or as a synthesis of systems theory and the vision of reality as socially constructed (Berger and Luckmann, 1956). Interestingly, if one thinks of organizations as cultural systems, one can argue that it may be easier (and more effective) to try to change the whole organization in some minor or major way than to attempt to modify some of its parts. The latter strategy is more likely to upset the totality than to transform it.

Can a concept of organizations as cultures help better to understand the way in which they change? Some people argue that culture may only be another of those passing fads. There are academics who argue that organizational culture is like a can of worms: if you try to understand a few cultural elements, such as symbols, you get a whole mess of taboos, values, heros, myths, rituals, and ceremonies, and then you wonder what to do with it all. Yet one could argue that an amateur surgeon would easily come to the same conclusion about the human body. Our understanding of organizations as cultures might thus be enhanced by borrowing the insights of experts.

Anthropologists are supposed to know something about culture. One of them (Geertz, 1973) defines culture as "the fabrics of meaning, out of which human beings interpret their experience and guide their action". From this perspective, organizations become fabrics of meaning. Organizational change becomes a process whereby new meanings emerge, leading to the reinterpretation of past experience and the reorientation of action along new lines, breaking away from repetitive cycles. The leadership of organizational change becomes a process of imparting visions which powerfully and coherently promote new lines of thinking and action. Resistance to change may sometimes be a legitimate reaction against attempts to change aspects of an organization's culture without saying so, a reaction against undeclared or hidden cultural engineering.

With this cultural perspective, we recognize that social systems are indeed symbolic systems, and that what counts in organizations is not so much what people do, their overt behavior, but more the shared meaning that is given by whole groups to these behaviors and actions. For instance, the behavior of bypassing the hierarchical line may constitute a legitimate and praised action in organization *A* and the most dreadful sin in organization *B*. The issue here is obviously not the behavior of bypassing the hierarchy but the institutionalized meaning of bypassing. Organizational change refers to the process by which new meanings get institutionalized.

Although the cultural perspective on organizations may be promising, it does include a few traps. One of these stems from the popular idea of "weak" and "strong" cultures. Organizations may die because of their strong cultures. The stronger is the culture, the more absolute the consensus on norms and behavior, so the more we can expect rigidity, conformity, and sclerosis, and the less we are likely to see innovation. At the other extreme, organizations may die from weak cultures. If everything has a different meaning for each organizational member and if everybody has different ideas on what should be done, creativity may flourish for a while; but the whole edifice is likely to collapse from lack of consistency, co-ordination, and direction. The concepts of strong and weak culture are no more useful than the concepts of strong and weak personality: "strong" does not necessarily imply effective. More conceptual differentiation is required.

Effective corporate cultures may be those that have developed a capacity to learn about themselves and their environments so as to monitor their own development. Effective organizations are those that recognize better the dual essence of culture as an inward and outward phenomenon. Corporate culture becomes a snapshot of the organization's ways of defining its environment, interpreting it, and transacting with it.

An organization's culture reflects assumptions about clients, employees, mission, products, activities, and assumptions that have worked well in the past and which get translated into norms of behavior, expectations about what is legitimate, desirable ways of thinking and acting. Following this line of reasoning, we can argue that large cultures like nations and civilizations do not and cannot change easily since they are embedded in deep seated assumptions about nature, reality and truth (Schein, 1984). But the same rationale does not hold for goal-oriented, more youthful, and smaller social organizations like commercial or industrial firms (Laurent, 1986). It is true that such organizations are likely to reflect the wider national cultural context in which they emerged; they are not likely strongly to modify the basic cultural assumptions of their social environments (Laurent, 1983). But these organizations do have the power and freedom to shape behavioral norms and to institutionalize preferred ways of acting towards clients, employees, products, and so forth. These norms of action constitute the heart of an organization's culture. They are the locus of its capacity for evolution and change. Such a conception of organizational culture makes it easier to understand major changes that some organizations have been able to manage. It allows us to view organizations as highly changeable.

However we define an organization's culture, both researchers and practitioners acknowledge that its culture has a profound effect on strategy, structure, results, and many organizational processes. After lengthy debates in the literature on whether structure follows strategy or the reverse, there seems to be emerging agreement that both assertions are correct, and that the dynamic interaction between structure and strategy is mediated and shaped by the culture of the firm. In this sense, culture is seen as the glue that holds the different parts of a firm together in a coherent, consistent, and meaningful way. As cogently expressed by Schein in Chapter 4 in this volume, this glue will serve different functions at different stages in the life of organizations.

There is however a gap between the growing awareness of the importance of organizational culture and our limited capacities to do something about it. If corporations recognize that their culture is so critical to their success, why is it that so little of the corporate budget is being invested in trying to find out more about it, so as to be in a better position to develop it, transform it? Few corporations are engaged in explicit and systematic attempts at diagnosing their own culture, its history, roots, evolution, positive and negative manifestations. Historians and social anthropologists are not as yet numerous on corporate payrolls . . . yet their expertise seems to be needed.

To be fair to the corporate world, one should also recognize that there is a similar gap among students of organizations, between their interest in the concept of organizational culture and the available methodologies for cultural diagnosis and cultural change. Everybody is aware of the presence of the elephant, but our method of investigation remains that of the blind man.

There is a long way to go for researchers, consultants and practitioners to fill the gap between awareness and action capability. Existing skills in transforming and revitalizing organizations need the support of new knowledge and approaches. The state-of-the-art in cultural change is probably to be found in those organizations that try to go beyond the limited folklore of corporate culture booklets, credos, or the "quick fix" consulting tricks. In any event, there is an indication that the interpretation of organizational change as a case of cultural change may enhance our understanding of the evolution of social organizations by re-establishing the evidence that change can hardly occur without a transformation of the actors' views, attitudes and beliefs (Pettigrew, 1985).

A CROSS-CULTURAL PERSPECTIVE ON ORGANIZATIONAL CHANGE

If the concept of organizational culture is relatively new, the concept of national culture has been around for quite a while. National cultures represent an important element of an organization's context, from which the firm draws its resources and with which it transacts. In spite of its obvious impact and in spite of the attention of the organizational literature to environments, this national cultural context has been grossly overlooked for many years. Unconscious parochialism and unfounded universalistic claims have marked the field of management and organization (Hofstede, 1980b). Approaches to organizational change have suffered from the same ethno-centric pathology (Faucheux *et al.*, 1982). Strategies for organizational change that were developed in one particular national culture continue to be viewed by many as perfectly appropriate for any other culture (Kreacic and Marsh, 1986). Management and organizational theorists persist in entertaining the comfortable assumption that their object of study, their observations, and their concepts are culture-free.

Yet comparative research has demonstrated that different national cultures hold different conceptions and assumptions about organizations and their management (Hofstede, 1980a; Laurent, 1983). Managers from different national cultures hold different assumptions about the nature of management, authority, structure, and organizational relationships. These assumptions shape different value systems and get translated into different management practices, which in turn reinforce the original assumptions.

For example, national cultures can be positioned on a continuum from those holding an instrumental view of organizations to those with a social view. In the first case, more typical of North America, the organization is perceived primarily as a set of tasks to be achieved through a problem-solving hierarchy, where positions are defined in terms of tasks and functions and where authority is functionally based. According to the social view, found particularly in Latin cultures, the organization is primarily conceived of as a collectivity of people to be managed through a formal hierarchy, where positions are defined in terms of levels of authority and status, and where authority is attached more to individuals than to their offices or functions (Inzerilli and Laurent, 1983).

The instrumental view looks at authority as a means to achieve tasks; relationships are instrumental to task achievement. The social view looks at tasks as means to establish authority; tasks are instrumental to the development of relationships (Amado and Laurent, 1983). Whereas the instrumentally-oriented manager is primarily interested in finding out who is responsible for what, the socially-oriented manager is more inclined to consider who has authority over whom. While these represent ideal types, there is some evidence that different cultures approximate such types to differing degrees.

In the same way that it has taken some time and the help of the Japanese mirror for American management writers to identify what is American in American management (Schein, 1981), so it has been difficult to recognize the cultural values that have inspired various approaches to organizational change. Such movements as "organization development" (OD) in North America, "industrial democracy" in Northern Europe, "institutional analysis" in France, and "quality control circles" in Japan are obviously not independent of the cultural context in which they have emerged. It should come as no surprise that the United States was the home of OD, with its instrumental focus on organizational processes as tools to be improved, while the Latin countries favoured institutional approaches that tried to deal with the social intricacies of human collectivities (Faucheux *et al.*, 1982). Nor should we be surprised that the OD movement has traditionally downplayed the importance of power issues in organizations, while institutional analysis has been obsessed by such issues.

If organizations reflect their social context (Maurice *et al.*, 1980), strategies for changing organizations obviously cannot ignore this. Different change strategies are likely to be needed in different cultural environments. A contingent approach to organizational change needs to be developed that takes national culture as a major parameter.

When a majority of German managers perceive their organizations as a co-ordinated network of individuals taking rational decisions based on their professional knowledge and competence, any process of planned organizational change in Germany will have to take this into consideration. When a majority of British managers view their organization primarily as a network of interpersonal relationships between individuals who get things done by influencing and negotiating with each other, a different approach to organizational change may be needed in England. When a majority of French managers look at their organizations as an authority network where the power to organize and control the actors stems from their positioning in the hierarchy, another change model may be called for in France.

These national caricatures, while based on comparative research in managerial assumptions (Laurent, 1986), are obviously oversimplistic, like any other caricature. They are intended to highlight the challenge of managing change that are faced by organizations operating across national boundaries.

Research indicates that the corporate culture and policies of long-established multinational companies do not reduce national differences in management conceptions (Laurent, 1983). While the corporate culture may lead to significant behavioral adjustment, it seems to leave intact the deep seated assumptions of the various nationals.

What are the implications of such findings for the management of change in multinational organizations? If the cultural change of organizations has to do with the creation of new meanings, how can this process be managed when different sets of meanings exist in the various national organizations that constitute the multinational enterprise?

In order better to frame this issue, we need to return to a number of points made earlier in this chapter. If we look at organizational change as a process of transformation of state A into state B, the easiest part of the management task may be to specify what state B ought to be. Most organizations do not encounter too many problems at this stage. Few organizations would be explicitly against the development of a total quality concept, against paying more attention to customers and personnel, against the improvement of competitive performance. Gospels on the corporate values distributed by companies to their personnel show more similarities than differences. Reaching consensus on such overarching corporate goals may not be too difficult, even in large multinational firms that have a high degree of cultural diversity.

Cross-national difficulties start at another level. Different national organizations are likely to favour different means in order to implement the desired changes, reflecting cultural differences in the art of managing and organizing. This may also reflect a completely different assessment of state A – that is a different assessment of what needs to be transformed in the first place. Effective strategic organizational change, at a minimum, requires the integrative management of a decentralized process if it wishes to avoid the pitfalls of ethnocentrism.

If the corporation is truly "multinational", it may actually try to learn from its culturally different constituencies, so as to transfer and adapt change know-how from these subsidiaries to headquarters, and between subsidiaries. In this way, learning and cultural synergy can be heightened. The international firm progressively acquires a true multinational identity through the deliberate use of its cultural diversity. However, this cannot be the result of a rational management decision. It requires an evolution in ways of thinking from a parochial and ethnocentric conception of management and organization to a world view. This may be one of the most important challenges in the strategic change of multinational organizations.

CONCLUSION

We have argued in this chapter that our understanding and mastery of organizational change may be enhanced:

- if we conceive change as a *true transformation process*;
- if we think of organizations primarily as *social inventions*;
- if we refrain from attributing to organizations properties of *individuals and societies*;
- if we accept the evidence that organizations have a *high capacity for change*;
- if we view "resistance to change" not as a property of organizations but as a *natural reaction of its social members* to cultural engineering;
- if we recognize that organizational change requires a *transformation of the viewpoints of its members* – a transformation that cannot be managed, only inspired by the compelling vision of spirited leaders;
- if we consider organizational change as a particular example of *cultural change*;
- if we clearly distinguish between *two cultural aspects* of organizational change: (a) the transient culture of the organization itself, rooted in changeable representations, images, and behavioral norms; and (b) the more stable culture of civilizations and nations, rooted in the deeper assumptions of its social members, and constituting the cultural context in which the national organization is embedded;
- if we develop our awareness and understanding of the shaping effects of both *national and organizational cultures*;
- if we can develop a capacity to build on the specific and unique insight of *our own cultures* (national and organizational), while minimizing the negative impact created by the blind spots of these cultures;
- if we can manage to develop organizations that can learn from the insights and wisdom of *other cultures* (both national and organizational).

Once we will have achieved all of this, the concept of culture will not be needed anymore to understand and master change in organizations, and we will be searching for a newer guiding concept.

The state-of-the-art of organizational change will have changed again.

Notes

1.   I wish to thank Michael Brimm and Paul Evans for their helpful comments on an earlier draft of this chapter.
2.   "*Fuite en avant*" is a French expression, meaning escaping forward; in other words, a tendency to engage in new activities or thoughts as a way of postponing the consideration of past and present problems.

Part III

Managing Human Resources in the Global Firm

Introduction to Part III

In the short space of twenty-five years, the arena of big business has moved from national markets with foreign exports to regional markets (Europe, Asia, the Americas), and on to global markets. "Globalism" has become a fashionable word.

For smaller countries like Sweden, Switzerland and Holland, national welfare has for some time depended on international markets, though this applies even to Germany and Japan. But internationalization reflects more than the search for opportunities and profits in other regions. In some industries, globalism is a necessity for survival. The massive investments in new technologies such as telecommunications cannot be justified unless the firm is sure that the resulting new products can be rapidly sold in most major industrial markets.

Local government restrictions have necessitated the setting up of plants in the countries where goods are marketed. And while recently trimmed headquarters may still be located in New York, Frankfurt or Gothenburg, centres of competence that were once the preserve of headquarter functions are now located throughout the world.

In the search for competitive advantage, we are beginning to see firms playing a global game. The company may explore new technologies in Japan, while development laboratories are in Italy; start-up production may take place with skilled German labour, and later be transferred to plants in Taiwan or Mexico. New business nations emerge: who would have predicted even twenty-five years ago Japan's presence in the world economy? How many people realized that Brazil would be an emerging leader in commuter aircraft, with Indonesia as a potential future challenger?

The implications of internationalization for human resource management are discussed in Part III of this book. Philips, the Dutch electronics multinational with only 6% of its sales in its home country, was one of the firms to recognize and respond to these challenges. *George van Houten* is a member of the top management board of Philips, and among his responsibilities is technology. In Chapter 6, he argues that the emerging global reality of business is challenging traditional management structures, ways of thinking, and assumptions. The world of international business is inherently matrixed, and Philips' complex four-way matrix organization has held them in good stead. Major adjustments to this matrix began in the late 70s, continuing today: the creation of international production centres and decentralized centres of competence, the management of interdependent technologies, and a wave of strategic partnerships. But at the same time as Philips has been decentralizing, there have been strong pressures toward greater centralization in the competitive industry of electronics, leading to clearer allocation of responsibility, mergers between divisions, the creation of regional management organizations, and a stronger role for top management. Constantly adjusting the balance between centralization and decentralization is the organizational challenge at Philips (the payoff from this is illustrated further in Chapter 11 with an account of Philips' compact disk innovation and its multiple applications).

Van Houten singles out management development as essential to getting this balance right. Key managers must be capable of operating in a complex and shifting game. They must have strong generalist capacities, international experience, and the cumulative knowledge of all aspects of a product division or divisions that can be acquired only by experience. He describes how the approach to management development at Philips has evolved and how it works, as well as some of the problems, concluding that the new macro-economic realities have brought human resource management powerfully into focus at the level of top management.

Chapter 7, jointly written by *Paul Evans, Elizabeth Lank* and *Alison Farquhar*, continues this discussion, distilling the lessons from practice of a score of other international firms. With varying degrees of success, attention in these firms has similarly been focused on integrating the decentralized or differentiated units of the enterprise. The term "integration" implies the use of subtle mechanisms rather than the more crude and traditional tools of hierarchic centralization. Building this "soft" cohesion is important to permit "harder" integrative devices such as strategic management and information technology to work effectively.

Five ways to provide cohesion to the disparate parts of a global firm are discussed: clear mission statements, the vision of the chief executive officer, group management training and education, project-oriented management programs, and the process of creating a corporate charter. All prove to have merits and limits, none of them being a panacea.

International executive development is a complementary way of building a deeper level of corporate integration, through the management of the assignments and careers of high potential individuals. Fifteen years ago, the rationale for international management development was to provide and develop individual competencies: expertise that was needed abroad, or talented managers for key positions. While the latter are even more essential today, the new motive is also to develop organizational capabilities to handle the challenges described in Chapter 6 by van Houten.

After contrasting the ways in which corporations in Japan, the United States, Germany, Latin Europe and other regions handle executive development, Chapter 7 goes on to discuss the practical problems of managing international executive development. How many managers should one focus upon? How and when should one identify potential? How should assignment and career decisions be reached? Perennial problem areas are reviewed – the risk of "cloning", of sacrificing performance for potential, and of not following a steady recruitment policy. Finally the lessons from practice in managing mobility are assessed. How can local managers be persuaded to release high potential persons? How can increasing resistance to mobility be overcome? How should the problem of re-entering the mother country after an extended expatriate assignment be tackled?

Internationalization has exploded the notion that there is one-best-way of managing, as this chapter also points out in its introduction. Management used to be synonymous with the American approach, then we discovered the different but equally successful Japanese approach, then the German approach. We began to suspect that there are as many approaches to management as there are national cultures, each with positive features and each becoming pathological if taken to the extreme.

This is one of the starting points in Chapter 8, jointly written by *Paul Evans* (Professor of Organizational Behavior at INSEAD) and *Peter Lorange* (Norwegian-born Professor of Management at the Wharton School in Pennsylvania, and an authority in the field of strategic planning). Complex international companies operate in different regions of the world, each with their own socio–cultural logics. They also operate in different product-markets which require differentiated management logics. And competition requires these firms to be more and more differentiated – how can the multinational handle these different logics? In this chapter, Evans and Lorange take up this issue from the perspective of corporate human resource management.

They show how the decentralized divisional structure has evolved to cope with the needs of differentiated product-markets, with three strategic tasks retained by corporate human resource management: executive appointments and succession planning, executive reward systems; and ensuring the cross-fertilization of functional and business experience. They then assess the implications of the moves towards closer integration between product-market units. This is leading to a heightened corporate HRM concern in a number of domains: for developing transferable, generalist, strategic human resources; for developing strategic management capabilities; and for greater human resource flexibility. They argue that although much of HRM should be delegated to business units, there is a newly emerging strategic role for corporate human resource management.

But the international firm must also cope with differences in socio–cultural logic, with concepts and practices of management varying from one subsidiary to another. Here Evans and Lorange map out two adaptation strategies, the polycentric and the global approach. The polycentric firm decentralizes the management of human resources to national subsidiaries, who build up distinctively local cultures. In contrast, the global firm rigorously controls the recruitment, socialization and development of people, selecting and retaining those individuals from different national cultures whose values match the corporate values. HRM is thus a local matter in polycentric firms, but a critical corporate function in global firms. They show how the disadvantages of either approach can be moderated.

Finally, Evans and Lorange discuss the balancing of product-market and socio–cultural logics. Product-market forces are leading some firms to more global HRM strategies, though this change is often difficult to manage. On the other hand, the global firm appears to risk losing some strategic flexibility, as demonstrated by the difficulties these firms face in managing major internal diversifications or acquisitions of related businesses. They conclude provocatively by suggesting that while most people would suggest that product-market logic should drive the business, perhaps its choice in opting for a polycentric or global culture may ultimately prove to be more important. Product-markets are increasingly ephemeral, shifting with competition and technology, while the deeper elements of organizational culture evolve more slowly.

What emerges from these chapters is that we have reached the limits of simple hierarchic concepts like "planning", "centralization versus decentralization", and "structure". They can no longer cope with the complexity of international organization. Such corporations are becoming networks of interwoven relationships, networks which are capable of achieving what no hierarchic organization can achieve. Attention to matrix structures is giving way to a focus on building matrix cultures and matrix attitudes in the minds of managers. Building the network in a carefully managed way, creating the matrix culture, emerges as a clear human resource management challenge, both for top management and for the corporate personnel function. The same message is reinforced in Part IV, which is concerned with fostering innovation.

The Implications of Globalism: New Management Realities at Philips

George van Houten

The last ten years have been perhaps the most volatile period in history for business and industry. Totally new world economic patterns have confronted the managers of companies, sweeping aside long-held assumptions about the way business is conducted.

Competition has intensified, not only between traditional competitors, but also with new entrants from developing countries. The "new competition" in turn has created demands for bringing innovative products to the market at an accelerated rate. Shortened product life cycles have brought spiraling research and development costs.

Following a period with the most open and unrestricted conduct of trade in modern history, the dynamics of trade have shifted towards tariffs, indirect barriers and a variety of retaliatory strategies.

We have witnessed a shift in the centres of economic dynamism from the Atlantic Basin to the Pacific Basin with the United States remaining the pivotal market. None too soon, Europe has started to understand the importance of presenting a unified, competitive front to the world and is beginning to integrate policies to this end. Meanwhile, world financial structures have shown themselves to be inadequate in dealing with mounting debt and distorted currency exchange.

The term "globalism" was coined during this period, and we began to talk about global companies, global products and global marketing. Company managers understood that a global strategy rather than a country-by-country strategy was the new imperative. This was especially true for those engaged in producing and selling products that demand large markets and economies of scale in production.

For multinational companies such as Philips, globalism has meant both good and bad news. The good news was that multinationals could capitalize on their experience in operating in foreign markets. An established presence in countries beyond the home country base provides, as it has in the past, a window from which to observe economic and social trends, new competition, new ideas. The feedback contributes to the innovative potential of the company and generates invaluable learning experiences. But the bad news was that the traditional structure and approach to management of the multinational company was no longer appropriate.

Philips has seen a progressive shift from multinationalism to globalism, leading to the deep structural and management changes presented in this chapter. An essential part of these changes has been the gradual tailoring of its management development system and human resource management processes to the realities of the new global organization.[1]

ADAPTING THE ORGANIZATION AT PHILIPS

A few statistics concerning Philips, the Dutch-based electronics company, will serve to illustrate its size and complexity. From its beginnings as a small electric lamp producer in Eindhoven in 1891, the organization has grown into the fourth largest electronics company in the world, operating in more than sixty countries and employing some 344,000 people around the globe. Its turnover in 1985 was almost 60 billion Guilders.

Along with Siemens, RCA, and Hitachi, Philips is one of the most diversified electronics companies in the world. The product scope includes lighting, small and major domestic appliances, and consumer electronics, which refers to the broad range of audio and video products. It also covers telecommunications and data systems, electronic components, medical equipment and systems, scientific instruments and software.

At Philips, the matrix organizational concept has served well for many years. Although it is a complex structure with multiple lines and layers of responsibility and accountability, the flexibility that the system offered was valuable. In today's global environment, that flexibility is even more critical for rapid response to changing situations. The changes made in adapting the organizational structure to global strategies have essentially been modifications to the basic matrix concept.

This complex breadth of activity is managed by a matrix organizational structure. There are four principal elements to this matrix structure:

1. *The board of management* is the policy setting body of the company. It is comprised of nine members, including the president. Each board member is assigned portfolios most closely related to his area of expertise. These are a mix of corporate functions, product policy activities and national organizations.
2. *Product divisions* are the second element. Products and components produced by Philips are grouped into major divisions, headed by senior managing directors with worldwide responsibility for their products. Product divisions follow the product categories described earlier.
3. *Corporate departments* are staff functions. Located at our headquarters in Eindhoven, these are twenty-three in number and serve the company worldwide. They co-ordinate such activities as finance, legal affairs, product design and development, marketing support services, and staff development.
4. There are *national organizations* located in the sixty countries where Philips conducts its business. Though the size of the national organizations varies in relationship to the size of the market, each national organization carries out the full complement of Philips' activities, including manufacturing and marketing and, in some countries, research activities.

Such a simplified description of the organizational structure fails to highlight the complexity of its management processes. This complexity arises from multiple activity interfaces.

If we take the example of a Philips factory manager manufacturing radios in Singapore, we can trace some typical interfaces. He is responsible to the Philips Singapore management. The consumer electronics division, in Eindhoven, develops product policy and strategy for the radios. Since the factory produces certain radio products for the global market, the manager must respect central management planning. Furthermore, design, development and component sourcing interface with staff departments and require co-ordination. The factory manager must thus not just be experienced in production operations. He must also be skilled in communicating with the numerous other people in the organization who have an interest in what happens in his factory. In other words, it simply isn't enough any longer for a factory manager to excel in the technical aspects of operating a factory. He must be skilled in managing the complexity that is inevitable today in a large, geographically spread company with a multiplicity of activities.

THE FRAMEWORK FOR A GLOBAL STRATEGY

Having sketched the basic structure of the company, let me now turn to the responses to these environmental shifts.

Philips anticipated the global concept some years before it was given a name and became a fashionable theme for conferences. Its global strategy began in the late 70s with a restructuring.

Over a ten-year period, worker productivity has doubled through factory modernisation, production, reallocation and workforce reduction, the latter achieved either through consolidation or transfer of factories to third parties.

A key element in restructuring was the establishment of *international production centres*. The revamped manufacturing facilities were assigned worldwide production of product lines. Microwave ovens for worldwide distribution, for example, are now produced in Sweden; office dictating equipment is made in Vienna; car radios are produced in Germany, and so forth.

Changes in the management structure begun in the early 80s continue today in parallel with evolving industry characteristics. The macro-economic shifts already mentioned have been intensified by specific developments within the electronics industry:

- The electronics industry is moving away from stand-alone products to systems and software-dominated operations. Technologies have converged, resulting in the integration of applications that were previously separate and discrete. Computers and telecommunications are one clear example, audio, video and data processing another.

- The consequence of such integration is to erase separations which existed for so long between techniques for communicating image, sound, text, and data. Industries formerly associated almost exclusively with the telephone, computer, audio/video and office equipment are now advancing towards one another, invading each other's market sectors. This means that companies are forced into areas of expertise in which they have little previous experience. In order rapidly to gain that expertise and also to share escalating R & D costs, individual companies are thus venturing into a proliferation of acquisitions, joint ventures and other forms of co-operative partnership.

- Competitivity has become the burning issue in the electronics industry. It is the theme of discussions about Europe's future economic viability; it is the centre of trade disputes between Europe, the United States and Japan; it is the crucial concern of every company in the industry.

- The concept of "centres of competence" is especially relevant to this industry. If a company wants to do business outside its home market, it must have a strong presence in the three key markets of the world: Europe, the United States, and the Pacific rim countries. Aside from providing the necessary markets, a focus of resources on regions ensures access to technological and commercial expertise, and provides an observation post for major social, economic and political trends.

For a European company like ours the shift in macro-economic power from the Atlantic to the Pacific rim also means planning and executing a major shift in resources. It is clear that the concentration of resources in Europe must be adjusted to reflect the market dynamism and technological strength of the United States and the Far East. Investment in facilities and people are still clustered in Europe. Of the total 344,000 Philips employees, more than half work in Europe. In the Netherlands alone, where they have a major concentration of investments for product development and research activities, Philips employs 22% of their total workforce for a share of 6% of total sales. Obviously, this is a major human resource management issue that has to be factored into strategic planning. Philips has developed new management strategies tailored to these situations and identified long-range human resource management objectives.

BALANCING CENTRALIZATION AND DECENTRALIZATION

One of the first changes instituted during the last five years was the consolidation of responsibility in the product divisions. Traditionally each product division had a commercial and a technical director. With the advent of a global strategy, lines of authority and accountability had to be defined more clearly. Effectiveness of decision-making and communication of goals had to be improved in order to minimize the product development to market time-lag. Defending the territorial conflicts between technical and commercial managers had to be eliminated.

Accordingly, all product divisions now operate under a single managing director, assisted by directors with a range of commercial, technical and financial expertise. This change reinforces a shift from a previously geographically-oriented structure to one that is more product-oriented, with its centralized product management team.

A second major change has been the recent integration of several divisions, reflecting the trend toward integrated product systems and the general convergence of electronics technologies. The audio and video divisions have merged to become the consumer electronics division; data systems and telecommunications are now integrated into a single division, as are science and industry and their electrical accoustics division.

In addition to these mergers, Philips also differentiates between the management of stand-alone product divisions and those that are interlinked. Stand-alone products divisions are those that neither depend for sourcing on other divisions nor benefit from marketing or technical synergy with them. Examples are the lighting, medical systems, and defense divisions.

Interlinked product divisions, on the other hand, depend on each other and the management of their strategies and decision-making must be co-ordinated. For example, the integrated circuits, displays and consumer electronics divisions must be effectively interactive. Within these integrated divisions there are coherently organized business units. In the consumer electronics division, for example, the compact disk or VCR activities are operated as business units.

The structure of national organizations is also becoming more integrated by centralizing management regionally where appropriate. The Nordic regional management has been formed for Scandinavian countries, and a Far East regional management team based in Japan.

These organizational changes – single-headed management of the product divisions, regional management, and the integration of divisions – signal a more centralized management of those activities that require continuity and close co-ordination. Centralization also corresponds to the evolution of the electronics industry toward integrated activities. But at the same time, we do not want to transform Philips into a rigid centrally controlled company. Not only would that be contradictory to the prevailing company culture, but it would jeopardize the flexibility necessary to compete in today's environment.

What is evolving at Philips is a balance between centralization and decentralization. While the actions just described are those that move Philips towards a more centralized form of management, there are also activities that stimulate the entrepreneurial potential of various units of the company.

For example, a new business unit has been charged with the responsibility for developing the entire program of what we call home information systems. The members of this team have co-opted colleagues from a number of corporate departments and divisions to create a multidisciplinary unit to develop everything from the concept to the product marketing strategy for the program.

And while product strategic planning is now centralized, the national organizations are too highly regarded at Philips to relegate them to a peripheral role of carrying out orders. Centralized planning and co-ordination are balanced with decentralized decision-making at the country level where the variables of different economies and socio-political factors come into play. Moreover, in sophisticated processes such as telecommunications or data systems, the added value of integral elements like software or service place new responsibilities on the national organizations. Major countries are identified in terms of their market size and turnover, and the top management of these countries play an important role in senior management meetings, product division planning and ad hoc task forces.

Multinationalism to Globalism

The diverse and conflicting pressures to co-ordinate global activities and at the same time be responsive to national differentiation thus force strategic choices. The choice between globalism and multinationalism is leading Philips to develop a third option containing elements of both concepts. Such a strategy is basically directed towards the simultaneous maximizing of economies of scale and other benefits of global co-ordination, such as product planning, while at the same time maintaining responsiveness to the cultural and market differences of countries or regions.

And so the balancing and tuning of centralized and decentralized activities is part of the management process. Management must decide which activities must be flexibly managed by the national organizations and which must be globally co-ordinated. The ambiguities of such a flexible system is part of the uncertainty to which managers must accommodate in their daily activities.

The most effective managers under such a system are sound professionals, having a solid understanding of basic disciplines such as finance, legal affairs, and R & D, and competence in both technical and marketing affairs. But this is also coupled with a broad understanding of how the company functions, and with the skills to maintain a wide internal network of relationships.

We also seek management candidates whose skills fit our requirements in the continuing search for competitive success. These requirements have become increasingly stringent with the years. In the 60s, efficiency was the basic requirement for corporate success. Quality was added during the 70s, and flexibility during the 80s. In this next decade, a company must excel in all three areas, but the winners will have to be creative as well. It is the creativity of the individual in the organization that gives impetus to innovation. And companies in this decade will have to be innovative in all aspects of their business to survive.

Tailoring a Management Development System to the Global Organization

Let me now turn to the subject of human resource management at Philips – developing the managers capable of operating in the environment I have already described.

The management development program at Philips has been evolving for over a decade. The result is a structured system for the evaluation, tracking and training of all managers worldwide.

The early goal of this program was to ensure the availability of a pool of capable managers at all times for the positions needed to be filled. The first action was to develop a human resource data bank so that we had information about human resource needs and availability. The data bank profile provided then, as it does now, an analysis of current manpower, anticipated needs at all levels of management and the time required to have people available to fill top level positions.

While the human resource management goal remains one of making certain that managers are available to move into the positions that need to be filled, that goal has been elaborated to reflect the organizational complexity in which the company must function. There are thus two new key elements to the goal:

1. Managers must have *a more generalized expertise* across all areas of Philips activities.
2. The management team must become *more international* in order to reflect our geographic scope of activity.

It is important to emphasize that these new elements constitute the focus of strategic human resource planning activity. Developing generalists versus the more narrowly focused technicians of the past, and internationalizing the management team differentiate the human resources needed for the future from the strictly operational planning needs.

Strategic human resource planning deals with the thorny question: how can we prepare for the functions we will need ten years from now when we cannot with any assurance describe what these will be? The pace of technology change and macro-economic shifts of the past few years have proven that change is the reality we must expect.

The HRM program is thus designed to develop managers with a broad overview of the company so that they can adapt their generalized knowledge to fluid situations. Cumulative knowledge of all aspects of a product division, from development to marketing, can be acquired through assignments to different areas of activity and levels of responsibility. The professionalism and management competences looked for should be developed by a combination of extensive experience within the division and an international overview gained from overseas assignments. The training of tomorrow's· generalists will not only include experience in countries of different cultures, but the new breed of generalist managers will themselves represent different cultures. The company intends to infuse people of diverse nationalities into as many staff, product and national organization groups as possible.

At the same time, the established operational planning program will provide the short-term management needs that can be identified with a fair degree of accuracy.

How the HRM Process Works

I would like to describe the human resource management process as it operates today. The entire workforce worldwide is ranked into twelve hierarchical levels and each employee knows where he stands. Management levels begin at level 60 (levels 10 through 50 are covered by bargaining agreements subject to national labour policies). 60 is the level at which recent university graduates enter. Levels 60 through 80 constitute the "middle management" group, the backbone of the company, and senior management fall into the 90 through 110 span.

The components of the system for ranking include performance appraisal and potential appraisal.

1. The *performance appraisal system* has become increasingly objective in an effort to assign demonstrable, job-related criteria to the evaluations. The emphasis on empirical and objective performance evaluation is spreading to include corporate staff functions which were previously thought to be "difficult" to evaluate in objective terms.

2. The *potential appraisal system* is more subjective since the outcomes are a combination of judgement and hypotheses about the future. However, it is the critical part of career planning and development for both the individual and the company.

3. The judgement of today's managers in identifying potential candidates for tomorrow's top management positions is crucial, and it is a responsibility that is taken very seriously. Responsibility for the management development program is therefore *spread throughout the entire organization*, with line managers shouldering the largest share, since they must perform the evaluations and appraisals.

4. Besides nominating those employees with high potential, potential appraisers are required to identify 2% of management staff capable of rotation to other divisions. For the sake of credibility, they are obliged to show some consistency between judgements on performance and potential. This effectively reduces the temptation to cheat the system and promotes an *equitable flow of human resources*.

5. Because the company is large, the records must be centrally co-ordinated and tracked. This is the responsibility of the *corporate staff bureau*, which also develops the procedures and monitors the system. And very importantly, it maintains a company-wide perspective on strategic planning and management requirements.

6. Because the function is considered to be so critically important to the company's future, the director of the corporate staff bureau reports directly to the *president of the board of management*. Filling the top 120 positions of the company is the responsibility of the president, the

board of management and the director of the corporate staff bureau. Other management positions must be filled by the various organizations themselves.

The Training Program

The final element of the management development program is training. *Job rotation* has always been the heart of Philips' philosophy of management development. It is seen as increasingly important in our efforts to develop interdisciplinary skills and an international perspective. The candidates considered to have the most potential for tomorrow's top management positions can be expected to be sent abroad for at least three or four years.

A recent variation on job rotation practice is the assignment of Philips managers to our ventures with other companies. Those posted to these assignments have the opportunity to experience company cultures and practices different from their own. Transferring people in and out of these ventures contributes both to the individual's professional growth and to the expansion of the company's perspective as a whole.

In short, at Philips, we consider on-the-job training, coupled with multicultural experience, to be the best development tool we can provide.

In addition to job rotation, we also provide a variety of supplementary formal training programs. Unique to Philips is the *Octagon Program* for young, high-potential managers. Those selected to participate work together in teams of eight on an assigned problem outside their area of expertise. The problems are real situations within the company, and the analyses and eventual recommendations by the Octagons are intended to provide input to company decision-making. The program is intensive – lasting about six to eight months. Its purpose is to broaden the scope of understanding of the company, to increase appreciation of the interdependence of functions and disciplines, and to provide a cross-cultural forum for working together and exchanging ideas.

Internationalizing the Management Team

These management development practices relate closely to our goal of internationalising management. The performance and potential appraisal systems allow us to identify the best people in different countries, placing them in jobs where they are needed most. The job rotation practice leads to a rich exchange of perspectives. When you send a Norwegian to Brazil, a Pakistani to Singapore, or an American to the Netherlands, the cultural influences that are traded are bound to result in an international point of view in the company as a whole.

There are of course problems in managing such intercultural exchanges. These range from different salary levels in different countries to the cultural shocks of adjusting to different standards of living. It is always difficult for someone who has become accustomed to a higher standard of living to adjust downward when transferring to a country where salary levels and standards of living are lower. Tax laws of different countries directly affect the expatriate, sometimes adversely. In Europe, the move finally to integrate policies will alleviate many of the problems experienced in the past in cross-border mobility.

The very notion of job rotation and its impact on internationalization of the company is not without its problems. The interests of centralized, strategic planning can conflict with decentralized interests. For example, a "fast track" candidate who has been sent to Brazil may be doing an excellent job there. The Brazilian national organization wants to keep him forever. But the corporate staff bureau in its effort to meet the strategic goals for the company says that it is time to move our candidate back to Eindhoven to a product division. There can be a pull and tug in terms of whose interests are being served: the national organization's interests, which of course serve company interests on a more short-term basis, or the company's long-term strategic planning interests.

The resolution of these issues is part of the complexity of balancing all of the interests of an international company. Successful interaction between centralized and decentralized functions means that our managers must have the skills to adapt to the give and take, to the flow of shifting balances, as new and often unexpected situations arise. Human resource management can be thought of as the lubricant to help achieve that kind of flexibility.

HUMAN RESOURCE MANAGEMENT: A CRITICAL MANAGEMENT TOOL

Human resource management is still in its infancy as a formal management tool within companies, including Philips. Until recently most companies tended towards reactive, "crisis management" of their human resources. New macro-economic realities and recognition (as a result of both external and internal pressures) that people are a company's most valuable asset, has brought human resource management urgently into focus.

Human resource management can never be an exact or predictable activity, because we are dealing with individuals, all of whom are unique. But we recognise that we must give careful attention to our human resource planning and processes. Such strategies must support the strategic planning of the company as a whole, since without the right people in the right places at the right time, the long-term goals of the company cannot be achieved.

For multinational or global companies, the dynamics of changing situations and organizational complexities demand nothing less than the excellent management of their human resources.

Note

1. Dr George van Houten is a member of the corporate board of management of N. V. Philips Gloeilampenfabrieken.

*Chapter 7*_____

Managing Human Resources in the International Firm: Lessons From Practice

Paul Evans, Elizabeth Lank and Alison Farquhar

No less than twenty years ago, the international operations of most companies were largely export activities of ethnocentric organizations. Expatriate assignments spelt career doom, distancing the exile from the headquarter politics of a successful career. Surveys in the mid-70s of Fortune 100 companies revealed that 90% of top executives had no foreign experience. There were of course a few exceptions, notably the corporations that were transnational by origin like Shell and Unilever, and firms with most of their turnover outside the smaller mother country. How many consumers realize that Nestlé is in fact a Swiss firm, though only 2% of its sales and 4% of its employees are Swiss-based?

Yet the banner words today are "international" and "global". Once-protected national markets have become regional and international. The virtual abondonment to the Japanese of consumer electronics and the semi-conductor industry that were once dominated by the United States became a symbol of what was happening. Economies of scale and the globalization of markets argued for the internationalization of the corporation. Cost imperatives and direct foreign investment necessitated by local protection-ism compelled the transfer of manufacturing into other regions of the world.

Yet the consequences of these continuing changes for human resource management have still to be adequately digested.

The main challenge for human resource management is the way in which it can contribute to resolving the conflicting pressures within the corporation of centralization and decentralization. The priorities are twofold: finding practical ways to create an overarching corporate culture that integrates decentralized subsidiaries; and formulating policies to guide international executive development. The latter in turn raises a host of operational problems in administering management development, where we can benefit from the experience of pioneers. These three issues constitute the basis for this chapter.[1]

But first, it is important to point out that internationalization has had deeper consequences, affecting the concept of management itself. Deeply rooted "one-best-way" thinking has been shattered by the awareness that there are different and equally effective approaches to management and organization.

BEYOND THE ONE-BEST-WAY OF MANAGEMENT

Twenty years ago, "good management" was synonymous with the American approach. The wave of concern for management development that spread through Europe, Japan, and other countries was a catch up campaign on the "American Challenge". Yet just a decade later, it was a surprise even for the Americans to discover that another concept of management and organization, the Japanese approach, was equally if not more successful. We then discovered the "German Challenge", and today there is growing interest in uniquely Swedish and Swiss approaches to management – perhaps in part because these are small but successful nations long dependent on international business. We appear to be in the process of discovering that there are as many different approaches to management as there are national cultures (Hofstede, 1980a; Laurent, 1986).

Professor André Laurent of INSEAD maintains that each of these nations has discovered and built upon some aspect of the complex reality of management, though often this concern becomes obsessive and pathological. Few nations are more results-oriented than the United States, and insights such as "management-by-objectives" and "pay-for-performance" are uniquely American contributions to management practice. Yet the results-orientation of American corporations often leads to a short-term "quick-fix" mentality, where corporate decisions are overly influenced by the imperatives of the next quarter's results, and where enterprises are in the throes of implementing yesterday's fashionable concept only to have attention shift to today's magic panacea. In contrast, one of the strengths of Italian firms is their innovativeness and adaptability; and yet a concentration on creativity and ingenuity often overrides the establishment of structure and systems that large firms require in order to commercialize innovation in a profitable manner. The German concept of management appears to be associated with technical and functional expertise (rather than American-type managerial skill), part of the explanation for the renowned operating efficiency of German industry. But the German concern for expertise creates hierarchic firms that are incapable of the rapid change that is required in a growing number of industries. If we want to learn how to improve the quality of working life in order to unleash the human potential that we know exists in our firms, there is probably no better laboratory than Sweden. Yet once again, this concern for human potential sometimes becomes obsessive, leading to what the Danes next door call "the Swedish disease".

The appealing "one-best-way" assumption about management, the belief that different cultures are converging at different paces on the same concept of organization, is dying a slow death. It is an assumption that is deeply rooted in our thought processes, and the "excellence" movement launched by Tom Peters' and Bob Waterman's all-time bestseller *In Search of Excellence* (1982) is an example of how deeply it is anchored.

In Search of Excellence was not intended to be a bestseller. It originated in a study of excellent enterprises commissioned by two European giants (Shell and Siemens) from the business consultants at McKinsey. They wished to learn from the lessons of leading American firms in order to guide the management of their operations in the United States. Neither Shell nor Siemens was particularly impressed by the results of the study, but the American companies themselves were fascinated, and this led to the idea of writing up the study as a book. Tom Peters himself was surprised by its success, explaining it with hindsight: American firms were so beleaguered by the threat of Japanese and foreign competition that the concept of a home-based excellence formula struck a chord in people's minds. Today, as many of those "excellent" firms struggle with competitive threats, he believes that the book has had a negative effect, falsely comforting Americans with the message that "things are quite healthy on the home front. After all, we have the formula for excellence, and we don't have to worry about those Japanese". Paradoxically, the Japanese and Europeans may be in a stronger position than the Americans. Scared early by the American challenge, they have fewer illusions about their innate superiority. Moreover, they have had the opportunity to assimilate the best of American management into their own indigenous approaches (the Japanese appear to have succeeded particularly well).

Where cultural differences have been recognized, they are typically seen as a nuisance, a constraint, an obstacle to be surmounted. "We're a truly international company – we accept that our managers have to be trained in 'How to do business with the Saudis' ". The notion that cultural differences might be exploited for strategic advantage is more controversial. It is not surprising that Philips, from that nation of Dutch international traders, is a pioneer here. Philips is establishing centres of competence, once the preserve of the Eindhoven headquarters, in regions of the world where the culture best matches that competence. For example, their centre for long-range technology development was recently moved from the United States to the Far East, where the time orientation was seen as more conducive to innovation than the "quick fix" mentality of North America. Some major research departments are located in Italy, which is seen by other firms as an impossible country for important facilities. Yet their Italian research laboratories are highly successful, as are the important R & D facilities of IBM and Digital Equipment Corporation (DEC) in the same region. All of them run in a uniquely Italian way, and they are left to do so since this appears to lead to their success. Manufacturing plants, needless to say, are likely to be located elsewhere – Germany, for example.

THE CHALLENGE: MEETING THE CONFLICTING NEEDS OF CENTRALIZATION AND DECENTRALIZATION

Whatever the reasons for internationalizing – being close to local markets, cheaper manufacturing abroad, building a global business, or creating multinational centres of competence – they share the same accompanying problem: the difficulty of balancing the conflicting needs of centralization and decentralization.

Differences in distribution systems, price controls, labor legislation, as well as local government and consumer attitudes and the interests of employee motivation, are strong arguments for presenting a local face. And one of the best ways of maximizing financial returns internationally is to put profit responsibility clearly in the hands of local general managers. However, there are equally strong arguments for corporate loyalty and strategic control – the need to optimize corporate priorities which may be at odds with subsidiary interests, the necessity for control over strategic objectives, and the need to mobilize subsidiaries for global competitive strategies. When local control goes too far, global decisions are blocked by intersubsidiary rivalries and the "not-invented-here" syndrome.

Corporate control is natural in the early stages of internationalization, since subsidiaries depend on headquarters for resources – capital resources, technological know-how, skilled managerial and technical resources. But as subsidiaries become established, they develop these capacities themselves, and the task of corporate strategic control becomes more difficult (Doz and Prahalad, 1981).

The resulting dilemma is frequently experienced as a conflict. Yet this is a misguided way of viewing the problem, and leads to disconcerting swings in the control pendulum. Local sensitivity and corporate loyalty are both desirable, in degrees which vary from one business to another. They are in fact complementary orientations. The challenge is to find ways of providing the necessary corporate integration, ways that do not compromise the local responsiveness of the national business.

Philips, Shell, Moët-Hennessy, Nestlé, Unilever, Honeywell, BP, IBM, Air Liquide, Peat Marwick, Hewlett Packard . . . almost all of the leading international firms are decentralized, and their country businesses are sometimes viewed by local consumers and authorities as national citizens. Often they behave sufficiently like a domestic firm for their foreignness to be forgotten – historically a strength of Philips and Nestlé.

Taking Shell as an example, its decentralized structure was introduced in the early 60s, with the central offices retaining a role as an investment banker and centre of expertise available to operating companies. "It is because of this structure – and not in spite of it – that the different parts of Shell have had the freedom to develop their businesses in the light of local circumstances", says Sir Peter Baxendell, former chairman of Shell International. "Companies identify much more closely with the aims and aspirations of the societies in which they operate". Yet Baxendell adds that "decentralization has to be balanced by some cohesive influences to prevent the Group breaking up into its component parts".

The matrix organizations adopted by many multinational corporations (MNCs) in the 70s were one attempt to reach a balance. Decision-making became the joint responsibility of local subsidiary and corporate managers (product division and corporate staff executives). The results were often disappointing, the matrix leading to slower decision-making, increased administrative costs, and widespread frustration at lack of clear responsibility. Many of our leading organizations still have such matrix structures or informal matrix overlays, though the search has been for other more "subtle" mechanisms (as Professor Yves Doz of INSEAD calls them) to provide cohesiveness and balance. In any case, we now realize that matrix structures require matrix minds and matrix cultures to make them function effectively.

Strategic management processes facilitate the balance, as do data management systems aided by powerful computers and the speedy transmission of information. But these "hard" tools of integration and control need attention to the "soft" aspects of integration to make them work. This brings us to the domain of human resource management. Attention in recent years has been focused, with varying degrees of success, on integrating the decentralized firm in more soft and subtle ways – first, through programs to create an overriding corporate culture, and second, through international executive development.

CREATING AN INTERNATIONAL CORPORATE CULTURE

The deputy head of personnel at Unilever sums up both the need for a corporate culture and the difficulties of creating it:

I don't think we could run Unilever without some kind of corporate culture. It is terribly important that people around the world feel themselves part of a Unilever culture without conflict with the fact that they feel fully Indian, Italian, Spanish or whatever. But I think that when you have reached the stage of having to articulate your culture and produce a sort of creed, you are a long way down a slippery slope. Culture ought to emerge from specific actions, and sometimes you have to take very specific actions to make it clear that you are changing the culture.

Academics refer to corporate culture as *normative control*, a form of control rooted in shared norms and values that is deeper and more subtle than administrative control mechanisms such as rules and reporting relationships. Yet creating these shared values is a difficult process. Five distinct elements of this process have emerged from the experience of the firms we studied:

- A clear and simple *mission statement*.
- The *vision* of the chief executive officer.
- *Management education*.
- *Project oriented* management programs.
- The process of building a *corporate charter*.

A *clear and simple mission statement* and corporate objectives that can be understood by all are important aspects of this process. ICL, the British computer company, strongly believes that policy statements should be short and general enough to accommodate local adaptation. The management development manager explains:

We were looking for a statement as brief as possible that would say something about ICL that would have meaning to people wherever they were in the world. The resulting mission statement was that ICL wanted "To become an international company dedicated to applying information technology to provide profitable high-value customer solutions for improved operational and management effectiveness".

With losses of £15 million in 1981, ICL was not far away from the wall. After a successful turnaround, top management felt that the foundations for a new corporate culture had to be created. A framework of ten management obligations were developed, published as *The ICL Way* and communicated throughout the organization. Some examples are:

- You must be as effective at managing people as you are at managing your business.
- You should encourage a "can-do" attitude, thinking of opportunities, not problems.

- You ought to strive consciously for improvement and innovation.

IBM also believes that simple and shared objectives are the crux of maintaining a corporate culture, though there is more emphasis at IBM on assessing the results. The company restricts itself to three basic beliefs and four goals. The goals, relating to profit, quality, efficiency, and growth, are all measurable, and numerical targets are used as benchmarks. As far as the human resource function is concerned, the principle of simple objectives is also followed. They number three – "attract, motivate and retain" – and for each a system of measurement has been defined.

Honeywell believes in "keeping it simple". Michael Bonsignore, President of Honeywell Europe, explains why:

> Our challenge is to overcome the cultural and communication differences that divide us, and ensure that every one of our employees knows how he or she can participate in the growth and prosperity of the corporation. To facilitate this sense of ownership at all levels of Honeywell, we have attempted to develop a corporate culture that accommodates the wide range of national cultures where we operate. For starters, we developed a statement of purpose that all employees could understand.

The *vision of a chief executive officer* (CEO) and his or her ability to communicate it is a second aspect of creating a common corporate culture (see Chapter 3). Examples of strong "vision" holders are John Harvey Jones of ICI, Carlo de Benedetti of Olivetti, Pehr Gyllenhammar of Volvo, Alain Chevalier of Moët-Hennessy, Jack Welsh of General Electric. But despite the fashionable concern with the vision of the "transformational leader", large international firms question how powerful this is in securing integration, since the CEO is a distant figure for most employees.

Company-controlled *management education* is a third tool, typically through courses where the objective is to create a common language and shared attitudes. IBM's policy of a minimum of one week per year of training and development for each manager has contributed greatly to its strong global culture. Ericsson and Olivetti have recently created management development centres where the participants are executives from all regions of the world; in both cases the centre is symbolically located in Britain rather than in Sweden or Italy. Honeywell's European Management Development Centre in Brussels also has the objective of shaping a common management approach to business. Kone, the Finnish elevator company, created an in-company top management program more than a decade ago as a vehicle to build a common culture from the diverse cultures of local companies they had acquired.

Indeed, it was the need for a forum for management education that motivated two leading multinational companies, Nestlé and Alcan, to sponsor the creation of IMEDE and IMI respectively (both in Switzerland) –

which with INSEAD constitute the three international management insti-
tutes in Europe. As the personnel director of Nestlé (himself a former
director of IMEDE) notes, the majority of their managers worldwide have
spent some time at IMEDE, helping to form an overriding corporate
culture. And the European Centre for Continuing Education (CEDEP) on
the INSEAD campus was founded in 1970 by a club of diversifying
enterprises in order to create a critical mass of managers sharing the same
language – or what we today would call a common corporate culture.

Project-oriented management programs go further than management
education in creating a common culture. The "strategic capability program"
at ICL is an example. As ICL came out of its crisis in the early 80s, a new
matrix structure of decentralized, market-oriented business centres was put
into operation. Making this work not only required new attitudes and a
shared vision, but also the drive to implement the strategy. The vehicle for
building that drive was the capability program, run and taught by academics
from London and Michigan. This four-tiered program of week-long
seminars, twenty people at a time, was targeted for the top 2,000 managers.
It was a major investment – but even the sceptics came to recognize its
worth. As a marketing director said, "It blew my mind at the huge gap
between where we were and where we needed to be. I came off it totally
hooked on what had to be done, but even more despairing than before at the
fact that ICL was in trouble and didn't realise it". The personnel department
saw the major benefit as the creation of a common language among
managers from different functions and countries, most of whom had never
even met before: "It has created much more cohesion in the way we deal
with strategic and organizational issues".

There appear to be four reasons why this ICL program has had such an
impact, all suggesting that there is no cheap solution to culture creation.
First, the program was actively led by the top, though the idea and
responsibility was that of the management development department.
Second, the academic team teaching the seminar immersed themselves for
months in ICL and its problems. Third, the seminar focused on key industry
issues and strategic concepts rather than on general techniques. And fourth,
it was attended by virtually all ICL managers, starting off at the very top, in
cascading tiers over an eighteen-month period.

Many companies have developed charters, credos, and cultural statements with the objective of creating corporate glue. All too frequently,
these are patched together by the executive committee or a working panel,
and the resulting statements have little effect. The ICL experience
emphasizes that it is the *process* that builds the culture, not the statements
themselves – and this was also the earlier experience of Lafarge–Coppée.

Diversification and internationalization in the late 60s had led to a loss of
identity at Lafarge, the world's third largest cement producer. With major
operations in Canada and Brazil and newly-acquired but loss-making

activities in sanitary ware and plaster products, what did the company stand for? In 1976 Olivier Lecerf, the new CEO, launched an eighteen-month round of discussions among the top hundred executives, leading to a corporate charter of values, missions, policies, and objectives known as "The Principles of Action". What these discussions above all achieved was a shared *modus operandi* for headquarters–subsidiary relations, which went beyond formally stated issues of structure (centralization of strategy, co-ordination of know-how, and decentralization of operations). Norms of persuasion and dialogue, as opposed to command or avoidance, were established by the process of mutual dialogue during these eighteen months, norms that have guided the evolution of the company since.

The most valuable lesson that came from this experience was the positive benefit of directly involving managers from both headquarters and subsidiary companies in the process of building a shared corporate culture. In the words of a senior Lafarge executive, "Those who were deeply involved in the development of the Principles, whether as supporters or initially as cynics, have translated the Principles into action. This isn't true for others who simply went through the motions".

Below senior management, each division or subsidiary was to develop its own Principles of Action, adapting policies and objectives around a core of common values. The process has been applied somewhat unevenly, and again the resulting cohesion and mobilization of action was proportionate to the investment in the process. The successful integration of a Brazilian subsidiary and of acquired companies in the plaster division illustrated the process working at its best. But in one country, the Principles were introduced at a two-hour meeting, and few were surprised to see that they flopped.

Overall, it is clear that the five elements summarized on p. 118 only scratch the surface of the problem of creating an overarching corporate culture. The "culture building" programs much in vogue in the early 80s led to disappointing results, and the intensive investment they require has typically limited them to senior management groups. Although cultural integration may be set in motion by programs such as those described here, it is only through careful attention to international executive development that this integration is achieved, step-by-step.

INTERNATIONAL EXECUTIVE DEVELOPMENT

Identifying and developing potential leaders is a particular priority for the international firm – recent surveys by INSEAD and by the Conference Board suggest that it is the top corporate priority for international human resource management these days (Evans, 1983).

Chief executives who espouse the importance of management development are perhaps in a majority today, rather than a minority. As Graham Corbett, senior partner for Peat Marwick's Continental European practice puts it, "We are on a fast growth track, and our major task is to attract and develop enough professional talent to enable us to support the growth rates we are experiencing". Even a sophisticated firm like IBM has found that the lack of management talent has been a major inhibitor in setting up businesses or developing new projects, in some cases actually preventing them from actioning projects which they mastered technically.

At firms like ICI, British Petroleum (BP), and Philips, board level attention to human resources has gradually shifted from a focus on industrial relations to a focus on international executive development. The corporate board of ICI has essentially two tasks today: major investment and strategic decision-making on the one hand, and the management of key human resources on the other.[2]

Expatriate assignments are notoriously expensive these days, and the reasons behind international executive development are changing, as Unilever's head of management development states:

> Over the years, the reasons for wanting expatriates have changed. Originally, the reason was usually that you didn't have a local who could do the job, so let's find somebody who has the skills. That still happens, but a further feeling has grown that the most able managers ought to get international experience because they are going to hold top jobs; therefore they need experience of working in different cultures. In recent years, I have had several product group directors who said that they would like an expatriate on the board of their local company. Not just because they haven't got a national, not just because it would be good for the expatriate, but because it would be good for the company to have a bit of challenge to the one-best-way of doing things.

The original need behind international transfers was for specific skills that local labor markets did not supply, complemented by control reasons. To this was added the need to find career opportunities for a new generation of bright and ambitious managers, no longer content to remain in their jobs until their bosses moved on or retired. This was reinforced in the late 60s as modern attitudes to management development took root. Paul Evans's own research has shown that a managerial orientation is best developed through mobility The authority of younger managers is typically based on the technical or functional expertise they have acquired. When cross-functional mobility leads them into posts where they assume responsibility for people with more expertise than themselves, they begin to develop the managerial skills and attitudes in "getting results through the expertise of others" that are indispensible in general management (Evans, 1975). The experience they acquire in different geographic regions, functions, and divisions also provides them with a hands-on feel for their businesses.

Management development will become more and more important, as Shell's Sir Peter Baxendell emphasizes:

> The word summarizing today's business outlook is uncertainty, and the response must be flexibility. For a complex, international, multifunctional organization like the Shell Group, the prerequisite for flexibility is a highly skilled, mobile, international body of staff.

International mobility appears to serve another less recognized, but vital, function. The research of academic scholars has pointed out the role of international transfers in developing organizational capabilities. Edstrom and Galbraith (1977) compared the transfer policies of four international firms, observing that one of the firms (Shell) was markedly different; it transferred employees in far greater numbers, more frequently, and at all levels. They observed that this had created what one might call a "nervous system" that facilitated both corporate strategic control and the flow of information throughout the firm. Widespread transfers had created an informal information network, a superior degree of communication and mutual understanding between headquarters and subsidiaries and between subsidiaries themselves, as well as a stronger identification with the corporate culture, without compromising the local subsidiary cultures.

Labeling this as "control through socialization". Edstrom and Galbraith contrast it with more traditional but cumbersome bureaucratic forms of control used by the other three companies studied – procedures, hierarchical communication, and surveillance. More recently, their observations have been reinforced by the findings of Prahalad and Doz (1987), whose studies of multinationals suggest that subtle, informal forms of control such as management development and conflict-resolution devices (task forces) are most effective in established multinational operations. International executive development not only develops the individual capabilities of managers, but also the integrative capabilities of the organization.

Chapter 8 in this book describes further how integrative pressures in many industries are leading international executive development to figure among the foremost priorities of strategic development. Meanwhile, let us turn to consider how companies actually manage executive development.

Cultural Traditions in Management Development

There is no established one-best-way of tackling management development. Focusing on the development of those persons with high potential, we can observe different traditions in different organizations, as Brooke Derr showed in an INSEAD-sponsored survey into the meaning of "potential" in European corporations (Derr, 1987). To map out these traditions, we have labeled them with national stereotypes – the Japanese model, the Latin European approach, the Germanic tradition, and the Anglo-Dutch model (see Figure 7.1). There is great diversity in American patterns, which are consequently omitted. These are only stereotypes, for some American firms are highly "Latin" in their approach, while other European firms follow the Japanese pattern.

The Japanese model that emerged in large companies like Matsushita, Sanyo, and Nissan after the Second World War is based on the recruitment of elite cohorts and a competitive tournament of elimination, leading the winners into executive positions. The educational system in Japan is a progressive filtering of elite achievers, and it is from the select few at Tokyo and other top universities that high-potential individuals are recruited. Management potential is thus identified on a person's entry into the company.

For the first five to eight years of the career, there is no further screening. The cohort (referring to the graduate recruits of a particular year) is rotated through various responsibilities (at Nissan they spend the first few months on the assembly line), complemented by intensive training. But the performance of these elite recruits is constantly monitored by a powerful corporate personnel office (this happens six times annually at Nissan). All are promoted equally on the basis of seniority; at this trial stage of the career, it is recognized that performance may vary with the ease or difficulty of the assignment or the boss.

It is after this early test and socialization period that the competitive tournament begins. In this next phase of the career, the competition follows a rigid schedule. Those whose performance and potential are assessed as highest will be promoted every four years, while the "failures" will receive that same promotion only after a longer period. To remain in the tournament, one must be promoted every fourth or fifth year. Indeed in many firms (with some exceptions like Honda), a single failure to be promoted after the fourth year implies that one is out of the running for a job as division head at the height of one's career – the maximum to which one can aspire is a functional position.

What happens to those who are promoted only after eight years, or who are promoted twice after a six-year period? This is tantamount to being labeled as a failure – one is out of the tournament. These persons become "staff managers", assigned to less important positions (in the extreme they are known as "window-watchers"). They are encouraged to leave the firm to make a career for themselves before it is too late in the "other" Japan – that of smaller or medium-sized industry, or in the foreign multinationals.[3]

It is a highly competitive system, where widely held beliefs about Japanese life-long employment and seniority-based promotion are distorted clichés of the reality. Most firms apply the system to their foreign subsidiaries, and if the shop floor climate of Japanese factories abroad has a favourable public image, the managerial development system tends to be viewed as alien.

It is the structure of management development in Latin Europe that most approximates that of the Japanese, though without the systematic tracking of cohorts. Taking France as an example, selection of potential top managers also takes place at entry, mostly on the basis of elite educational qualifications. Studies have shown that the graduates of the three top "Grandes Ecoles" (the elite engineering schools) who chose an industrial career had a 90% probability of landing up as president of a company: the only open question was the size and importance of the company (Granick, 1972; Sainsaulieu, 1977). Laurent (1986) discovered that even in the French subsidiary of an American multinational, being labelled early as an individual of high potential was viewed as *the* critical career success factor, whereas success in other countries was more linked to personal qualities or achievements.

The career progression of these individuals is a tournament as in Japan, though one that is more political and without systematic norms. It is a competitive struggle of achievement, selling of oneself, and building alliances that is captured by the social game theory of the French sociologist Michel Crozier, though subtly combined with the camaraderie of association with a mafia of fellow peers.

The Germanic tradition (embracing to some extent Switzerland and certain Scandinavian and Dutch firms) is different, with a tradition of formal apprenticeship and more attachment to functional career paths. Apprenticeship is a well-rooted historic Germanic tradition for skilled and blue-collar employees: a two- to five-year period of on-the-job training, courses on company practices and policies, and training in partnership with local technical or trade schools. Yet even graduates undergo a two-year "apprenticeship", a period of job rotation through the enterprise accompanied by training. This has the dual purpose of providing broad exposure to the company and of finding the function or type of job most suited to the individual. In his late twenties, the person will be guided into the appropriate function, where he acquires progressively greater and greater expertise, moving up through that hierarchy. For those with the depth of education that is provided by a doctoral diploma in particular, this may ultimately lead into a board level position.

But just as there are two industrial Japans, the Zaibatsu concerns and the lesser firms, so there are two Germanies, that of the large established firms and that of the smaller sized companies; and two Frances, that of the establishment and that of the self-made entrepreneurs. In Germany, our research has shown that certain individuals find the functional or technical orientation of "big business" to be unattractive, leaving for positions in

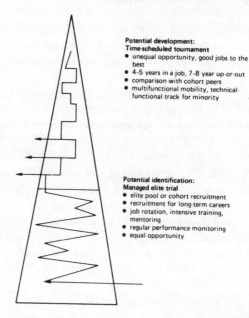

FIGURE 7–1a
Elite Cohort Approach to Management Development: the "Japanese"
Model

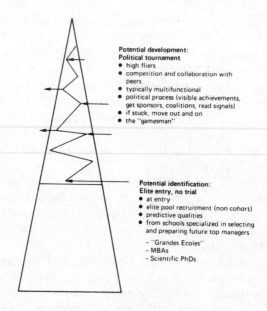

FIGURE 7–1b
Elite Political Approach to Management Development: the "Latin" Model

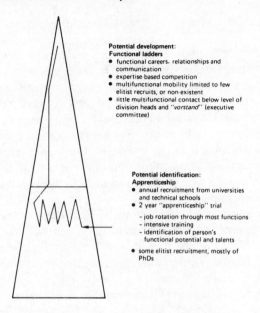

Potential development:
Functional ladders
- functional careers, relationships and communication
- expertise-based competition
- multifunctional mobility limited to few elitist recruits, or non-existent
- little multifunctional contact below level of division heads and *"vorstand"* (executive committee)

Potential identification:
Apprenticeship
- annual recruitment from universities and technical schools
- 2 year "apprenticeship" trial
  - job rotation through most functions
  - intensive training
  - identification of person's functional potential and talents
- some elitist recruitment, mostly of PhDs

FIGURE 7–1c
Functional Approach to Management Development: the "Germanic" Model

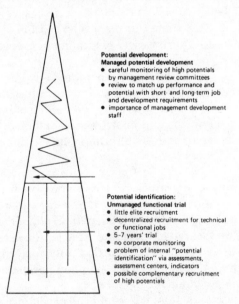

Potential development:
Managed potential development
- careful monitoring of high potentials by management review committees
- review to match up performance and potential with short- and long-term job and development requirements
- importance of management development staff

Potential identification:
Unmanaged functional trial
- little elite recruitment
- decentralized recruitment for technical or functional jobs
- 5-7 years' trial
- no corporate monitoring
- problem of internal "potential identification" via assessments, assessment centers, indicators
- possible complementary recruitment of high potentials

FIGURE 7–1d
Managed Development Approach to Management Development: the "Anglo–Dutch" Model

smaller companies where responsibilities are more generalist in nature.

The generalist notion of management development is most rooted in the Anglo-Saxon culture, and in some Dutch firms, joined more recently by the Scandinavians. Entry is less elitist, with most graduate employees being recruited for specific technical or functional jobs. At Shell, some 80% of the graduate intake have technical qualifications, with a slightly lower percentage at ICI or Exxon; 99% of all IBM executives have come from non-management entry positions. Entry on a "Germanic"-type job rotation program is favored by some other firms recruiting for life-long careers (though today this runs into problems in that the best graduates appear to want to begin with a real job).

During the early career years (about the first eight years at ICI), these graduates are expected to perform and climb in their functional or technical hierarchies. At Marks & Spencer, it is a climb up to the position of store manager, a job that every senior manager in principle must have proven that he or she can master. Performance evaluation in these western countries is less systematic than in Japan, and the parallel notion of a testing period is implicit rather than explicit.

Around the age of thirty, after these testing years, the human resource management problem is to identify those individuals who have "potential", usually synonymous with some notion of generalist or general management potential. Since Japanese-style systematic performance appraisal is less traditional and less appropriate (for there is no concept of tracking an elite cohort), companies resort to a variety of techniques for the identification of potential.

The age at which potential should be identified is a problematic issue. On the one hand, individuals should have time to prove themselves in the technical or functional ladders where they entered. Yet on the other hand, the experience requirements for tomorrow's generation of executives make a persuasive argument for early identification, as a senior executive of IBM puts it:

> This early identification is critical because if you work backwards from the chief executive job or any other key job, recognizing in our case that executives retire at sixty, then you have to get them there in their early fifties if you want them to have a reasonable period in that job. You can work backwards and you have to say that if they have not got beyond a certain stage in their career by a certain point in time, then you have to assume they will not attain the top jobs.
>
> It's not age discrimination, it is what I call experience discrimination. I have looked at all the top people in our corporation, and they have all managed major divisions while still in their thirties.

Managers are often so strong about defending people in their function that in fact they defend them out of the executive system. By holding them too long they have deprived them of the opportunity, because you physically cannot get the necessary experience in the time that is left.

Exxon learnt the same lesson when they discovered that the majority of their executives had started their careers at one of their two refinery breeding grounds in the United States. Why was Baton Rouge supplying a disproportionate amount of executive talent? Did it have something to do with their policies and practices, with a work climate or structure that was more propitious to management development? In fact they found only one difference between the two refineries – at Baton Rouge, management potential was being identified at the age of twenty-seven to twenty-eight, while at the other refinery it was identified in the individual's early thirties. The result is understandable: imagine that there are two talented candidates for a country manager position, each in their early forties and each with outstanding track records. However, one of them has eight years of international and multifunctional experience, while the other has fifteen years. Who does one naturally choose . . . ?

The understandable trend in the United States since the late 60s (and more recently in Britain and among some continental multinational companies) is toward earlier identification of potential, even at entry level. For some US firms, the MBA diploma has become an entry ticket into the high-potential development ladder, thus leading toward the elitist entry pattern of Japanese and Latin companies. Other firms have invested in assessment centers, a concept pioneered by AT&T: two–three day simulations of managerial situations where the performance and qualities of aspirants can be observed and evaluated by pyschologists and trained managers. These have developed widely in Britain, and in 1983 were being used by some 17% of major British firms (Hunt, 1984). The National Westminster Bank uses them to identify "E" or "exceptional track" graduate banking recruits. Marks & Spencer, faced with the need to develop rapidly a more analytic and dynamic generation of executives for the turbulent retailing industry, was sceptical about recruiting MBAs with high levels of ambition but little hands-on retailing experience. They chose to invest £2 million in developing a selection centre to screen graduate recruits for faster track careers. Meanwhile, recruitment is booming at the three European MBA programs of INSEAD, IMI and IMEDE.

The tradeoffs between potential identification at entry level or after some years of proven technical or functional experience are hotly argued, and there is little hard data that allows one rationally to take sides. While the experience logic is clear, the cynics argue that early assessment is inevitably faulty, likely to lead to a significant number of problem cases, mid-career failures trapped in "golden cages".

The development system for those who have been identified as having potential varies considerably among these Anglo-Saxon, Dutch, and Scandinavian firms. In some companies the timetable for success is more programmed than in Japan: at Exxon, the individual changes jobs every eighteen–twenty-four months and must have reached a certain level of responsibility by the age of forty. At others it is far less programmed. The development structure may be elitist, leading to the politics of promotion among "walk-on-water golden high potentials" that has been well analyzed by Rosabeth Kanter in her *Men and Women of the Corporation* (1977). At others, it is intensively managed by a management review process.

Managing the Development of International Managers

Administering the development of managers in international firms is fraught with operational tradeoffs and problems. Some important lessons can be learned from the experience of some of the leading edge companies mentioned in this chapter.

How many managers to focus upon?

The task of managing managers is typically focused upon key position holders and those with the potential to occupy such positions. But how do we define a "key position holder", and how widely should the potential dragnet be spread?

The scope of corporately monitored international executive development varies widely. Philips was one of the European firms who recognized the importance of this early on (in the late 60s), and its Corporate Staff Bureau focuses on all senior managers above a certain level – some 2,000 key positions in a firm of 340,000 employees – with particular attention paid to the top 150 persons. Additionally, the system monitors all managers at the level immediately below senior management plus those who have the assessed potential to reach this level of responsibility: some 6,000–7,000 "high potentials". There is also a special monitoring responsibility for all 1,500 expatriate managers and professionals.[4]

"Executive resources" at IBM encompasses all general managers and the people who report directly to them, as well as major function heads. The succession plan dominates the process at IBM, and the potential net is less widespread; in a firm of a similar size to Philips, about 2,000 managers out of 400,000 (less than 1% of total employees) are closely tracked.

Shell, with its 140,000 employees, monitors the careers of perhaps the largest percentage of managers with a corporate group of personnel planners. Shell strongly believes in the importance of multifunctional and international experience, and broadly speaking the aim is that every member of an operating company management team should have had international experience and that each such team should include at least one expatriate – recent examples being a Columbian production manager in Spain, a Malaysian general manager in Saudi Arabia, and an Omani chief engineer in Norway. About 10,000 individuals are centrally monitored on the reference list, which links with 5,000 expatriates. A major part of the work of the personnel planners is to keep these opportunities open in the face of increasing constraints, such as reduced mobility of staff, more complex chains of moves as operating and service companies become leaner, and difficulties with local work permits.

At Unilever management development encompasses the top 2,000 (plus increasing monitoring of those lower down with high potential), while the numbers are smaller at other firms – 600 individuals at the divisional manager level and high fliers with that potential at BP, 300 at Migros in Switzerland, 400 executive level persons (many of whom have international experience) at ICI.

The arguments for extensive international management development must be balanced by considerations of cost, both the direct costs of expatriate expenses and the considerable administrative costs. But there is another argument for conservatism. If at a mid-career stage the individual proves not to have the necessary motivation or skill, a "golden cage" may have been created, problematic for both that person and the firm.

The "golden cage" is our term for the dilemma of the forty-year old high-potential manager who has typically worked in four countries and two divisions of the firm, with experience in three different functional areas. Paradoxically, this person's career may have become locked into the company. Half of his or her knowledge and skill is company-specific, unsaleable on the outside labor market if employment is terminated. By contrast, the "lower-potential" functional manager who has worked only in one country and one industry is more likely to have a saleable toolkit of expertise and knowledge that can readily be transferred to a smaller competitor in the community.

The evaluation of potential

During the trial period of management development in what we have styled the "Japanese" model, the focus is on rigorous performance assessment, leading to an initial evaluation of potential. This is different from most western approaches, where there is an ingrained distinction between performance and potential. Rightly or wrongly, and justifiably or otherwise, the "Peter Principle" is widely accepted as a truism in western cultures: since the management structure is intransitive (the skills required at one level differ from those at the next), high-performing individuals at one rank will not necessarily be competent two ranks above.

Consequently, the notion of "ultimate potential" – a prediction of the ultimate level which a person is likely to reach at the height of his or her career – is more widespread in the west. The individuals assessed as having high ultimate potential are placed on generalist development tracks, and this judgement is confirmed or disproved by their performance in the subsequent tournament. This raises the question: what success factors or personal qualities are good predictors of ultimate potential?

One firm that has rigorously tackled the question of defining success factors is Shell, where "currently estimated potential" (CEP) is regularly reviewed. An executive, Dr Herman Muller, undertook in the late 60s a careful study of the qualities associated with ultimate potential, in collaboration with the Dutch psychologist David Van Lennep. They used evaluations of the CEP of nearly 3,000 Shell managers and separate assessments of the same people on 28 personal qualities that are often associated with potential.

The results were striking. Much of the variation in judgements about an individual's potential boiled down to their assessments on four qualities:

- a sense of imagination;
- a sense of reality;
- the individual's power of analysis;
- the "helicopter quality", or capacity of the person to envision facts and problems in a wider context.

What appeared to distinguish the high-potential individuals at Shell was their capacity to see the big picture, to imagine the latent possibilites in a given situation, and yet at the same time to grasp detailed facts, realities, and constraints – linking the two through their analytic skill into constructive action (Muller, 1970). The so-called "helicopter quality" was the strongest correlate of estimated potential.

Shell's system for identifying management potential has been adopted in a pure or modified form by many organizations, including the Singapore Government. However, other enterprises either prefer a more open process or one that is less closely related to the notion of ultimate potential. Shell today is also moving toward a more open conception, involving a wider range of qualities and competencies.

Philips is a case in point, where four criteria are used to guide (though not slavishly restrict) managerial judgements of potential:

1. *Conceptual Effectiveness* (vision, synthesis, professional knowledge, business directedness).
2. *Operational Effectiveness* (individual effectiveness, decisiveness, control).
3. *Interpersonal Effectiveness* (network directedness, negotiating power, personal influence, verbal behavior).

4. *Achievement Motivation* (ambition, professional interest, emotional control).

In most firms, the basic judgements on the potential of a person are made by the bosses, the middle managers who know the individuals best. Whatever the success criteria used to identify potential, Edgar Schein of Massachusetts Institute of Technology maintains that middle managers have little realistic knowledge of the requirements of distant executive positions. He argues against the prevailing concept of ultimate potential, advocating two-step suitability for promotion as a more operational and pragmatic concept: the appraised ability of an individual not only to occupy his boss's job, but a job one level above this. And indeed the Exxon Corporation has moved in recent years toward such a concept, where potential is assessed as one, two, or three promotability levels.

In the complex discussion about guiding success criteria, a basic, pragmatic question is sometimes forgotten. Potential often boils down to willingness to be transferred. Indeed, with the developmental emphasis on mobility at Shell, this is an important supplementary criterion in the estimation of potential. At Marks & Spencer, the contract is clear; high-potential individuals have to be willing to move home and family to a department store in a different geographic region each year if necessary. And if you don't like that contract, then M&S is not the firm for you.

How should the judgements of line managers be assimilated into final evaluations as to who has what degree of potential? Whatever their differences, a common feature of IBM, Philips, and Exxon is their attachment to a comparative ranking system.

Exxon advocates multiple appraisal in reaching judgements about potential, arguing that the collective judgement of many individuals is more reliable than the judgement of a few, even guided by the "best" of criteria. The way the ranking system works is that each manager receives a stack of cards once a year, each indicating the name of a subordinate or working colleague – there may be fifty or more such cards. The manager has to rank these cards in order of appraised potential of the persons. A computer analysis of these judgements is undertaken, providing the initial input into a more qualitative management review process.

Seriation rankings are employed by Philips, where high-potential managers in positions of comparable responsibility are ranked in groups of six on the four criteria mentioned above. On the basis of a summary, the appraiser is asked to give a final ranking to the six people. A similar process is undertaken for other comparable groups of six employees, leading then to the ranking of the six "number ones", which ultimately becomes the basis for the review process.

The management review process

In these Western organizations, the crux of potential management is the review process where senior line managers meet with the appropriate personnel staff to consider the progression of high-potential individuals and to decide upon appropriate assignments or development actions. Without such a review process, the quantitative rankings would become mechanical. Without it, the judgements on assignments would become haphazard or political.

In large firms this is a formalized committee process, with a cascading tier of committees going down the hierarchy, starting with the top corporate committee chaired by the CEO. At Shell, for example, the key strategic group is the Committee of Managing Directors, who meet once a week to decide upon major investments and strategic plans. However, once a month this group turns itself into the Management Development Committee in order to discuss human resources, including a review of the progress of key people and discussion on succession planning for senior positions. In this way, the Committee can also focus on the *implementation* of its strategic plans. At IBM, the analogous body is known as the Executive Resources Committee, at Exxon it is the Employee Development Committee. Pragmatically, the question of who has potential boils down to those individuals who are subject to review by these committees.

A common pitfall for firms that are beginning to tackle potential identification and development is that this review task lands up as the functional responsibility of the personnnel department. The responsibility for management development *must* lie with line executives, as in these review committees (with the management development officer playing a support role). Where there is uneven or token acceptance by senior line executives of the importance of management development, the system is unlikely to function effectively.

Indeed, management development involves tradeoffs that only line managers can decide upon – tradeoffs between investing in potential and in performance, between the operating needs of today and the strategic needs of tomorrow, between the conflicting needs of different subsidiaries and divisions for scarce qualified human resources. For example, there may be a tough choice between two candidates for a position as purchasing director. One is a purchasing specialist who would retire in this position, but who might quit the firm if not offered the job. The other is a high potential manager whose effectiveness as a possible division head would be increased by two years in this role. The line executives in these review committees are intimately familiar with both the operating and strategic plans of the firm, and they alone are in a position to make the necessary tradeoffs and choices on dilemmas such as this.

Major assignment and developmental decisions are the result of such a review process – getting the right people into the right place with long-term strategic goals as well as short-term imperatives in mind – and the committees typically come to constitute the arena for organizational planning and human resource policy making.

Three Problem Areas in Executive Development

The cloning danger

Success in the task of developing executive resources creates its own problems. The firms that are most professional in dealing with these issues face the risk of cloning, of becoming over-professional in developing managers, a problem of which Exxon, IBM, Unilever, Hewlett–Packard, Shell, and ICI are today fully conscious. As an Exxon manager put it, the people who move into senior executive positions all come to behave and think alike, each one a clone of the other. The organization is in danger of losing the variety and diversity of views among its managerial ranks that is the lifeblood of vitality, change, and dynamism.

Many people today advocate strong corporate cultures, the glue which unites the people in its far flung operations. But Hewlett–Packard feels that this can go too far. Research by INSEAD's André Laurent suggested that among dozens of firms he studied, Hewlett–Packard was the company that demonstrated the strongest corporate culture, to the point of virtually overriding national cultural differences. Far from being flattered, the firm seems to have interpreted this as a danger signal of over-homogenization, particularly in the light of the difficulties it faced when it attempted to move from its business base in instruments to the new field of computers.

We discovered a similar concern at IBM in the late 70s, when IBM began to send managers to INSEAD executive programs after a decade of absence. When asked why, they told us that feedback from their managers indicated that there were symptoms of sterilizing inbreeding, as a result of their policy of in-company training. Their managers were coming to INSEAD again not so much to share our academic pearls of business wisdom, but more to trade views with managers from other corporate cultures, nations, and industries – in one phrase, to be "positively contaminated"!

Sacrificing performance for potential

There is also a risk, especially in firms which choose to develop ultimate potential, that success here leads to sacrifices in performance. In focusing on the "critical few", the development of the 90% of solid performers with more limited potential may be compromised. The majority start to feel neglected as second-class citizens. Separating the management of performance from that of potential, and learning how to develop the valuable individuals who do not have high ultimate potential, is one of the major current challenges.

The dangers became strikingly clear for a major international company as the result of an internal study of the relationship between performance and age. The results showed that the appraised performance of senior managers peaked on average in their early forties and declined thereafter, while that of engineers reached its ceiling in their late thirties! Does this imply that most individuals reach the limits of their capacities at so-called mid-career, if not before? Does it mean that engineers are obsolescent after fifteen working years?

Closer examination showed that this was not the explanation. What had happened was that over the years the corporation had come to be driven by an obsession with developing executive potential. The interesting projects, the top training programs, the incentives and rewards, the praise and attention were all being channeled toward those individuals with high ultimate potential. This resulted in a damaging tautology, where the forty-five year old employee with lower "potential" than the thirty-five year old, being nearer the peak of his or her career, saw the rewards, the interesting assignments, and the training go to the younger individuals, and felt like a second-class citizen. The result was a self-fulfilling prophecy, whereby actual performance began to suffer through demotivation.

It is a danger that Tom Allen comments upon later in Chapter 10, with some provocative data from engineers, scientists, and managers. We may over-estimate the number of people who have hierarchical and managerial ambitions, he argues, and create viscious circles of our own making. In focusing too narrowly on developing executive potential (a role that is attractive to only a small minority of professionals), we may compromise the development and the performance of the vast majority of professional employees in our firms.

At this same multinational, the growing criticism of middle managers initiated a process of change. They complained that their inputs on individuals tended to be disregarded in the development plans unless the person appeared at the top of the potential lists. The result has been a total separation of the two assessment and development systems relating to job performance and management potential respectively. Judgements on job performance should be based on a comparison of the individual and the job requirements, while potential evaluations should be based on comparing the person with others. At this firm, the former is based on supervisor judgement, while the latter is founded on multiple assessment. The evaluations of job performance are not normalized, while potential judgements are reached through ranking and are normalized. Job performance appraisals should be communicated and shared, while potential is a more secretive judgement, communicated only on request in compliance with local legislation.

Steady recruitment

Statistics in most firms undoubtedly show a strong relationship between annual operating results and recruitment. One recruits when one has the cash, when the going is good; when there is a downturn, the first budget to be cut is often that of recruitment and headcount.

As a senior Philips executive sees it, this short-term logic leads to longer-term problems:

> We've been through a major reorganization where Philips has been split up into strategic business units [SBUs]. One of our big problems is that we have no general managers for these SBUs – we've generally had to give the jobs to our commercial types. We should have recruited today's general managers in the 1974 recession, when in fact we were not hiring because of the squeeze.

IBM, Hewlett–Packard, and Shell have come to a similar conclusion, and Shell's Sir Peter Baxendell summarizes the current policy:

> Shell has a firm policy to the effect that recruitment at the graduate level should NOT be altered in an effort to correct short-term imbalances in staff members. It should be directed towards matching the long-term needs of an organization as identified through the techniques of staff and structure planning. Maintaining a steady intake of graduates each year rather than short-sighted overreaction to swings in the business cycle gives a more consistent standard and makes for smoother integration of the new recruits into the organization. It also avoids transmitting misleading messages through the university recruitment systems.

MANAGING MOBILITY

In these leading international concern, some of the most time-consuming, worrying, and intractable problems have to do with the management of mobility. Some of these problems crop up time and time again.

Getting Talented People off the Local Management Leash

In companies where potential is identified after five to seven years of technical or functional job experience (as opposed to identification at the time of recruitment), a serious problem for corporate human resource management is enlisting the co-operation of local managers in identifying and releasing persons with potential. There is little natural incentive for them to do so: their most talented individuals will be creamed off by the corporation, disappearing into other subsidiaries or parts of the world. Moreover, it is not uncommon for an unscrupulous manager to subvert the system by using it to dump a subordinate. A manager can rate a poor performer as superior and appraise his potential unrealistically high, thereby making it easy to transfer the subordinate to another unit.

Getting managers to understand the importance of mobility and the strategic reasons behind it is part of the solution. But the distinguishing characteristic of the leading companies is that they put their money where their mouth is. Management development is not only a verbal concern, not only a corporate function – the corporate measurement and reward systems are also behind it. In the words of a senior IBM executive, "In our company nothing seems to move unless there is an objective, and nothing gets done unless you are measured against it. So unless people feel they are going to be measured, they will not do it because there are plenty of other things they are measured on".

The measurement and reward system at Philips works in this way:

What we did is to officially announce to all managers responsible for larger units that they have an obligation to make available for corporate purposes a certain number of people. So the boss of the audio division gets a letter from the president telling him six months in advance that "You will make ten people available this year". Now if they don't, the remuneration of this boss is affected. Instead of getting a 100% bonus on the basis of his results, he may only get 80%, and the argument will be given to him that the 20% is missing because he didn't supply the people.

It is not so long ago that local managers said that they were responsible for their own operations, not for the rest of the corporation. Today it's a different story. When you can feel it in your bank account, your reaction is different.

Many stories are told of companies with task forces that wallow in the complexities of management development. Yet when the objectives and bonuses of general managers are linked to this task, action is finally mobilized. The greatest problem in fact is to get top management consistently to back and reward management development and mobility.

One of the practical objections of middle managers is that in releasing people, sometimes at short notice, they lose the expertise that they need to deliver the operating results for which they are accountable. Philip's answer is what they call "the corporate pool". This is a pool of mobile individuals representing more than 50 nationalities, people with at least five years of experience and in the top 20% of performance, and all financed on a corporate budget. The pool itself is constituted in a similar way to the potential list. Having a replacement immediately available (despite the admitted cost of settling a new person) has apparently increased the willingness of managers to make high-potential employees available, introducing more flexibility in the deployment of human resources.

Nevertheless the problems remain, requiring hard-nosed negotiations on the part of the corporate management development staff. Entrepreneurially-oriented operations managers inevitably have a short-term, focus of attention, out of tune with the longer-term thinking and global perspective of corporate staff.

Coping with Increased Resistance to Mobility

Individual resistance to mobility is certainly on the increase. A great deal of time is spent spotting potential and asking whether people can do the job abroad – yet when it comes to the crunch, the question is often whether they *want* to do it. "Personal and family reasons, often genuine though sometimes an excuse, are certainly the greatest inhibitor to moving people", says an IBM executive. "And it is increasingly so with the dual career situation. We calculate in our company that 85% of our Swedes have working partners, and it is very difficult to move such people unless you can do something for the spouse". As mentioned earlier, the readiness to be transferred becomes an important criterion of potential.

Compensation obviously becomes an important area of policy and practice in firms where geographic mobility is needed. For many individuals, working abroad may be undesirable, but it is a question of price. Expatriate remuneration is an increasingly complex and specialist domain, involving finding a balance between national and expatriate equities, between simplicity and complexity, while minimizing the ad hoc incentives that are sometimes needed. Most multinationals have developed a multi-tier salary structure, and that of Unilever is an example. The first component is a local base salary, more or less equivalent to that of a national. The second is a percentage of the equivalent home country salary, paid locally. Third, a bonus is paid a the end of the assignment, varying with the unattractiveness of the location and the difficulties of finding suitable candidates.

Clear norms and expectations regarding mobility appear to reduce resistance. Mobility is the norm among high-potential executives at Exxon, where 65% of the moves planned during a recent five-year period were realized; the others did not occur either because of business changes or personal family reasons. At IBM, there are several such formal and informal norms. First, individuals are expected to change job once every three to four years. Second, international experience is indispensible for those aspiring to senior positions. Third, if you are serious about your career and are proposed a particular job, only very specific and concrete reasons are grounds for refusal. On the other hand, expatriate assignments tend to be of short duration so that people will not be forgotten by their local companies.

Personnel managers often advocate warning people well in advance about international assignments, a practice resisted by line bosses on the questionable grounds that this may compromise their motivation in their existing job. When the norms are clear, and better still when there is advance notice of the assignment, it is surprising how adjustable individuals and families are.

Preventing Failures on International Assignments

However, the other side of the coin is that undue pressure on managers to move may increase the costly failure rates on international assignments. Failure signifies having to repatriate the manager before the projected end of the assignment because it is not working out; and it also implies the unmeasurable costs of poor decisions, lower operating results, or even irretrievably damaged local operations. The mobility problem is resolved, the people have moved, but at what expense to themselves and the corporation?

What are the reasons for failure on such assignments? It is widely recognized that expatriates should be technically skilled – the expatriate job is rarely a promising role for someone's first experience. But research suggests that the major reason for failure on such assignments is the failure of the family to adapt (Evans and Bartolomé, 1979). Sometimes the spouse is virtually coerced into the move; or the couple have been inadequately prepared for the problems of settling into a new culture. If severe family stress is added to the inevitable tensions of settling into a new job abroad, the degree of stress frequently reaches a point where people cannot cope. Either the marriage breaks down, or job performance suffers – decisive people become impulsive, while those who find it more difficult to take decisions become paralysed. Under such stress, people fall back on their weaknesses.

Failure rates are significant. Surveys of American Fortune 500 companies reported rates averaging 32% in the early 70s, declining to a still important 23% in the 80s (Tung, 1984). European multinationals, more sensitive to the problems and more experienced in preparing expatriates for such assignments, report failure rates of 10–15%.

The Re-entry Problem

According to some experienced executives, fears about re-entry are what worry expatriates most. The expatriate assignment is of limited duration.

Even on longer assignments there is a desire to return to the mother country as the children grow up: research has shown that resistance to geographic mobility peaks for families with teenage children.

Top management may emphasize the necessity for international experience, middle management may understand the reasons, but it simply takes a few well-publicized stories of re-entry into empty staff roles or at demeaning cuts in salary for the barriers to mobility to rise. Conversely, when top jobs go to younger managers who proved themself abroad, senior management is being consistent with their words.

The expatriate manager is far from the inevitable jockeying for key positions that goes on at headquarters. Whatever the person's performance, he or she is a distant commodity. Even Japanese expatriates see extended foreign assignments as destining themselves at best for roles in the international division at the height of their careers.

Systematic management reviews may alleviate this problem, but the longer the assignment the more there is a risk of being discounted, indeed forgotten. Even such a systematic enterprise as IBM has been obliged to tackle this problem directly. Expatriates are always on loan from the home country so that they have a guaranteed return ticket, at least at the level at which they left. Policy is that these "international assignees" should go out for three years and a maximum of five, for it is difficult to retain someone on the succession plan beyond this time. After five years abroad, the exceptions become "international careerists", whose careers are managed centrally. However, 99% of the people overseas are assignees and only 1% careerists.

The obligation to take people back at their initial level of responsibility is a non-negotiable issue at IBM. However, the positional guarantees are only chipping away at re-entry problems: "The actual reentry job is never perceived by the international assignee as satisfactory, partly because we have built up the person's expectations and because the foreign assignment itself often creates delusions of grandeur that are out of line with the perception of the person by the mother country", says an IBM executive. The international assignment is often excitingly developmental, sometimes with significant managerial responsibility at an early age. The return assignment seems lacklustre in comparison, a step backwards.

Successive expatriate assignments at Shell may span over much longer periods than at IBM, and the company tackles this by ensuring that each manager has a "parent function", typically the function or business where one began one's career. This parent function has the responsibility for the manager's long-term career welfare, even during the lengthy generalist assignments to other businesses or functions. The career "home" is thus a business function rather than a geographic place.

Return jobs are often into headquarter or staff roles, where international experience is needed in the mother country. Philips experiences particular problems here with its Dutch returnees:

The closer high potential people come to headquarters, the more difficult their career becomes. For people who operate excellently far away, the corporate bureaucracy seems to hamper development, in part because you have to be a good politician. So typically a high potential fellow with excellent performance on the other side of the world gets rated much lower when he comes to headquarters.

Research on Canadian and American returnees (Adler, 1981) leads to the conclusion that "reentry shock" poses far more severe problems than the more widely publicized difficulties of psychological adaptation abroad that are known as "culture shock". Returnees are advised to expect the worst, to discount the cosmopolitan experience of living abroad when returning to the milieu where daily concerns are strictly local. The long-term returnee's problems are aggravated by wider difficulties of social reintegration. Expectations have been created by short visits and summer holidays, where the expatriate is a focus of attention during the short stay. Returning home for good, the airport looks somehow more untidy and disorganized than expected, the taxis seem inefficient, and the problems of finding a house unreasonable. Friends and relatives who were eager to see the couple during the home leave now put off their visits until tomorrow. Socially, that comment about one's experiences in the river market in Bangkok leads to a discounting "Oh, you lived abroad for some years, did you?", as the conversation returns to more parochial banter on politics, football, and community scandal, topics that are now distant from the expatriate's repertoire of interests. In fact, Adler shows that returnees who have spent more than seven years abroad typically spin into a state of depression and self-questioning that takes five to seven years to work through – the time that it takes to become "local" once again, forgetting about one's life elsewhere.

CONCLUSION

International management development, despite its complexity and its time-consuming problems, is the crux of human resource management in the multinational enterprise. We will return to this domain in the concluding Chapter 12, where it emerges as a key to building the capabilities of such complex firms. But in the meantime, Chapter 8 leads us on to a broader review of the corporate role of HRM in the global enterprise.

Notes

1. This chapter was written by Paul Evans (Professor of Organzational Behavior at INSEAD), with Elizabeth Lank and Alison Farquhar (respectively Research

Assistant and Research Associate at INSEAD). It builds upon the experience and views of numerous executives (in particular Kees Krombeen, senior director of the Corporate Staff Bureau at Philips; Sir Peter Baxendell, managing director of Shell International; and John Stanley, general manger for the Areas Division of IBM). The assistance of other executives is gratefully acknowledged: Michael Bonsignore, president of Honeywell Europe; Graham Corbett, senior partner, Peat Marwick Continental, now KPMG; Luigi Dusmet, director of personnel, Nestlé; Ray Fields, management development manager at ICL; Tom Glynn Jones, manager for the human resource division, British Petroleum; Junichi Imakita, head of Pacific development division, Air Liquide: Claude La Peyre, employee relations manager, Essochem Europe; Jurg Marx, director for personnel and administration, Migros; Paul Smith, head of personnel, Marks & Spencer; Edgar Vincent, group personnel manager, ICI; Anthony Vineall, deputy head of personnel division, Unilever.

2. Perhaps in part due to their international orientation, several major European corporations have always made executive development a priority. This is shown in the structure of responsibilities, where the function of executive development reports directly to the CEO rather than through the personnel department, as is typical in the US. This is the tradition at Philips (with its Corporate Staff Bureau), at Ciba-Geigy, Unilever, BP, and until recently at Montedison – and also at IBM, whose executive resources department is separate from the personnel department.

3. The description of the Japanese management development system is based on the studies of Dr Mitsuyo Hanada (Professor at the Sanno Institute of Business Administration in Japan) and Dr Vladimir Pucik (Assistant Professor at the University of Michigan).

4. The management development system at Philips is described in some detail in an INSEAD report by Harold Rush, *Managerial Career Development in a Multinational Giant* (INSEAD, 1984).

Chapter 8

The Two Logics Behind Human Resource Management

Paul Evans and Peter Lorange

Multinational corporations (MNCs) often operate in many different product-market segments. The employees in their far flung geographic operations represent very different social cultures. The policies and practices for human resource management that are effective in managing one product-market may not be the most appropriate for another; those that work well in one cultural setting will not necessarily function in another.

How can a firm operating in different product-markets and diverse socio-cultural environments effectively establish human resource policies? What principles should guide corporate management of the complex MNC in the management of its human resources? In assessing the orientation of human resource management in the corporation, we believe that it is necessary to examine the implications of these two logics both separately and together. These are the issues discussed in this chapter.

PRODUCT-MARKET AND SOCIO–CULTURAL DIVERSITY

Most multinational enterprises administer a portfolio of products, some of which may serve multiple markets. Some of their operations may be in mature business segments while others are in growth settings.

The first complexity for the MNC is that these different product-markets require appropriately adapted approaches to human resource management (Fombrun, Tichy and Devanna, 1984; Lorange and Murphy, 1983; Gupta,

1986). Subsidiaries with products at different stages of the product life cycle may require very different types of general managers to run them, and correspondingly different approaches to personnel management. Mature business typically depend upon efficient cost-conscious management; general managers require strong integrative skills, while appraisals and rewards may be linked to operating targets. In contrast, emerging businesses require more adaptive entrepreneurial capacities on the part of general managers, and rewards that provide a stake in business growth. The orientation of personnel management is likely to vary in these businesses. Recruitment may be a critical success factor in one setting, management development in another, while labor relations may be the key personnel problem in a third. An important aspect of strategy implementation is adapting HRM to specific product-market requirements.

The second complexity for the MNC is that the social, legislative, and cultural environment varies from one country of its operations to another. Differences in labor legislation are obvious. Going further, Hofstede (1980a) has established that strong cultural differences exist between nations, criticizing American management theories and personnel practices as being too culture bound. Laurent (1986) shows that the concept of management and organization may vary significantly from one national culture to another, even among employees within the same MNC. Germans, for instance, tend to have a concept of management based on competence, Latins a more social conception, while an instrumental notion of management typically prevails in the United States (see Chapter 5). Both he and Hofstede argue that management methods may succeed in one culture but backfire in another. For example, management-by-objectives and pay-for-performance are quite natural in the United States and Germany, but they have been widely rejected in France and other Latin cultures.

What principles should guide the formulation of human resource policies in a multiproduct-market, multinational enterprise? One set of principles can be induced from research and practice based on applying product-market reasoning, the logic of business dynamics. Another set of principles follow from the logic of socio–cultural analysis. Let's take a look at these two logics in turn.

HRM Based on Product-market Logic

The multidivisional organization has emerged to cope with the challenge of managing a complex firm which operates in different product-market environments. In such a firm, one can distinguish between three levels of policy making:

1. the *corporate level*, concerned with the strategic management of a portfolio of enterprises and the integration of these firms;

2. the *divisional level*, where strategic and operational concerns meet in a family of enterprises with common product-market characteristics; and

3. the *business unit* level, where operational plans for each product-market are translated into functional policies and practices to achieve them (Lorange, 1980).

Within this structure, human resource management should be largely decentralized to the divisional and business unit levels. Human resource policy is typically general and non-contingent at the corporate level, progressively becoming more specific and operational as one descends to the business unit level. Indeed, the major challenge is to obtain a better matching of the strategic and operational plans of the division and business unit with the human resource practices to implement them.

From this business perspective, human resource management and the personnel function has not traditionally been regarded either as a strategic task or a critical corporate domain. However, there are at least three important tasks for corporate and divisional human resource management, the importance of which is reinforced by increasing needs for corporate integration.

The first task is human resource allocation, *key executive appointments and succession planning*, which is analogous to investment and other resource allocation decisions. Strategic decisions are in part implemented through decisions on general manager appointments, as well as through selecting people for key functional positions. The appointee should have a profile that matches the desired strategic development and the product-market logic in the business unit concerned – be it an entrepreneurial person, someone with desired functional competencies in marketing or engineering, an integrative generalist, or someone with experience in the rationalization of a declining business, as the case may be.

The second task is the *design and management of appropriate incentive systems*, intended to align managerial rewards with the strategic tasks of these individuals. The incentive package for managing a mature product-market setting may thus emphasize efficient, result-oriented management, while the incentives for managing a more entrepreneurial growth business may stress building business strength for future payoff rather than the "bottom line".

The third task is that of fostering the *cross-fertilization of functional and business experiences*, so that important lessons of experience in particular subsidiaries and divisions are communicated rapidly to others, as are relevant developments outside the corporation. The principle tools here are management education and training, as well as the organization of functional meetings for the sharing of experiences.

Increasing Needs for Corporate Integration

While the principle of decentralization of HRM applies to all but the most simple of firms, many industries have witnessed product-market trends leading to a heightened need for corporate integration, particularly since the late 70s. We might highlight three such trends. The first is the globalization of industries such as chemicals, many types of industrial equipment, computers, and pharmaceuticals. The driving forces behind this are increased economies of scale in production and R & D, decreasing costs of transport and communication, and intensified international competition, as well as a progressive homogenization of markets. Even traditionally country-based, consumer-type industries, such as retailing and food products, are beginning to feel the pressure to develop global strategies (Levitt, 1983; Bartlett and Ghoshal, 1987).

The second trend is an increasing interdependence in certain industries between subsidiaries and even divisions, particularly where marketing imperatives dictate the provision of a system type service to client. Consumer electronics, computer and telecommunication industries are notable examples.

The third trend is a need for increased flexibility in the deployment of resources, especially where product life cycles are shortening and competitor reactions sharpening.

How can this integration be provided in an effective manner? In the early 70s there was a search for structural matrix solutions involving dual or multiple direct reporting relationships. However, the costs of communication and ambiguity often outweighed the benefits of such complex structures.

The alternative was to provide integration through an overlay of management processes – and notably strategic management processes (Lorange, 1980). Strategic objectives need to be established and reconciled. These are translated into strategic programs at corporate, divisional and functional levels, programs to realize the objectives (acquisition, negotiation of joint-ventures, new business development, cost reduction, development of a stronger market orientation, quality improvement, and so forth). These strategic programs then need to be concretized as action plans and strategic budgets. Reconciling the objectives, programs and budgets at the levels of the corporate portfolio, the divisional business family, and the business unit levels requires an interactive and iterative process, such as the one illustrated in Figure 8.1 – a top-down and bottom-up process of negotiation and tradeoff between different perspectives.

In recent years, we have discovered that one of the major constraints in the functioning of these strategic management processes is human. Three human resource factors begin to act as constraints:

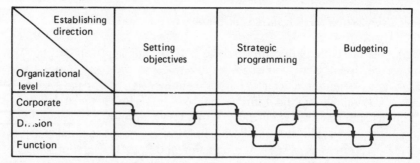

Source: Vancil, Richard F. and Lorange, Peter (1975) "Strategic Planning in Diversified Companies", *Harvard Business Review* (January–February) 81–90.

FIGURE 8–1
Strategic Management as an Interactive Process to Develop Both a Corporate-wide Plan and a Business Plan

1. the lack of strategic human resources effectively to implement global strategic objectives and programs;
2. weakness in terms of the strategic capabilities of managers in the firm (which is often particularly difficult for such managers open-mindedly to acknowledge); and
3. the loss of flexibility that stems from otherwise necessary differences in personnel systems between divisions and operations.

A recent Conference Board survey of 277 chief executives from multinational corporations in different regions of the world showed that the first two of these issues were their top human resource management priority (Shaeffer, 1985). Consequently, human resource management is today often becoming a strategic priority of the corporate management team, providing a new focus for the corporate and divisional personnel functions. Let us briefly discuss these three emerging management challenges.

Developing strategic human resources

Any implementation decision ultimately boils down to a question of staffing: the effectiveness of implementation depends on having the right people in the right place at the right time. The limits to strategy implementation are thus largely set by the resource pool of key strategic human resources.[1] To overcome this limit, the corporate concern with executive appointments and succession leads to a wider concern for the development of strategic human resources (as discussed in Chapter 7).

A strategic resource, human or otherwise, is a resource that can be transferred from one business strategy application to another (Lorange,

1980). For people to constitute strategic resources, their talents must be transferable to other business settings. Flexibility and mobility (in an inter-functional, inter-divisional and geographic sense) are thus essential criteria.

Strategic human resources are therefore associated with some concept of "generalism" – although this is a misleading term since it denotes general managers, who constitute only one type of strategic human resource. "Generalist managers" is the label used by Philips, "executive resources" by IBM, "corporate property" by Citibank and other firms. They are the occupants of key strategic positions (most general management roles, and key functional or staff roles), as well as the people deemed to have the potential to occupy such positions. Employees with such capacities are known as "high potentials".

The transferable expertise that characterizes strategic human resources is proven and honed above all through managed experience in different functions, in strategically important businesses, in different geographic regions, in headquarters and operating roles, complemented by management training and project assignments.

The forum for taking these development and mobility decisions is typically a *management review*, as described in Chapter 7. In large MNCs a cascading series of interlocking review committees may exist at corporate, divisional, and major business element levels. The "inputs" into the review are the needs of the organization based on its strategic and operating plans, together with the inventory of strategic human resources or high potentials. The outputs are assignment and developmental decisions, though the review process may lead to discussion of changes in human resource policy or organizational design. This review process can in fact become an intrinsic element of strategic management, constituting an arena for a general management dialogue on the tailoring of strategic and human resource management.

It is important that this management review process be driven and chaired by senior line management, supported though not usurped by the personnel department. It is in this resource allocation process that important strategic tradeoffs are made, decisions that can be made only by the line: decisions to assign key people to certain divisions rather than others, tradeoffs between the strategic needs and the operating needs, and between the different geographic areas of operations. This leads us to the second strategic challenge for HRM.

Development of strategic management capabilities

One of the lessons of the 70s was that strategic management is the responsibility of line management, be it corporate, divisional or business unit level of the firm. It cannot be entrusted to corporate staff – strategic planners, marketing co-ordinators, human resource managers, and the like. Nor can one expect any CEO in situations short of turnaround crisis single-handedly to direct the process of strategic management. As described earlier, strategic management is an interactive process involving dialogue and negotiation on complex tradeoffs, so that a broadly shared sense of strategic direction can emerge among the management team.

This requires capabilities that few line managers, with their predominantly operational orientations, traditionally possess. First, it requires a capacity to think strategically, analytically to size up a business situation with its threats and its opportunities, all with a sense for competitive, market, and technological dynamics. Second, it requires the ability to adopt perspectives other than one's own – the perspectives of other functions, higher corporate levels, and perhaps even other divisional areas. Strategic management programs often involve working in ad hoc teams with a deliberately diverse set of managers, calling for open-mindedness, give-and-take, and tolerance. Without a high degree of teamwork, the process of strategic negotiation breaks down. And third, it requires the ability to work in two different attitudinal modes – a strategic mode (oriented toward change, adaptation and development), and an operating mode (oriented toward realizing the operating budget of the particular business unit). This ability to wear two hats is not easily understood or developed.

Pierre Borgeaud, the CEO of Sulzer (one of Switzerland's leading industrial firms), talked about this challenge in an interview with Paul Evans:

> We have to tackle the task of preparing the firm for its longer term future in different ways. Long-range planning has lost its credibility in an uncertain world. Will we see open trade or a return to global protectionism, recession or growth? What about inflation and exchange rates? Will the Gorbachev revolution in Russia continue or not? What about competitor reactions? There are too many uncertainties to permit anything but the planning of broad scenarios.
>
> And yet preparing Sulzer for the 1990s is one of my major responsibilities as CEO. What this implies is that its leaders and managers and its organization must be prepared to face whatever business and economic circumstances we turn out to confront ten years in the future.
>
> This is going to require a significant change in way of thinking and behavior on the part of our executives. We have managers who are excellent at running their business and delivering today's operating results. That's vital, but they have also to be capable of preparing their businesses to deal with the changes and shifts that we know lie ahead.

The process of executive development should assist managers to develop these strategic capabilities. Exposure to different jobs within the MNC is likely to foster an analytic perspective, while establishing necessary personal communication networks and developing a broad feel for the corporation as a whole. Although management development decisions are typically made in order to staff jobs and develop individual potential, the development of strategic capabilities appears to be an important "hidden" benefit (Edstrom and Galbraith, 1977).

The development of strategic capabilities may be supported by management training. One such example is ICL, discussed in Chapter 3. After a successful turnaround in the early 80s, the CEO realized that the future of the firm would depend on the capacity of executives to manage a constant process of strategic change. A successful series of executive training programs were organized in order to sensitize senior management to this reality, which for many of them turned out to be an eye-opening experience.

Increasing human resource flexibility

The necessary differences in human resource management policies and practices from business unit to another can create major obstacles to mobility and flexibility. The managers who constitute strategic human resources will therefore typically be governed by a separate corporate compensation and employee management program. Ensuring that the mobility of key managers is not constrained by locally favorable conditions is a complex specialist domain of personnel management.

Where strategic developments require great flexibility, one may see further corporate centralization of human resource policies and practices. IBM certainly seems to believe in this, with the corporate-level attention it pays to personnel management. As described later in Chapter 11, the fact that their successful independent venture unit in personal computers was not allowed much autonomy in the area of personnel policy and practice facilitated the ultimate integration of this unit into the mainstream business, where it was needed to satisfy the market for network systems. IBM also has a corporate policy that managers should spend no more than three to four years in a particular job, a policy which also facilitates flexibility in the strategic deployment of human resources.

Overall, while most operational human resource practices are being decentralized to divisions and business units, the pressures of global integration and the related challenge of making strategic management processes work more effectively are leading corporate human resource management to an important strategic role in the domain of executive management and development. Let's now change perspective, moving on the implications of socio–cultural diversity.

HUMAN RESOURCE MANAGEMENT BASED ON SOCIO–CULTURAL LOGIC

The business units of the multinational enterprise are typically based in geographic subsidiaries, and the firm also has to contend with another source of diversity, that of managing employees from different social and cultural environments. As mentioned earlier, there are two strategies for adapting to socio–cultural differences between subsidiaries: the global and polycentric approaches to human resource management respectively.[2]

1. The *global enterprise* typically manages its global workforce in a relatively centralized, co-ordinated way. Corporate policy on human resource management tends to be quite specific and influential – there are numerous guidelines, procedures, principles, and guiding corporate values. Examples of such procedures are worldwide policies regarding recruitment and promotion criteria; "single status" policies; a uniform stance toward unions; standardized procedures for performance evaluation; global compensation policies; uniform monitoring of human resource management through opinion surveys; a code of corporate values guiding the indoctrination of newly hired recruits. It goes without saying that corporate and divisional personnel officers typically have powerful roles in global enterprises. Such firms are also seen as having "strong" organizational cultures.

    IBM is perhaps the most well-known global enterprise, as are Hewlett–Packard, Procter & Gamble, and Unilever. Many of the companies upon whom the book *In Search of Excellence* (Peters and Waterman, 1982) is based are indeed such firms, and the global approach to human resource management (building the strong worldwide culture) is currently much publicized.

2. The *polycentric enterprise*, on the other hand, decentralizes the management of human resources to its subsidiaries. Corporate co-ordination, to the extent that it exists, tends to be loose and informal. There are few guidelines, policies are typically quite vague, and there is little specification of desired practice – all of these tasks are left to the subsidiary or business unit general manager and his or her personnel staff. The role of the headquarters staff is limited to tasks such as executive recruitment and advice on key appointments, and the organization of occasional meetings of subsidiary executives to exchange lessons of experience. Examples of polycentric enterprises are Holderbank (a Swiss firm that is the world's largest cement company), American Express, Britain's GEC, Sweden's AGA, Schlumberger, and Nestlé.

Two Strategies for Socio-cultural Adaptation

These two approaches constitute different adaptive strategies for coping with the heterogeneous social, legislative, and cultural environment of a complex multinational firm.

One theoretical model for organizational adaptation is known as the variation–selection–retention model, loosely based on Darwinian theory of natural evolution and applied by a branch of organizational theory called "population ecology". The argument is that among the natural *variation* of any phenomenon, environmental forces will favor the *selection* of certain types, leading these to be retained or to become success models (i.e. subsequent *retention*) until environmental forces change. Population ecologists have applied this to analyze how old forms of organization die when the environment changes, while new organizational forms come into prominence. Let us apply this model in a different way to explain how the global organization copes with its heterogeneous socio–cultural environment.

The global organization, with its centralized or co-ordinated policies and practices, selects and retains those people in any given country who most closely fit with its own cultural values. It adapts to different local environments by controlling selection; indeed, recruitment (complemented by socialization and management development) becomes a core function of such a firm.

This represents one way of adapting to socio–cultural differences. Deep differences in values, attitudes, and conceptions of management do exist between cultures, as researchers such as Hofstede and Laurent have established. But those differences are stereotypes, statistical differences in means between the normal curve distribution of values and attitudes in any given national population. Certainly, Germans are different from Americans who are different from the French. But *some* Germans are very American in their attitudes, and *some* French are more similar to the "average" German than to their own compatriots. When a globally-oriented company, for example Hewlett–Packard, is recruiting a German manager for a career at their plant near Munich, they are not simply seeking any technically qualified German manager; they are looking for a German whose personality matches Hewlett–Packard's cultural values. Global enterprises adapt through selection. In turn, those persons who are promoted into positions of power are individuals who most closely conform to these core values (i.e., further internal selection).

Polycentric enterprises, on the other hand, adapt in a more direct way. As pointed out, adaptation to local socio–cultural circumstances is the task of the local subsidiary, at best loosely circumscribed by corporate guidelines. Thus, the German subsidiary is likely to have markedly stereotypical German properties, the United States subsidiary different American characteristics, and so on. Socio–cultural adaptation is the task of local management, rather than that of the corporation.

The Importance of Internal Consistency

Leaving product-market logic aside, neither adaptation strategy is intrinsically superior to the other. Effectiveness in adaptation to socio–cultural differences appears to be largely a function of the internal consistency of human resource management policy and practice. Inconsistent policies and practices can lead to disruptive uncertainties about the rules of the corporate game, typically perceived as disconcerting swings in the centralization–decentralization pendulum. Inconsistencies mean that the energy of managers and other employees are drained away by internal politics rather than channeled into the market place. Indeed, in complex organizations it is advisable to keep the basic ground rules simple and coherent – the importance of simple form in a complex firm.

Internal consistency of policy and practice is easier to ensure in the polycentric enterprise. It implies a slim corporate staff with the limited role of ensuring executive succession and the cross-fertilization of experience. Divisional staff may have a co-ordination role, but real power lies in the hands of subsidiary line and staff executives. Inconsistencies arise if, for example, a strong-willing corporate vice president is appointed, armed with a mission to co-ordinate tightly policies and practices throughout the subsidiaries. This message is likely to be ignored or defeated by local subsidiary managers, entailing disruptive political infighting.

Internal consistency is more difficult to attain in the global firm. The attention paid to selection has to be complemented by retention policies, by socialization and management development practices to build corporate as well as national loyalty. IBM could perhaps be taken as an example, not because of the widely discussed content of its approach to human resource management, but rather because a high degree of internal consistency has developed over the decades. Even in its recent headcount reductions, IBM has taken pains to try to preserve that consistency.

In firms like IBM, individuals are rigorously and selectively recruited in national labor markets for careers, not jobs. The early career years are marked by indoctrination experiences to test the loyalty of the individual. The young manager is guided by a transparent code of corporate values and conduct. Such firms may have relatively high turnover rates among their graduate recruits during the first two years of socialization; these individuals discover that their own values and needs do not match those of the firm, and they quit – a desirable result for both the firm and the individual. After the early career years, a variety of policies exist to ensure the retention of these carefully groomed employees, so as to obtain a payoff from this investment in human capital: salaries well above the industry average; close attention to welfare policies; safety valve and grievance procedures such as an open door policy, and morale monitoring in the shape of opinion surveys; and a policy of transfer to new positions every few years, ensuring that individuals develop firm-specific rather than labor-market competencies.

Perhaps the most frequently cited and enduring example of a global organization is the Catholic Church, whose recruitment and indoctrination procedures for the priesthood (i.e., selection and retention), and whose rigorous adherence to an "organizational" credo of values will soon pass the two-thousand year test of adaptability.

In contrast, other firms espousing global philosophies have less consistent policies and practices. Selection procedures are less rigorous, socialization is neglected, less attention is paid to retention management. The external labor market often steals the capable individuals at the time in their careers when the firm's investment in human capital is beginning to pay off. The company is saddled with the investment costs of aiming to be global but without the benefits. It may then be obliged to recruit local talent into senior positions from the outside labor market, individuals who, however technically competent, do not necessarily share the values and attitudes of the global corporation. Consistency is further compromised since disruptive clashes can break out with these newcomers.

The *costs and benefits* of these two adaptive strategies also differ. The global firm gains in terms of corporate integration, but the price is the heavy cost of selection and retention. The polycentric firm gains in terms of lower overhead costs (relatively little time and energy devoted to human resource management; salaries linked more closely to local labor market rates), though it typically loses out in corporate integration.

Modifications to the Extremes

In a highly competitive environment, companies are obliged to minimize the disadvantages of the chosen strategy. But how can the firm do this in such a way as not to compromise the necessary internal consistency? Our observation is that effective firms do this with "subtle" management processes; in contrast, less effective firms tend to use overt management actions that disruptively compromise consistency.

Examples of disruptively overt management actions in the polycentric firm are new centralized corporate guidelines, closely monitored corporate programs, and the appointment of mother country nationals with little foreign experience to subsidiary general manager positions. Disruptively overt management actions in the global firm are sudden cut-backs in corporate or divisional human resource budgets, corporate programs saying "drop everything except the bottom-line results", and forced and rapid nationalization of the managerial workforce in a developing country.

Subtle management processes, to use the term of Doz and Prahalad (1981), can achieve the same ends without compromising internal consistency. Let us provide some examples of subtle countervailing mechanisms in the polycentric and global enterprises respectively.

A major problem for polycentric firms is how to introduce a degree of corporate integration into the otherwise decentralized firm. Doz and

Prahalad have mapped out mechanisms for this, which they call data management, conflict management (e.g., ad hoc task forces), and manager management. Limiting ourselves to the latter, manager management involves above all paying careful attention to the development of key managers for subsidiaries or business units (see Chapter 7). Other devices exist. Both Holderbank (the Swiss-based cement corporation) and the French multinational Generale de Biscuits make use of corporate "trouble-shooters", members of the executive committee who take over troubled or rampantly independent subsidiaries until they have been realigned. There are the periodic "jamborees" and meetings where subsidiary and corporate executives get together to discuss policy, problems and experiences. Corporate worldwide executive training programs have become an important integrative tool for many polycentric firms.

Turning to the global enterprise, the heavy costs of selection and retention cannot be radically cut with ease. However, over time, corporate and divisional staff can usually be thinned, as has occurred at IBM. Line management, socialized through their own experience into the global corporate norms, can gradually take over the responsibility for selection and retention. A global culture probably takes at least one or two decades to create, though gradually more freedom can be given to subsidiary line managers without compromising globalism. However, a major risk for the global enterprise is that of "cloning", as discussed in Chapter 7.

BALANCING PRODUCT-MARKET AND SOCIO–CULTURAL LOGICS

Human resource management is all too often guided by black-and-white generalizations or fashions, by the imitation of competitors or today's "excellent companies". We believe that human resource policies should instead be guided by two logics: the business logic of products and markets and the socio–cultural logic of geographic spheres of operations. But although we have presented them separately, these two logics are of course *not* independent (see Figure 8.2). Whereas the dictates of product-market strategy may sometimes be consistent with the chosen socio–cultural adaptive strategy, in many instances there may be serious friction between the two logics.

Compatible Strategies

For some firms, product-market logic and the chosen socio-cultural adaptation strategy may be quite compatible (cells 2 and 4 in Figure 8.2). The current concern with product-market integration has, in particular, led firms with global adaptation strategies (cell 4) to be much in the limelight –

SOCIO-CULTURAL LOGIC

	Global ·adaptive strategy	Polycentric adaptive strategy
Independent country-based businesses with low integration	**Cell 1** Potential conflict between HQ and subsidiaries	**Cell 2** HRM largely decentralized to subsidiaries
Interdependent businesses with high integration	**Cell 4** Strong corporate policies guiding HRM	**Cell 3** Potential conflicts between divisions and subsidiaries and loss of competitive performance

PRODUCT-MARKET LOGIC

FIGURE 8–2
The Relationship Between Product-market Logic and Socio-cultural Logic in Determining the Orientation of Human Resource Management in the International Firm

the human resource systems of companies like IBM and Hewlett–Packard have frequently been upheld as models.

Many firms have in fact developed *mixed human resource management strategies* in the sense that human resource management is global and centralized for senior executives and those with such potential (as discussed in Chapter 7), though for all other employees the human resource management approach is polycentric, decentralized, and country-based. In such firms, the decision to label someone as having "potential" constitutes the critical selection decision that was discussed earlier. This trend to dual human resource cultures seems to be developing into the typical pattern; it is also consistent with the emerging strategic integration forces that were discussed when considering product-market problems above.

Incompatible Strategies

In other firms, human resource management can be a more problematic domain (cells 1 and 3), with unresolved tensions between the forces of centralization and decentralization. The competitive evolution in a particular industry may argue for closer integration between product-markets units or divisions, which clashes with their polycentrism. This is the case for certain firms which had a technological speciality in a particular niche (of electronics, for example), and which expanded their international sales rapidly by setting up polycentric subsidiaries. Local entrepreneurs were hired, sales agencies were bought up, and the autonomy given to these subsidiaries indeed stimulated rapid growth in the early stages of market development. Today, however, competitive pressures and technology shifts necessitate closer product-market integration, which is resisted by the managers of now established local fiefdoms.

Conversely, product-market decentralization is important in industries based primarily on differentiation rather than integration (e.g., retailing, food products, and consumer durables), which would clash with a global adaptive strategy. For example, Marks & Spencer has a tradition of global-type employee management which has been outstandingly successful in Britain, and which they regarded as one of their distinctive strategic assets (Evans and Wittenberg, 1986). This was applied abroad when they opened stores in France and Canada, partly accounting for the disappointing results of their internationalization (see p. 39 for details).

The subtle management mechanisms described earlier may be employed to combat these problems, either providing more diversity within globalism or providing a measure of integration to the polycentrism. But these subtle mechanisms take time to have any visible effect – five to ten years is a good rule of thumb – and this may be too long to ensure survival if competitors are moving fast or if the industry structure is changing rapidly. In this case, the firm logically has one of two choices: either to modify its approach to human resource management, or to modify its product-market strategy. At first sight, the former seems to be the obvious choice, though experience suggests that it is difficult to achieve in a short time frame. Typically, it is only via the trauma of turnaround that one can change the basic approach to human resource management since this involves the deep transformation of organizational culture that was described in Chapters 3 and 4. Companies will naturally avoid this unless crisis forces it upon them.

The aphorism "stick to your knitting" may well be the appropriate guide for firms with global management philosophies. Such enterprises should restrict their strategic development to related businesses that share a similar product-market logic, rather than engaging in strategic diversification, however appealing that diversification may be. While there is little empirical data to substantiate this, our experience is that global corporations find it difficult to manage diversified product-markets, where the global human resource philosophy clashes with the need for differentiated approaches to human resource management in these product-markets.

Examples of this dilemma are Hewlett–Packard, Ciba–Geigy, and IBM, all corporations with global management philosophies. By origin an instruments business, Hewlett–Packard ventured into computers during the 70s. For a while, this led to a widespread loss of identity, internal confusion, and a clash between different cultures in a firm noted for its single value system. The choice was either to compromise those values or to get out of computers, and Hewlett–Packard has chosen a variant of the latter. Symbolized by changes in top management as well as in business strategy, the firm is resetting its path as a global instruments company, with computers as a strategic support to the mainstream business.

Ciba–Geigy, the Swiss pharmaceutical and chemical multinational, has had a similar experience. It ventured into consumer products with the acquisition of its Airwick division. After a decade of clashes and conflicts, Ciba–Geigy's top management concluded that they may never understand the values and dynamics of such a business, leading to the sale of the division. Furthermore, IBM diversified into telecommunications, but has recently decided to sell off its Rolm acquisition in a partnership deal with Siemens. For the global firm, it may be that strategically necessary competencies can be best obtained via joint-ventures and strategic partnerships rather than through outright acquisition or internal diversification. Research on the difficulties in acquisition integration provides at least indirect support for this view (Haspeslagh, 1983).

Polycentric enterprises, on the other hand, have more strategic flexibility; they do not have to stick to their knitting. It is easier for them to acquire businesses in new product-markets or to develop them internally. Their difficulty is in exploiting the synergies between these businesses, or in building on the interdependencies between businesses that may develop with the evolution of product-markets. Diversified polycentric firms are well advised to introduce a measure of integration by focusing attention on international executive development, particularly in newly-created divisions of interdependent companies. However, as noted, this takes time; where the cultures of competitors are better equipped to exploit these synergies rapidly, the polycentric firm may be forced into selling off businesses that it acquired.

The Longer-term Perspective

This analysis of balancing product-market logic and socio–cultural logic is admittedly tentative, based on our observations of a limited number of companies. But it does lead us to a provocative conclusion.

Intuitively, most businessmen will say that product-market logic is far more important than socio–cultural logic, and that it should drive strategic decisions in the firm. Classic strategic management theory and practice has also tended to draw uniquely on product-market reasoning. In the short term, where most attention is focused, this may be true. However, the above observations suggest that socio–cultural logic constrains strategic development more than most people believe when it comes to the long term.

The choice of a basic socio–cultural adaptive strategy (global or polycentric) is typically taken on the basis of managerial values and the perception of product-markets at a particular stage in the evolution of the firm. If we assume that this choice, while perhaps not irrevocable, takes at least a generation to modify (global organizations cannot easily become polycentric or vice versa), then the firm is implicitly deciding on its long-term way of adapting to a competitive environment that *will* inevitably change. This implies that while product-market logic may indeed be the important consideration behind short-term competitive strategy, socio–cultural logic is the more important consideration framing the choice of long-term strategic arenas.

Let's return to an insight provided by the population ecologists. The polycentric firm can be viewed as a "population" of loosely integrated entities. Over time, some are likely to die and others are likely to expand. Some will be sold off, and others brought up. If a film of the polycentric firm is speeded up to show decades in minutes, it will be seen to be constantly changing boundary, shape, and form. The "organization" loses its identity.

The global organization, on the other hand, is more likely to endure as an organization with relatively stable boundaries, precisely because of the attention paid to selection and retention of its human resources. Over the decades it will certainly change markets and products, it will go through good times and bad times, but as an "organization" it is more likely to retain its basic identity.

Borrowing from the perspective of a sociologist, one might point out that product-markets are essentially ephemeral. Markets shift and products change with increasing rapidity. Though varying from industry to industry, market forces argued for centralization in the 60s, decentralization in the 70s, integration in the 80s . . . and the catchword of the 90s may be some variant on deintegration, or global niches facilitated by new technologies.

However, social cultures do not change so quickly – quite to the contrary. It takes decades, if not centuries, to achieve even small changes in the deep fabric of society; similarly organizational cultures change slowly and painfully – such was the message of Part II of this book. Thus in choosing one socio–cultural adaptation strategy or the other, a decision that perhaps was arbitrarily based on product-market logic at a particular point in time, the firm may have fundamentally determined how it will adapt to currently unknown forces in the future. From the long-term perspective, as many have suspected, what is ultimately important is a cultural choice reflected in a basic stance on human resource management.

Notes

1. It is worth pointing out that this is one of the central arguments of a classic work in microeconomics, Edith Penrose's *The Theory of the Growth of the Firm* (1959). In analyzing what limits the growth of an organization, Penrose concludes that the limits on the growth of a firm are set not by factors such as

technological diseconomies of scale: "the capacities of the *existing* managerial personnel of the firm necessarily set a limit to the expansion of that firm in any given period of time, for it is self-evident that such management cannot be hired in the market-place" (Penrose, 1959, pp. 45–6).

2. The "global" and "polycentric" concepts are based on the pioneering work of Perlmutter (Heenan and Perlmutter, 1979). What we call "global enterprises" may, in his terms, be either ethnocentric or geocentric (respectively, policy centralized from the home country, or developed on a worldwide basis). The term "polycentric" is taken directly from Perlmutter, though such firms may be regiocentric (co-ordinated at a regional rather than at the subsidiary level). However, for the purposes of this chapter, Perlmutter's distinctions between ethno- and geo-centric, and between poly- and regio-centric, are left aside.

Part IV

Innovation Through Human Resources

Introduction to Part IV

In today's world of change and competition, innovation is obviously one of the keys to success – and often to survival. But "innovation" is a broad term. In the minds of most people, it refers to the development of new products and services (in some industries, more than 50% of the revenues are generated by products introduced in the last five years). But innovation also means creating an organization that is capable of rapidly commercializing those products in all major markets of the world. It means improvement of what exists, incremental improvements to quality and customer service. It refers the introduction of new technologies and new processes so as to get things done in more cost-effective ways. It means exploiting the opportunities that the new technologies of computers and telecommunications open up.

More than anything, innovation means doing things differently. The economist Schumpeter pointed out more than fifty years ago that innovation is inherently destructive – it destroys the status quo. As Stanley Davis argued in Chapter 2, this is a fact that has not yet been digested by industrial management.

Indeed, the three chapters in this section challenge a number of widely held assumptions: that only small firms are innovative, that organizations are necessarily hierarchic, that new technologies reduce our reliance on labor, that "intrapreneurship" is the key to innovation, that the decentralized divisional structure is best for international firms, that older scientists and engineers inevitably become obsolescent. These chapters also challenge conventional thinking about reward systems, performance appraisal, dual career ladders, and the role of top management.

And these challenges to our orthodoxies continue. A report in *Business Week* (May 1988) questions conventional accounting procedures. Despite the cost cutting and rationalization of the 80s, the productivity gap between the United States on the one hand and Japan and certain European countries on the other has increased rather than diminished. Obedience to traditional accounting practices leads only to short-term productivity gains, correcting the ills of the inefficient past. Sustainable productivity increases come from defying those accounting practices, investing in the future through quality improvement, customer satisfaction, and the creation of more responsive organizations. Fundamentally new rules to account for capital investment are being developed – innovation strikes even here.

Schein and Laurent pointed out in Chapters 4 and 5 that deeply ingrained beliefs and assumptions are the major obstacles to organizational change and to its corollary, innovation. Indeed, this is a thread that runs through the three chapters in this section, which tackle different aspects of innovation. Chapter 9 looks at the impact of new technologies on internal operations, and the development of new products or services, and it examines the need for greater responsiveness to changing markets. It is based on the lessons of practice of a score of international firms.

New technologies, symbolized by automation and information systems, are changing not just factories but entire industries. For example, as the judgemental element in bookkeeping is mechanized, so the audit profession is transforming itself into an industry of consultants. A frequent obstacle to such transformation are erroneous widespread beliefs, for example the belief that new technologies reduce the reliance on labor. In fact, the new technologies increase reliance on people's skills, and the training and development of human resources is becoming a corresponding priority. A recurrent preoccupation is that our educational systems may be unable to supply sufficient people equipped with skills that will be needed in the future. This applies to most business sectors, and not just to those popularly labeled as "high tech".

In the subsequent discussion on how to foster an innovative organization, the central issue is that of balancing autonomy, individuality, differentiation, and bottom-up management with teamwork, cohesion, integration, and top-down management processes. For some firms, the specific challenge is to build individuality into the bureaucracy in order to release the creative potential of employees. Other organizations have creative and innovative track records, but they lack the management systems and corporate cohesion needed to commercialize their inventiveness.

The experiences of organizations like IBM, Digital and Volvo in building individuality into the organization are reviewed. This leads to a discussion of ways of minimizing social distance, of unorthodox training approaches which foster positive criticism, and of how to inject diversity into overly-conformist enterprises.

But individualism needs to be channeled, and this implies strong leadership. Channeling creativity in the interests of the firm means establishing and communicating the desired goals and directions, and using subtle means of control rather than traditional crude mechanisms. Devices used by these firms to channel individualism are discussed, such as the use of symbols, the education of employees in the strategic and operating realities of the enterprise, and the alignment of reward and other management systems.

Chapter 10 looks at another aspect of innovation, namely the management of scientists and engineers. It reports provocative research by the widely esteemed Technology Management unit at MIT's Sloan School of Management, presented by Professors *Tom Allen* and *Ralph Katz*. Based on their studies of thousands of engineers and scientists, their focus is on how to reward, motivate and develop the careers of professionals, and on the worrying problems of the obsolescence of their knowledge.

Starting with questions about the effectiveness of dual career ladders for engineers and managers (firms with the most experience here find such ladders to be of doubtful utility), their key finding was that nearly half of these persons were neither interested in technical promotional ladders nor in managerial ladders. What motivated them above all was the opportunity to work on challenging projects.

Allen and Katz argue that in the changing face of science and technology, management must provide challenging, stretching work assignments and the motivation constantly to update knowledge. Their data also suggest that much of obsolescence is an artificial problem, created by a false management assumption that engineers will inevitably become less creative with age. They are therefore given less challenging jobs and become demotivated and obsolescent in fact – an example of how assumptions lead to self-fulfilling prophecies.

This chapter implicitly points out the dangers that arrive if top managers who have successfully climbed the hierarchies of their corporations project their hierarchic thinking onto others in the firm. Flatter, leaner organizations, with more horizontal communication and more self-organizing capabilities, are seen as the way forward, but clear goals and organizational commitment are also needed to prevent diversity and autonomy from turning into disorder.

It's a cultural juggling act, and in Chapter 11 *Yves Doz* (Professor of Business Policy at INSEAD) assesses how the innovative firm manages it. Taking a top management perspective, he conceptualizes how the necessary diversity and creativity can be managed and channeled, based upon his studies of firms such as Philips, IBM, Ciba–Geigy, and Matsushita. His key argument is that large and complex international firms are potentially no less innovative than small companies. However, in order to capitalize on their innovative potential, top managers in multinational corporations have to learn how to manage a paradox, that of controlling diversity.

Fostering innovation in these firms calls for much more diversity and differentiation – more debate and communication between people with different perspectives, more diversity in resource allocation channels, and more diversity in different ways of organizing within the umbrella of the corporation. This leads Doz into a discussion of ways to manage this diversity: creating networks through increased mobility; communication channels that bring people with diverse perspectives together; facilitating the meeting of solutions with problems; creating a climate for constructive dissent; the engineering of resource shortages; the use of multiple funding channels to test the commitment of sponsors; careful design of physical layouts; and separating innovative ventures from established businesses while maintaining the interdependence that is needed.

But if innovation is to lead to viable commercial results, the organization needs control, fixed poles, and cohesion. Top management must set broad but clear visions, leaving the means sufficiently open to inspire and attract able people. Performance expectations must be mapped out, and reward systems should emphasize results but tolerate justifiable failure. The norms for dissent within the network must emphasize analysis and business interests rather than power and vested interests. And "hands-on" top management is needed, executives who get involved in the substance of innovation rather than simply focusing on management processes like planning and budgeting.

Doz argues that the guiding metaphors for innovative organization are paradoxes like "controlled variety", "managed diversity", and "ambiguity by design". He concludes that the greatest challenge to innovation in product development and the exploitation of technological progress is the need for innovation in our deeply ingrained concepts of management and organization. It's a conclusion which is implicit throughout the whole of this book.

*Chapter 9*_____

Fostering Innovation Through Human Resources: Lessons from Practice

Paul Evans, Alison Farquhar and Oliver Landreth

> Let us look at the market place now as far as banking is concerned. We have to respond to fluid markets. The financial services industry within the UK is experiencing tremendous change, at a speed we have never seen previously. Traditional markets have been eroded. We find that retailers, building societies, saving institutions, post offices via the national Giro, are all fishing in what has been our traditional pond, facilitated by new technologies. Deregulation is moving apace, removing the barriers, and we face competition that we have never seen before. International markets are also getting increasingly competitive, and the so-called "big bang" of capital markets is eroding our traditional margins.

This statement from an executive at Britain's National Westminster Bank underlines the volatility of today's markets in the financial sector. Such rapid change is not confined to this one area, though the pace of change varies from industry to industry. If the automobile industry had undergone the same rate of technological change as in electronics, when we would now be able to buy a Rolls Royce for £1, run it for 50,000 miles on a gallon of petrol, and pay annual maintenance costs of less than £10.

In these changing markets and with these new forms of competition, innovation has become an increasingly important instrument for competitive success. Hewlett–Packard, for example, derives 50% of its sales volume from products introduced during the last two to three years. The secret of its success is a continuous flow of products, and the prerequisites are innovation, creativity and entrepreneurship. The new technologies that firms like Hewlett–Packard are providing are in turn creating opportunities for organizational innovation in other firms – in their manufacturing, office and other functions.

This chapter discusses separately the impact that new technologies are having on the internal operations of the firm on the one hand, and the process of innovation that leads to new products and services, and responses to changing markets on the other. However, organizational and product innovation are in fact closely interwoven processes. And the lessons of experience in recent years clearly indicate that both the source of innovation and the obstacles to innovation stem more than anything else from human resources.

THE IMPACT OF NEW TECHNOLOGIES

Information technology, particularly in the shape of the computer, has begun to revolutionize the workplace during the last two decades. This has necessitated radical changes in attitude on the part of employees and managers alike, and daily tasks have been transformed.

Take for example the bookkeeping function in a business. Technological evolution has required substantial changes in mental approach. Prior to the widespread use of the computer, bookkeeping was principally governed by legal concerns. Decisions about account postings were made a according to the rules of jurisprudence, and this meant that personal judgement was necessary where the legal frame work was unclear. With the advent of the computer came the age of the predetermined framework in which personal judgements were no longer the order of the day. Account postings are now ruled by computer programs, and employees are asked to exercise rigor rather than judgement. This is leading to changes in the accounting industry, in the Big Eight audit firms. On the one hand, the auditor's work now requires less judgemental skill. Conducting an audit becomes more routine, and competition becomes fierce as audit procedures become systematized. Yet on the other hand, new skills are required and new opportunities are created. The auditing profession is changing its role as the competitive skill becomes the design of audit and financial systems rather than the conducting of an audit; the improvement of the quality of financial management within the client firm rather than the verification of its books according to statutory criteria; expertise in the interpretation of financial standards rather than the mere application of financial standards. Firms that were traditionally seen as accountants are now becoming consultants, and the catalyst for this process is technological change.

Hewlett–Packard's manager for management development points also to the similar impact of the micro-computer that has appeared on office desks. In the old days, a systems analyst would write a carefully designed program for one's particular needs. Today, one uses a universal tool like a spreadsheet program. The attitude that is now required from users is mental curiosity. A spreadsheet program has infinite possibilities and capabilities. What is needed is the curiosity to find out how to use those capabilities.

Upgrading the Skills of the Workforce

New technology has brought about a need for different skills and higher qualifications in the workforce. In the words of Hewlett–Packard's manager:

> Someone who used to be an assembly worker might now be replaced by someone who is overseeing the operation of a whole automatic chain for insertion of components. The people are now operators of a system, and that requires different skills. You need to understand the whole process, not only one part of it. This requires learning and communication skills that are different from those the workers had before, which were hand and experience skills. The assembly worker has become a mini business manager.

Automation and new technologies were once seen as threatening job security and devaluing the quality of work. At least in terms of the latter, the reverse has happened. The challenge is to build operator competencies, to unleash and channel the human potential in the factory.

Bottling water seems like one of the lowest of low technologies. But the possibilities of new technologies are being exploited by Evian (a company within the French BSN group). Water that used to leave the factory in standard glass litre bottles is now shipped in hundreds of variants of plastic and glass containers, each adapted to the requirements of an airline, a hotel or supermarket chain. This trend led Evian in the early 80s to envisage a flexible but highly automated "factory of the 90s". Evian's first steps in developing this project were focused on the human factor, in parallel with technical feasibility planning. The thousand-strong workforce was subjected to assessment and psychological testing in order to determine who had the qualities required for the new factory. The skills of those who did were then broadened via rotation through different tasks, supplemented by technical and economic training (a difficult challenge since this preparatory training is often abstract until the new plant is a reality). The number of workers without such qualities gradually declined through retirement and attrition, while others where transferred either to the simple jobs that would still be required in the new plant, or to a smaller plant that would continue to use traditional technology. Today, that new factory is being smoothly run in, aided by five years of advanced attention to human resources.

Volvo's CEO, Pehr Gyllenhammar, points out that the time has gone when poor jobs simply went south or east to where they could be done by cheaper labor. Hit by a cost squeeze and competitive pressures in 1977, Volvo decided to continue the task of building its manufacturing base in Sweden rather than siting it elsewhere. It was in Sweden and not in the Third World where there was the combination of technological expertise, human competence and an entrepreneurial spirit that Gyllenhammar felt was needed in the auto industry. He points out that high technology is mistakenly associated with the suppliers of that technology, not with the users. Whereas the auto industry is labeled as "mature", its technology is in fact as complex and evolving as that used by NASA to send men to the moon. It is typically dynamic firms in industries such as this which specify the standards and requirements for the suppliers of high technology.

Indeed stereotypic labels such as "high" and "low" technology are misleading if not dangerous. What could be lower on the popular technology scale than the cookie-business? Yet an executive in the European biscuit industry points out that factors such as the shelf life of a biscuit are distinguishing between the winners and losers in a toughly competitive market. Innovations in the technology of gases that are injected into packets allow the leading firms to extend shelf-life from weeks to months, thereby gaining competitive advantage.

Most organizations have only just begun to digest the consequences of new technologies, where formerly unskilled workers become sophisticated systems operators, supervisors become business managers, factories have leaner structures, and where the role of middle management needs to be redefined.

Training and Education

In companies such as Hewlett–Packard, Volvo, Wärtsila, and National Westminster Bank, these consequences are recognised in the increasing importance of human resource development. For example, retraining an assembly group leader into a new role as a business manager at Hewlett–Packard is an investment of some 700 hours of training. Yet the failure to recognize the need for upgrading the skills of the workforce and the failure to make the necessary investments may lead to costlier problems – witness the months of disorganization and strikes when France's Credit Lyonnais bank converted to computerized processing of cheques without the prior investment.

The types of skills and qualities that these organizations are seeking to recruit among their workers are changing. The companies that are actively involved in introducing new technologies feel that this will place new demands on national educational systems. What is needed is not school leavers with specialized knowledge, but school leavers equipped with the learning skills that will be needed in a world of continuous education.

Wärtsila, a successful Finnish engineering company, believes that the basic education system could cater better for industry's needs by revising the methods of teaching rather than the school syllabus. The pressing need is for developing study skills, a heightened capacity for learning.

As explained later in this chapter, Wärtsila places a great deal of importance on the ability to learn as a lever for success in its own internal programs. This is tied in closely with the strategic priorities of the company:

> We want to link closely our strategic and development actions so that there is not much difference whether people are operational or in training. We give our most difficult strategy questions to the participants to solve during the training programs, so that they develop the capacity to learn. It is important for the future that organizations develop learning capacity. Then the changes we face are not so difficult.

For Hewlett–Packard, the general education of recruits is essential. Governments will have to realize that it is going to be necessary to lengthen the whole cycle of the average citizen in training. For example, in France the elite engineering schools select their students primarily on their proven aptitude in theoretical mathematics – too narrow a criterion for the future. Business administration is slowly percolating into the engineering syllabus, rather than being left to business schools. And Norwegian engineering schools are experimenting with standard courses in the social and management aspects of engineering.

On the other hand, companies should not merely delegate this role to governments and professional educators. If a gap exists between industry and education, then companies have an equal responsibility for closing it. Only industry can define the skills which it requires and which today's education systems fail to supply. Honeywell Europe believes that as recruiters of graduates, business can also foster co-operation by elevating its attractiveness to universities. To this end, they have promoted a "European Futurist Essay Competition" which has the combined value of pushing students to think in a manner relevant to a high technology firm and revealing quality candidates.

However, there is a tendency to inertia since those who have survived the old system see little personal gain in pushing for change. Hewlett–Packard is keen to fight this:

Universities sometimes complain that in fact industries are not putting enough effort into going out into schools and telling them what they think they should have. There is the attitude, "I went through that myself – too bad for my successor, he'll have to go through it also". But if we keep going that way, it probably won't work in the future. Companies probably have to take a more aggressive attitude in trying to express our needs to schools.

The Skill Gap

On the other hand, certain jobs which require very low qualifications will also survive. This stems from the paradox that the simplest and least interesting jobs in the work place, such as machine feeding and cooking hamburgers, are precisely those which are the most difficult to automate. As a consequence, the gap between the lowest jobs and the first level of skilled work is widening.

Assembly operations in particular are unlikely to be much affected by technology this century, in the view of Volvo. Volvo's response to this paradox was the use of semi-autonomous work groups in car assembly, tried out initially at the plant in Kalmar. Cars are transported from work group to work group on electrically driven carriers or compressed air conveyors rather than on the traditional assembly line. Yet at Kalmar, it still takes 60 people to finalize a new car. The concept of the future, they believe, is that of the flexible product workshop: a core group of fifty people or less putting one car together, with the flexibility to add more people and to experiment creatively with new methods and procedures.

The New Plants

Volvo's Kalmar was the first major factory in Europe where an attempt was made to pioneer a new match between the workforce and technology. At the time, in 1971, there were many people within Volvo who were suspicious, while outsiders said, "It will never work!" Today, with its semi-autonomous assembly groups, its high degree of automation and creative use of technology, and its lean managerial structure, it is one of the most efficient car assembly plants within the Volvo group.

Its success unleashed a wave of innovation within Volvo. While automation has been applied to sub-component manufacturing, ten other assembly plants have been built since, each factory design team attempting to apply certain basic principles but also to improve upon them.

There are four common principles. First, maximum delegation of responsibility to the working team, and second a corresponding principle of minimizing the number of levels in the organization. The plant design group typically spends several years running in the new plant, and in the newer plants there are incentive systems for the work groups gradually to assume planning and control functions that would traditionally have been assumed by management. The third principle is the matching of the technical and social systems, and the fourth is the search to maximize plant flexibility in both design and operations, leading in the future to modularized plant designs. Volvo believes that this flexibility, coupled with their ability to channel the creativity and entrepreneurial spirit in the work force, is the key to further developments in the future.

Volvo naturally considers detailed productivity information on their new plants as confidential, indeed strategic, information. However, reports suggest that although direct productivity per operating worker is not much higher than in traditional plants, there are three important benefits: first, a capacity for continued and organic productivity improvement that does not exist in tradition low skill plants; second, a degree of flexibility that in the long-term has a high economic value; and third, substantially higher overall plant productivity owing to the leaner organizational structure. This latter benefit is important when one considers that 40–60% of the payroll cost in traditional plants may go to cover the salaries of managers, supervisors and engineers, and other indirect employees.

The Structure of the Corporation

So far we have referred mainly to the impact that new technologies have on the lower status jobs within an organization. The implications are, however, much further-reaching. The coming years will bring significant changes both to the overall structure of large companies and to the roles that managers play within them.

Traditional relationships change. The once clearly delineated tasks of manager and secretary, for example, are already becoming blurred. Through direct use of his desk top computer, increasingly sophisticated word processing programs, and electronic mail systems, the manager is in some senses becoming his own secretary. He devotes time to tasks which used to be performed for him, but on the other hand this saves duplication of effort by avoiding retyping and proof reading. This has repercussions for the role of the secretary who must free the manager up by playing the role of personal assistant.

Some managers have been slow to adapt to these changes. At Hewlett–Packard, instances are cited where managers have their electronic mail printed out and put in their in-trays!

New technologies lead to the upgrading of operators' skills, which in turn creates the necessity for *hierarchies with fewer levels* – in itself often desirable for reasons of cost and flexibility. The new generation of operators have a lot more autonomy and are expected to exercise more initiative, as Hewlett–Packard points out. Multiple levels of supervision and staff are incompatible and inconsistent with these requirements, and the firm wishes to reduce the ten supervisory levels between John Young, the president, and the lowest handyman.

Indeed, the traditional hierarchic structure is becoming a hindrance, says Hewlett–Packard's director of management development. In support of this he cited a recent French study which had concluded that computerisation had not generally improved the productivity of government services; he suspected that the major explanation for this was that the hierarchically bureaucratic structure had not changed. Indeed, in such organizations, people who achieve something have to go *against* the structure. His vision of the future company was one of a composite of semi-autonomous groups with rotating leaders, appointed according to the skills needed at that stage, and with experts available when needed on a particular task. Management in such a firm means creating the magnetic field which orients the efforts of these changing group cells. Far from today's realities? Not entirely. That vision is based on the Japanese Kanban production system, also used by Hewlett–Packard.

Perhaps the most significant implications for the producers of these new technologies are the implications for the internal structure of the corporation. Hewlett–Packard, for example, is built on the notion of the divisional unit handling a maximum of 500 people, with a triad of functions: research and development, marketing, and manufacturing. Though several divisions may be in the same building, each conducts its own business, and each is a profit centre. Senior management tries to mimimize overlaps and internal competition. This structure fosters the creativity needed in a company generating a majority of its revenues from new products, and has led an instruments company first into pocket calculators, then desk top computers, then technical computers, and now mini-computers. Today's customer wants all of these products to talk to each other via the technology of data communications. And this of course challenges the concept of the division. How can research and the affairs of twenty different divisions be co-ordinated in order to meet this customer need? Hewlett–Packard, Philips, and other such firms are today wrestling with this question.

Externally, too, structures are changing. Forced by international competition, the rapid increase in co-operative partnerships and joint-ventures means that companies who would never previously have dreamed of disclosing technological know-how are now banding together.

As technology becomes more complex, managers have to demonstrate more leadership than in the past. Honeywell's European president Michael Bonsignore, believes that establishing and communicating the objectives of the firm or the business unit will be a fundamental role of the manager in the future, an observation echoed throughout this book. This was also brought home when the president of Hewlett–Packard commissioned an internal study of "good managers" in the company. The interviews with these individuals led to the conclusion that their distinguishing capability was that of establishing objectives or a mission statement for their group, and the ability to communicate that sense of mission and purpose to its members.

DEVELOPING THE INNOVATIVE ORGANIZATION

Few managers would dispute the place of innovation among the keys to competitive success in today's rapidly moving markets. But what can an organization *do* to enhance its innovative capacity? There is no straight-forward answer. Each company has its own culture, and the formula for success in one may well spell failure in another.

Before looking at the approaches of some leading edge companies to developing an innovative organization, two generalizations can, neverthe-less, be made. First, no company can be innovative without its people. They are the key to the process. Second, the development of an innovative organization involves finding a subtle balance between top-down manage-ment processes on the one hand (that is to say direction, control and systems), and bottom-up creative processes and the encouragement of individual initiative on the other.

For many large organizations, the major challenge is to build room for individuality into the bureaucratic culture, to free the creative potential of the employee. This is the challenge which typically underlies today's concern with innovation. All too often, the hierarchical structures of large corporations stifle the individuality they would like to develop. Yet the problem of other organizations is the reverse. There, the organization is only a loose framework in which creative and autonomous individuals pursue their own goals, with little sense of collective purpose. For example, the inbuilt strength of many Italian firms is their innovative and creative track record; yet their weakness is often the lack of formal management systems and organization to commercialize their inventiveness.

It's analogous to the centralization–decentralization dilemma. If Hewlett–Packard is trying to co-ordinate decentralized divisions in order to meet customer needs, as described above, Honeywell Europe under Bonsignore's leadership has been stimulating initiative by pushing respon-sibility down from its centralized Brussels headquarters to product-oriented "centres of excellence".

The constrasting experiences of Len Peach illustrate these opposite challenges. Peach is currently on secondment from IBM to the British National Health Service. At IBM, he was director of personnel for the

British company, becoming first personnel director for the NHS with its one million employees, and recently its chairman.

IBM is somewhat monolithic as an organization. Despite its ground principle of "respect for the individual", it has a culture which expects a degree of conformity. Recruitment policies and reward systems have traditionally encouraged employees to "fit in". Hence the popularly quoted company quip that "IBM likes wild ducks – as long as they fly in formation!" To unleash innovative individuality in such a strong culture requires a great deal of leadership on the part of management. The fact that "respect for the individual" is one of IBM's three basic corporate values is a permanent reminder of this challenge.

IBM is renowned for the commitment of its workforce, but there is also a high degree of commitment in Peach's new organization, the British National Health Service. However, whereas commitment at IBM is to the corporation as a whole, the NHS commitment is to the patient. The NHS has the opposite problem – too many individuals. Within its fourteen regions and 192 districts, each with its separate local board, there is constant reinvention of the wheel. There are few economies of scale, and messages from the centre are rejected with equal and opposite force as an invasion of individual freedom. As Peach says:

> The problem in the NHS is not the creativity of the individual. It's very much how you can make the individual feel part of a large organization and use his or her creativity to the benefit of others.
>
> The idea of loose–tight in *In Search of Excellence* is important; you have to get the balance right. The NHS doesn't have the balance right. And its Management Board doesn't have the balance right when it talks about devolution [decentralization]. It should not be devolving, it should actually be deciding what areas it wishes to hold tight to the centre, where it wishes to give clear direction, and what good practice it wishes to disseminate.

This is a pertinent reminder that innovation is only one side of the coin (see Chapter 12 for a further discussion of this issue). Let us consider how an organization can build individuality into its formal practices and systems by reviewing the actions of some leading corporations.

BUILDING INDIVIDUALITY INTO THE ORGANIZATION

In large business organizations, the IBM problem is more frequent. How can one successfully build individuality into the firm in the interests of innovation?

Minimizing Social Distance

The multilevel hierarchies and formal reporting systems of large firms effectively widen the social gap between senior management and the bottom line. Such structures send clear messages to employees not to operate out side their brief, and they tend to stifle innovation at source. Many companies now recognize the danger of such a situation and take active steps to reduce the social gap. "Single status" is the term that is often used in policy discussions.

The successful British retail chain, Marks & Spencer, has a strong tradition of the most senior people talking directly to the most junior. Popularized today as "management-by-walking-around" (the term used within Hewlett–Packard), it has long been common to see the chairman of Marks & Spencer in a store asking a sales assistant for his or her ideas about product ranges and what could be improved. This helps minimize the distance between centralized merchandising operations and the 260 stores spread throughout Britain.

All this is reinforced by the fact that academic qualifications are not an indispensable requirement for reaching the top at Marks & Spencer. Communication groups have been set up at the lowest levels to provide a formal channel through which staff can express their views. Encouragement of employee input is made clear from the start:

> 250 to 300 graduates join the company every year, starting their careers as sales assistants. From a very early stage they are encouraged to look at the company, to look at their own training program, and to criticize and innovate.

A senior manager admits that at times, perhaps, people are asked to criticize from the basis of ignorance. The value of this particular approach lies as much in the symbol its represents as in its output – speaking up is not only allowed, it is encouraged by the system.

IBM is equally keen to reduce the social status gap in order to have more employee input. However, it is not blind to the difficulty of the challenge:

> Single status is often seen as trying to put people in the same cafeteria or having the same conditions at work. My view of single status means accepting the person on what that individual can contribute to the organization. But I find among professional engineers, for example, statements which mean: "He's a blue collar worker, so how can he have ideas? I'm a professional engineer, I have the ideas!" That is a problem.

Titles are played down at Shell to avoid creating unnecessary communication barriers. Titles such as "director", "vice president" and even "manager" are avoided in preference for more neutral labels such as "head of department"; the top executives heading the major functions or businesses are known as "coordinators". Even official office paper at Shell bears only the name and address of the individual, not his or her title.

Digital Equipment Corporation (DEC) is also concerned about the inhibiting influence of social distance on innovation. At the same time, it is conscious of how difficult it is to minimize this distance in practice. This goes far deeper than giving your secretary the right to call you by your first name. A senior manager confesses: "It is hard to have much creativity unless you minimize social distance. We try to do so, but there is still way too much, much more than we would like to see".

"Push Back" in Decision-making

Certain norms, embedded in the culture of the firm, may facilitate (or handicap) innovation. DEC, the world's second largest computer company, is a firm with a strong track record in product and organizational innovation. One of the cultural norms that appears to have fostered that track record is known as "push back": the encouragement of contributions and criticism from each and every employee. The norm has its origins in the methods and values of Ken Olsen, the founder-engineer of the firm. What it concretely implies is explained by a Digital executive:

> "Push back" means that anyone from any level is expected, when an idea is presented, to push back if they have a different view or opinion. The way it is supposed to work is that this is welcomed, even though it is sometimes painful. It's an organizational norm, and in effect people will get criticized for not pushing back. That can be even more painful.

Explaining how the concept functions in practice, he cites an example which challenged his own openness of mind. With a hectic schedule ahead on a business trip from the United States to Europe, he and another senior vice president decided that they would be justified in flying Concorde, despite company policy of not even traveling first class. Instructions were accordingly given to his secretary. However, when he came to collect his ticket before leaving for the airport, he discovered that he had been booked on a regular flight with the explanation, "Mary and I decided it was too expensive!" Honesty forced this executive to admit, "At one level, I was really angry, but organizationally I was pleased as hell. I was proud that I was lucky enough to have her as a secretary!"

Another Digital norm, "doing the right thing", stems from the view that the firm can never foresee all situations, nor tell an employee how to react when faced with the unexpected. Personal judgement has to be exercised.

Sometimes an individual employee will have superior knowledge to that of the person who has given him instructions. In such a situation, he should do what he judges best, that is "the right thing".

Norms such as "push back" and "doing the right thing" have advantages and disadvantages. On the one hand, they bring vitality, creativity, and a healthy irreverence for bureaucracy. On the other hand, they can be messy. Following such norms can become a justification for flying in the face of authority, unless it is realized that some issues cannot be pushed back, that certain instructions cannot be overruled by personal judgement. The line between the two is cultural and implicit.

On the whole, however, DEC has been encouraged by the results, and in the words of that executive: "I don't know of organizations that have fantastic innovation without a little bit of messiness".

New Approaches to Training

The majority of large corporations agree that an innovative attitude can be thoroughly instilled only through training. And then only when the training is constant, consistent and given at all levels of the company. But traditional training fosters norms of obedience and conformism, so the concern for individualization leads to new approaches.

Volvo has been successful in activating middle management by involving them directly in the teaching process:

> We believe that maybe one of the best means of learning is to teach. If you have to teach, if you are in a teaching position, you have to prepare yourself . . . If you switch this down all the way to the supervisor level, you get a very interesting picture.

At first, this policy evoked considerable fear of failure, but with support from the human resource function many supervisors are now carrying out tasks they had never previously attempted, gaining self-confidence and a range of new skills in the process. Leadership has improved and supervisors now tend to communicate with their departments as a whole and not on the one-to-one basis of the past.

Since risk is an indispensable part of both company and individual growth, Wärtsila in Finland does not believe in traditional classroom teaching:

> In the learning situation, people need demanding real situations. They really want to do their best, they do not want to sit as pupils . . . We have tried to give more difficult tasks that we believe they can solve for themselves so that they really can grow. We have used active learning especially for the high fliers so that they can show what they are capable of and be first from the start.

Wärtsila has instituted "action learning projects". Different units within the company are requested to submit development projects which they would like to undertake and for which they would like to borrow a project manager from another unit. Then, high-potential managers on the program are indentified as possible project leaders. Finally, projects are paired with project managers to the benefit of each side. To date nearly forty managers have been assigned to such projects and gone on to successful careers afterwards. Philips has an analogous training system where eight-person teams of high-potential managers are assigned to "Octagon" projects, the results of which may be presented to board members (described on p. 110).

Marks & Spencer also uses special projects as a means of stretching its managers. A "programme of scrutinies" has been designed in which managers are given six weeks to two months to pull apart a certain operation in the company and make recommendations for improving its efficiency or reducing its costs. These projects are usually outside the managers' normal domain and so provide useful breadth of experience. A system of mentors or sponsors also exists. Managers are assigned to a senior director in another field to help brainstorm any problems he or she may have. Besides the value of having a mentor, this again gives managers experience outside their usual field.

Structuring for Innovation

IBM, like General Electric and many other firms, has chosen to play on structural form in its encouragement of innovation:

> We recognize that we are a bureaucracy to some degree and therefore the important development in the last five years has been the creation of the independent business unit, the IBU. It recognizes that the business itself imposes restrictions. It puts these on one side and says, "Here's the money, there's the people, now get on with it".
>
> The great success of the IBU was the PC itself. The PC was developed by a Independent Business Unit and brought to the market very much more quickly than this could have been done in the main structure of the corporation. So you can indeed take organizational action to take the pieces away from the business to prevent the bureaucracy from getting their arms around it.

IBM has not forced its monolithic culture on companies it has acquired. When it purchased Rolm Telecommunications, for example, it was recognized that the informal "jacuzzi and beer" culture of California was far removed from that of IBM. That was allowed to continue, though admittedly it disturbs IBM managers.

Leaving an acquisition alone for the time being, a new interest in joint-ventures, establishing research links with universities, sending executives on business programs outside the corporation where they will work with peers from other firms, involvement in projects such as the EEC's *Esprit* – all these are indications of IBM's recent desire to allow new ideas to percolate into the corporation.

And within the corporation, management spillover is essential. When people successfully develop new ideas, there must be rapid cross-fertilization to other parts of the corporation. Indeed, this is one of the strengths of the IBM culture. Where there is a good idea, the general attitude is "Well, let's take it, copy it, and do better". Very different from the "not-invented-here" syndrome of other more individualistic organizations, with the opposite problems of how to channel that individualism and creativity.

Encouraging Entrepreneurship and Injecting Diversity

The term "entrepreneur" is associated with those people who, on their own initiative, start up new businesses from scratch, often risking personal capital in the process. However, it could equally well be applied to those who use their initiative in following up opportunities they have spotted, even when doing so could mean failure. This form of entrepreneurship has its place not only in start-up concerns but also in the mainstream of large organizations. A certain amount of risk is healthy, and many corporations are encouraging this by trying to reduce the negative consequences of failure.

The new chairman of Marks & Spencer himself sends clear messages down through the organization to this effect. The executive group, set up two years ago with the intention of brainstorming various problems, was pushed to "be radical, be revolutionary, but be well reasoned in the presentation of your ideas". Managers are incited to entrepreneurial action by another of the chairman's well known exhortations: "Bring me solutions, not problems!"

Many organizations feel a need to inject new blood, diversity, and new ideas into the organization through recruitment, even though this may be difficult at senior management levels. After a long tradition of "growing its own management", Marks & Spencer has started to recruit middle managers in order to reap the benefits of new opinions and operating styles. The recent recruitment of some three hundred university graduates is also seen as an injection of innovative spirit, particularly since they are encouraged to speak up from the start.

Marks & Spencer has traditionally exposed its own managers to other work cultures through secondments to public organizations or community projects. In contrast to other firms, these secondments are often of key employees, regarded as part of their management development. Indeed, the current chairman, Lord Rayner, spent many years on secondment first to the Heath government and more recently to Margaret Thatcher, with a particular assignment to streamline the British Civil Service. In recent years, senior executives have been on study visits to other successful corporations to explore their approach to management and organization. Volvo has permitted several high-potential managers to leave the firm temporarily in order to work elsewhere for several years, and has been so encouraged by the payoff as to endorse this in the future. Indeed, one practical vehicle for injecting innovation into senior management may be to keep track of managers who left the firm earlier, re-recruiting these "hybrids" into senior positions.

Volvo and IBM have reinvigorated the old idea of the suggestion scheme, now backed by financial rewards for successfully adopted, cost-saving ideas. IBM awards 20% of the first year's saving to the suggestor. Moreover, awards are also made to suggestion investigators, to overcome the problem of such investigations always remaining at the bottom of the engineer's in-tray – through recognition schemes or participation in a lottery for some luxurious holiday. Volvo's plant level suggestion scheme led to some 700 suggestions each year in the past. A different approach was recently developed, resulting in 7,000 suggestions in the first year.

The idea of the suggestion scheme tackles entrepreneurship on a small and low-key scale. But it should be borne in mind that major innovations often have humble origins. Much that lands up being labeled as innovative originates in modest achievements and small breakthroughs rather than in grandiose visions – indeed in a trial-and-error process where the successes are gradually built upon while the failures, though not punished, are either left to wither or are ignored.

The development of Marks & Spencer this century is a good example of how experimentation or trial-and-error can lead to success. Experimentation is a value that is built into the culture of the firm. They do not believe in marketing surveys or high-powered analysis to determine the merchandising range. Instead the approach is to try out new wares; if they sell fast, stock up (this is facilitated by the firm's close relationship to its manufacturing suppliers), otherwise forget it. And each store manager has the authority to try out experimental goods.

It is this practice of trial-and-error (and not strategic marketing) that has successfully led Marks & Spencer from its base in clothing to high value-added food products, and more recently into profitable lines of homeware. For example, more than a third of off-the-peg men's suits sold in Britain are bought at Marks & Spencer – a merchandising line that was not even part of its business ten years ago! The origin of this innovation was a local store experiment in selling jackets and trousers made from the same cloth, ostensibly for reason of economy. They sold out in no time. What the customer was in fact doing was choosing an appropriate size in trousers and then finding the right fit of jacket, thus walking away in a "tailored" suit. Recognizing what was happening, although it was by no means what had originally been intended, the formula was rapidly built upon. Within five years, Burtons, the men's clothing chain that had hitherto led this retailing sector, had been driven completely out of this line of business!

Another example is Volvo's successful diversification over the last fifteen years. Although viewed by the public as an auto manufacturer, in fact more than 20% of the group's turnover comes from profitable activities in energy, food, and strategic shareholdings. While the decision to move into each new area has been a carefully assessed strategic move, the actual approach to diversification has been more experimental – to try out a number of ventures on a modest scale. Volvo's top management does not believe in taking one single option, no matter how good it looks on paper. "We believe we have to apply a sort of trial and error method", says a senior executive. "For instance, when we moved into energy we tried all sorts of things – we even had a project on solar energy". The result in each case was gradual learning from both successes and failures, and a progressive refining of the successes.

It is worth remembering that the values behind today's successes were initially produced by successes that were often random. What innovation, as opposed to imitation, implies is rediscovering the mechanisms that led to those initial successes. And as Peter Drucker points out in his book on *Innovation and Entrepreneurship* (Drucker, 1985), the origin of those original successes is typically in problems, handicaps, and difficulties combined with a random component of luck and good fortune. Allow creative deviance, introduce diversity in the firm, bear in mind that innovations are often things that weren't supposed to happen, view problems and handicaps as potential opportunities, don't kill that spirit by punishing failures – and then keep eyes and ears open for the successes, for what works, and build upon them rapidly. This is today's formula for innovation.

THE CHANNELING OF INNOVATION

With books such as Rosabeth Kanter's *The Change Masters* (1983) and Tom Peter's and Nancy Austin's *A Passion for Excellence* (1985), a great deal of attention has been focused on revitalizing individuality, creating entrepreneurship, and inducing informality into organizations. But there is another aspect of innovation that has received less popular attention, namely how to channel innovative behavior in the interests of the firm. After all, few organizations are in the business of innovation. Innovations should serve a commercial, money-making objective, in line with the business mission of the firm.

The channeling of innovative behavior, the alignment of such behaviors with the strategic and organizational interests of the enterprise, requires the use of *subtle* mechanisms of control. Overt mechanisms such as formal plans, centralized procedures, and formal authority would undermine innovative behavior. Individualistic organizations such as the British National Health Service tend to reject with hostility the attempt to align people through such overt means.

What are the subtle mechanisms that allow for individuality and yet nevertheless channel such behaviors towards a superordinate organizational interest? One such mechanism, though less than subtle, that has long been investigated by the scientists of group behavior is external threat, a threat of crisis proportions to the survival of the organization and its members. This mobilizes a collective purpose, the superordinate goal of collaboration for survival. Since management may be powerless and certainly reluctant to induce a real crisis, in practical terms this often means "selling the crisis" before it comes real (see Chapter 3 for a fuller discussion of this).

Apart from this, there are three subtle mechanisms that emerge from the practice of the firms we have studied: the use of symbols, the alignment of reward and other management systems, and education in the strategic and operational realities of the firm.

The Use of Symbols

Berth Jönsson, vice president at Volvo, believes that an innovative organization needs leadership that can create powerful symbols which are visible to the whole organization. An example of this is the way in which Volvo has promoted the creation of lean administrative structures in the group. This started at the top of the company in 1971. The headquarters at the time consisted of 1,500 people and powerful fiefdoms. Top managment decided that this was one of the largest headquarters in the world, and they wanted the smallest. Within one year, it had been cut back to a hundred people, its size today. Although this was not the conscious intent at the time, it became clear that this lean headquarter organization served as a powerful message to keep administration very thin in the various Volvo companies.

The widely publicized Kalmar plant, discussed earlier in this chapter, became another symbol of the type of innovation that Volvo's top management endorsed. It promoted a whole new attitude toward innovation within Volvo. Berth Jönsson remembers engineers, quality controllers, and maintenance managers coming up to him at the time and saying, "Well, I thought of these ideas before, but no-one at the top was interested. I have this idea about truck assembly, but I thought that no-one cared". Thereafter, the selection of plant managers became partially self-selecting in the sense that young engineers whose ambition was to become plant manager had to prove themselves by trying something new.

In a similar way, Volvo has begun to use an employee attitude survey called "Monitor". This new tool in their management information system complements traditional economic and financial statements. But its purpose is also symbolic, to communicate in a tangible way that people are the most important asset, and that complementary information is needed by each manager in the type of company that Volvo is becoming.

Such symbols allow Volvo to maintain the decentralization that innovation and responsiveness to specific product markets require, and yet to guide and channel behavior at lower levels toward the corporate interest.

The Alignment of Reward and Other Management Systems

Pay, promotion and rewards must also be seen to recompense the qualities and achievements which management wishes to encourage through other symbolic processes. The company's basic reward system has to be aligned with the types of innovative behavior that management requires.

The following story is told of the late Douglas McGregor of MIT, well-known for his Theory X and Theory Y models of work motivation. McGregor was called in to advise the CEO of a company who wished to ensure that his vice presidents and middle managers paid more attention to employee development. The CEO felt that the long-term future of the firm depended on this. After ensuring that the CEO was committed to this goal, even if it meant modest short-term compromises to earnings, McGregor simply suggested that a substantial part of the bonus of the vice presidents be linked to achievements in this area. And indeed within a year, a wave of programs, innovations, experiments, new systems and policies had been set in motion, bringing about the attention to personnel development desired by the CEO.

IBM pays great attention to rewards, and not only via bonuses and salary. Few other organizations make more use of ceremonies, lotteries, luxurious holidays for the innovators and high performers, and special awards. And ICI's Harvey Jones reportedly sent a crate of wine with a thank-you card to employees when he heard that the person had made some outstanding or innovative contribution, something that required risk or bucked the system.

Honeywell makes use of such reward systems, and its European president Michael Bonsignore conducts quarterly "state of the business" meetings for all headquarter employees, where outstanding performance is recognized with champagne and gift certificates. He also stresses the importance of what he calls "strategic rewards" which emphasize the importance of the employee to the company over and above his or her current job – invitations to sit on high visibility task forces or to participate in customer or community interface projects.

Education in Strategic and Operational Realities

The third mechanism for aligning innovative behavior and for increasing organizational flexibility is educational. Traditionally, strategic information on products, markets and competition has been the preserve of top management. But the forces of both decentralization and technological innovation are leading this information to be disseminated throughout the firm.

If the metaphor for yesterday's organization was the machine, where the individual is a cog, the metaphor for tomorrow's organization is the hologram, as Stanley Davis pointed out earlier (see Chapter 2). A blue print of the entire organization – its values, missions, problems, and opportunities – is contained in each and every employee. The "organization" is found in the mind of each person, and in this way the organizational imperatives are balanced with those of individuality.

Volvo's current "Dialog" program is an example. Its purpose is to spread knowledge about the firm throughout the organization: knowledge about its products, its markets, its history, its values, its threats and its challenges. Volvo believes that it is not only management that has the right to understand the nature of the business, the competitive environment, and the future of the corporation. Everyone should have some knowledge about the direction of the company, right down to the most humble plant worker.

For example, the volatility of international markets for cars and trucks means that Volvo must find ways of increasing flexibility in manufacturing operations. However, the plant workers and engineers are far removed from these markets. Through "Dialog", the intention is to help these people to understand that 80% of their production goes for the export market, that these markets are highly competitive and change rapidly, and that manufacturing operations must be more business-oriented. The hope is to instill a dialogue which will on the one hand encourage bottom-up innovation in line with organizational and market imperatives, and on the other facilitate important internal changes and developments.

Dialogue is indeed built into the methodology of the program, thereby symbolizing the type of behaviors to be encouraged. Each company and each geographic unit is encouraged to personalize the program to suit its own needs: "What do you wish to communicate to your people that fits this program?" Although aided by powerful audiovisual supports, the managers and supervisors themselves are the teachers in progam, rather than corporate staff specialists. The assumption is that one of the best means of learning is to teach, that when the supervisor meets to commmunicate with the team of workers there is constructive dialogue on directions, problems and solutions.

CONCLUSION: LIVING WITH INTELLECTUAL TENSION

Executives from innovative companies appear to agree that the development of an innovative organization involves creating and living with an atmosphere of intellectual tension. "We need to look for balance", they say; but this is a dynamic balance rather than something static.

Mechanisms have to be found to reconcile centralization and decentralization, the contribution of the individual and the constraints of the organization, individualism and teamwork, the formal with the informal, the loose with the tight. As one manufacturing executive put it, "You need people who will stand by standard practices from shift to shift and produce a consistent product and a consistent result, but still be able to think about that process and suggest better ways in which it can be done. And it is quite difficult to achieve that balance".

Paul Smith, personnel director for Marks & Spencer, makes this comment:

> One of the dangers in the current climate of exciting developments is that if you are not careful, you spend all your time innovating and in task forces and working parties, and very little doing the job you are employed to do. Creativity, like any other resource, has to be managed. And it has to be commercial. In a retail organization, it is one thing to stimulate creativity. But you cannot have three thousand new product lines coming on show in a season – it has to be managed. The paradox is that if you lose control of creativity, you lose your sense of direction as a company.

This question of how to balance the intellectual tension that this implies is another pervasive theme in this book – from Ouchi's "hard" versus "soft" to the centralization–decentralization dilemma of multinationals, and now to what one might term the paradox of business innovation.

Note

1. This chapter was written by Paul Evans (Professor of Organizational Behavior at INSEAD), Alison Farquhar, and Oliver Landreth (respectively research associate and research assistant at INSEAD). It is largely based on the experiences of the following persons: Pierre Ardichvili, manager of management development for Hewlett–Packard; Michael Bonsignore, president of Honeywell Europe; Sheldon Davis, personnel and organization advisor, DEC

Europe; Berth Jönsson, vice president for human resources at Volvo; Philip Norcross, manager for management development with the National Westminster Bank; Len Peach, director of personnel for the UK National Health Service; Paul Smith, head of personnel at Marks & Spencer; Anneli Valpola, vice president for management development at Wärtsila; and Yves Doz, Michael Brimm, Manfred Kets de Vries, and Arnoud de Meyer, professors at INSEAD.

*Chapter 10*_____

Managing Engineers and Scientists: Some New Perspectives

Thomas J. Allen and Ralph Katz

Until very recently, management theorists paid scant attention to problems that are unique to the managing of engineers and scientists. Most research in management has been directed toward understanding the needs and behavior of blue collar and clerical employees. To the extent that engineers and scientists were even considered, it was assumed that principles developed through research on these other employees would apply to engineers and scientists as well.

In recent years, a number of groups in the United States, Britain, Germany, and Sweden have begun research directed toward the problems of managing research and development organizations employing engineers and scientists. This research shows clearly that there are many problems that are unique to these organizations and their highly educated employees. Such enterprises have to be managed differently than production or clerical organizations.

This comes as no news to the managers of research and development organizations. They have long recognized the unique position of their enterprises, and they have responded to this uniqueness by being very innovative in developing new organizational structures and management techniques.

Most of these have been effective. As might be expected, however, there are some managerial assumptions that have not stood up entirely to the test of rigorous empirical research. Among these false assumptions are several which cluster around two areas of human resource policy, namely in the domains of reward systems and the obsolescence of an employee's knowledge.

Concerning the first of these, *reward systems*, it has been assumed that engineers and scientists in industry, like their academic counterparts, are more interested in peer recognition than they are in organizational advancement. Under this assumption, it is believed that engineers and scientists are not interested in becoming managers, and that they do so reluctantly only after seeing that it is the only path to higher pay and status in most organizations. These assumptions form the basis upon which management developed a new form of reward system known as the "dual ladder".

The second set of assumptions which have not held up to empirical scrutiny concern the *inevitability of obsolescence of knowledge* in fields in which new knowledge is being rapidly developed. In such fields, education alone does not prepare a person for lifelong performance. The knowledge a person gains in school or university quickly becomes obsolete, supplanted by new knowledge. To keep up to date, people must constantly renew their education, so to speak. This is very difficult task and one that, according to the assumption, becomes increasingly difficult with age.

It is these two sets of assumptions that we will address in this present chapter. In the light of recent research, we will examine both to determine the extent to which they hold true and, where this is not the case, the degree to which management policy should be adapted to empirical reality.

THE DUAL LADDER

The effectiveness of "dual ladder" career systems has long been debated in industrial and academic circles. The idea was conceived somewhere in the dim past by a research manager or personnel administrator who hoped to increase the number of career opportunities available to high performing technical professionals, and thereby to sustain their motivation.

The underlying assumption was that productive engineers and scientists were being "forced" into administrative roles in order to attain higher salaries and more prestige. Their technical talents were thereby lost to the organization. Yet the basis for this assumption is exaggerated. Studies since have shown that productive scientists and engineers in industry are often not "forced" into management–a high proportion see their career paths from the outset as progressing into management. For example, 20% of first year MIT students choosing engineering majors cited management as their ultimate career goal.

Nevertheless, there remains some proportion of the technical staff of most organizations who prefer technical problem-solving, and for whom management has no attraction. These people might find a technical ladder career to be attractive.

How large is this proportion remains an open question, and companies vary widely in their estimates. Some firms restrict technical ladder entry severely, while others promote a relatively high proportion of their staff into this career path. Companies also vary widely in their enthusiasm for the concept. A representative of one firm told us that when his company was recently considering the possibility of such a system, he informally polled the management of thirteen other firms with such dual ladders. Most reported varying degrees of satisfaction, but when asked if, given the chance, they would do it over again, twelve out of thirteen replied definitely not.

There are several problems underlying the dual ladder concept. First, prestige is associated in most cultures with managerial advancement. Vice presidents are accorded high prestige, while someone working for an industrial organization with the title of "senior research fellow" is not accorded the same degree of prestige by society. As a result, technical staff begin very early to think about eventually attaining a management position. If told that they have been selected for promotion to a technical ladder position, they interpret this as feedback that they will not make good managers. The technical ladder promotion becomes a consolation prize, and often demotivates an otherwise productive member of the staff.

Second, despite attempts to equate pay and perquisites for the two ladders, there is one key ingredient of the managerial ladder which is missing from the technical ladder, namely power. As an individual progresses on the managerial ladder, the number of employees reporting to that person generally increases. When that manager requests action, those subordinates generally mobilize to accomplish the action. Yet as an individual progresses on the technical ladder, neither the number of subordinates nor the visible power increases. Hence a technical ladder position is viewed inside the organization as less important than its supposedly equivalent management counterpart.

Finally, organizations tend with time to diverge from the initial intent of the system. For the first few years, the criteria for promotion to the technical ladder may well be followed rigorously, but they gradually become corrupted. The technical ladder often becomes a reward for organizational loyalty rather than technical contribution. Equally damaging is the prevalent tendency to use the technical ladder as a repository for failing managers. Either of these practices will destroy whatever reward value there may be in the dual ladder system.

We are faced with two key questions. First of all, what proportion of a laboratory's technical staff will find the technical career ladder to be attractive? Second, for those others who will never be promoted to the limited number of managerial positions, and who are not necessarily inclined toward the technical ladder, what can be done to reward them and maintain their motivation?

To address these questions, we surveyed more than two thousand technical staff in nine public and industrial organizations. Along with other questions, these people were asked whether they would prefer to progress up the managerial or the technical career ladder to a higher level position. The survey question also provided a third option, that of working on challenging and exciting research projects, irrespective of promotion opportunities. The respondents were asked to rate these three alternatives on seven point scales.[1]

A Third Career Option: Challenging Projects

The 2,157 respondents were of all ages, averaging forty-three, and they included both management and technical career ladder employees. 1,495 of the respondents indicated a clear preference for one of the three options.

Of these, 33% preferred the managerial ladder over the two other alternative career paths, while 22% preferred the technical ladder. And a surprising 46% reported a preference for having the "opportunity to engage in those challenging and exciting research activities and projects in which they were most interested, irrespective of promotion".

We wondered if this unexpectedly strong response was simply the result of this third alternative having been worded in an unintentionally attractive way. Would the results change if we focused on those with very clear cut preferences for one option over the others – by a margin of two or three preference points on the seven point scale? But the proportion of those preferring interesting projects did not decrease. In fact, there was a higher percentage of engineers with a strong preference for interesting projects in comparison with those preferring the technical or managerial ladders. We concluded that the wording was unlikely to have caused great bias, and this has been supported by recent independent data which echoed our findings, despite a more mildly worded third alternative.

As one might expect, we found that career preferences were significantly related to *age*. As engineers grew older, they reported an increasing preference for interesting projects (see figure 10.1), perhaps explained in part by the fact that they see fewer opportunities for promotion on the managerial and technical ladders. However, a high proportion of those in their twenties chose this option. In fact, it is the most preferred alternative for all engineers, save those in the twenty-five to thirty age range.

In contrast, the technical ladder career attracts the smallest proportion of engineers in all ages. The proportion with this preference hovers around 20%, with only a mild peak among those in their thirties. The proportion preferring a managerial career peaks in the late twenties and declines steadily thereafter.

We were not surprised to find that managers reported a distinct

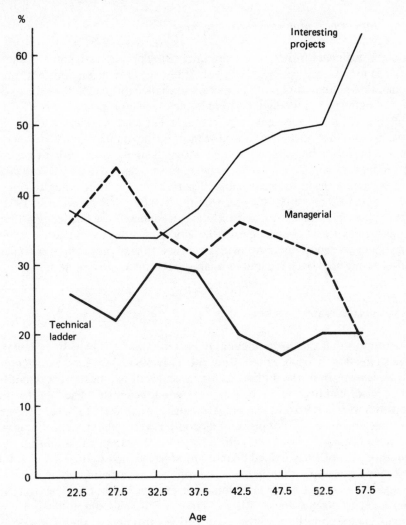

FIGURE 10–1
Career Orientations Reported by Engineers and Scientists in Nine Organizations as a Function of Their Age (*N*=1,402)

preference for a managerial career. With age, this decreases slightly and there is a corresponding interest in challenging projects. But only for a brief period in their late thirties do managers show any interest in the technical ladder.

Even for engineers who are on the technical ladder, the technical reward system is the least preferred. Younger engineers tend to prefer management over the technical ladder. Older technical ladder engineers show a preference for interesting projects.

How Management Motivates Older Engineers

If older engineers truly desire more interesting project assignments, and if after some twenty years on the job, they see less attraction in formal promotion systems and more attraction in challenging work, then the usual way of managing older engineers is completely inappropriate.

In making project assignments, management tends to operate under the assumption that technical obsolescence is inevitable. Older engineers should therefore be assigned to the least challenging tasks. Other research has indeed shown that these older engineers are assigned less complex tasks, believing that they are less capable of performing on more complex, more challenging assignments (see, for example, Dalton and Thompson, 1971). This, of course, leads to a self-fulfilling prophecy. Less challenging tasks require less current knowledge and thereby remove any motivation for older engineers to renew their knowledge. An artificial problem of technical obsolescence has been created by a largely erroneous assumption.

COMBATTING OBSOLESCENCE

The notion that engineers inevitably become obsolescent with advancing age stems largely from a book from the early 50s called *Age and Scientific Achievement*. In it, the author, Lehman, showed that most great scientific discoveries had been made by relatively young scientists. The fact that his statistics were flawed and that great scientists are unlikely to behave as very average engineers has not prevented people generalizing from his findings.

Recent research, however, calls the age – obsolescence relationship into question. People may indeed be more productive early in their careers, but this need not imply that age is to be equated with fading ability. As we suggested above, it is organizational constraints and not advancing years that lead to obsolescence. All too often, companies simply do not give engineers the chance to contribute effectively throughout their careers. At General Electric's research centre, studies have not demonstrated any clear link between an engineer's age and his value to the company. Recent academic research is in total agreement.

A substantial and growing body of research leads us to the conclusion that what is important in maintaining long-term professional performance is the provision of challenging work assignments and the accompanying motivation to constantly update one's knowledge. Professional development depends upon what one does, on actual job activities, and this is of practical importance for a company's human resource policies. In general, job related problem-solving has been found to be the most important aid in helping professional personnel keep abreast of developments in their fields. It has been argued that unchallenging engineering jobs must be redesigned and enriched so as to force the professional engineer to remain current.

Studies of the first job experience have demonstrated the importance of the challenge and perceived significance of the first work assignment given to newly hired college graduates. This has been found to have greater influence on later performance and career success than the challenges and demands of succeeding years. Those with limited challenge are likely to become frustrated, reduce their aspirations, and perhaps leave the organization.

The feeling of being underutilized has serious consequences not only as far as obsolescence is concerned. Individuals whose capabilities are not constantly tested may question their relationship with the company. They see little incentive for high performance, and are discouraged from keeping abreast with the latest technology in the field. Researchers have been led to advise managers as to the importance of capturing their subordinates' enthusiasm with increasingly challenging tasks, thereby motivating them to update their knowledge. Clearly, if no advantage is perceived in doing so, there will be little interest in further learning.

The motivation to update one's knowledge is particularly important. Studies back in the 60s showed that managers will not be stimulated to further learning unless they perceive real advantages in keeping up to date. And a recent review of the literature concluded that the perceived importance of keeping up-to-date is perhaps the single most important factor affecting obsolescence (Cooper and Jones, 1980).

The Importance of Staying Current

We had the opportunity to explore these issues ourselves with an anonymous survey among the research and development personnel of a major US electronics manufacturer. A total of 3,036 technical personnel, just over 75% of the total, responded to the survey, covering several types of work (research, product design and development, systems development, software engineering, manufacturing engineering, and sales engineering) and various organizational levels (engineers, supervisors, and managers). The ages of the respondents were quite evenly spread, with just over a third in their forties.

Jobs vary in the degree to which performance requires staying abreast of current technology, though a clear majority of all respondents saw technical currency as being essential. However, only a minority of the respondents viewed management as emphasizing the importance of staying current (see Table 10.1).

Staying current was viewed as slightly more important for those with managerial responsibility, perhaps because they saw their bosses as placing greater emphasis on this need. In contrast, only 29% of the engineers saw management as stressing this.

Respondents were also asked to estimate their own levels of currency on a

TABLE 10.1

Perceptions of Importance of Staying Current and Managerial Emphasis on this as a Function of Position

	Proportion perceiving	
Hierarchical position	high importance of currency %	high management emphasis %
Engineer	76	29
Supervisor	80	35
Manager	83	41

percentile scale, their ability to keep abreast of developments in their field. The respondents were divided into two groups – those who were above the median on perceived technical currency, and those below the median who, relative to others, perceived their obsolescence as higher.

Given the contradictory opinions concerning age and its relationship to technical obsolescence, we were interested to see whether responses did indeed vary with age. Our own feelings on the issue were supported when we found that there was absolutely no relationship between age and reported obsolescence.

If obsolescence does not go with age, is it related to the perceived importance of staying current in one's field, as other studies have suggested? With one hypothesis supported, we were keen to test another. Is it true that when technical personnel perceived a strong need to remain up-to-date, they take active steps to do so?

The survey clearly supported this (see Table 10.2). 64% of those stating that staying current was "highly important" in their work reported that they were relatively up-to-date. In contrast, only 28% of those who saw currency as being of less importance in their jobs described themselves as being

TABLE 10.2

Perceived Obsolescence as a Function of Importance of Keeping Abreast of New Technology

Importance of staying current in present job	Proportion perceiving low obsolescence %	N
High	64.4	2,279
Low	28.3	688
Total		2,967

$X = 261.3; p < 0.001$

current. Individuals who consider technical currency to be of low import-ance are thus more likely to be those who experience a higher degree of obsolescence.

Another important finding came out of our survey. It seems that the *climate created by management exerts considerable influence on obsolescence.* A critical aspect of this climate is the degree to which management emphasizes keeping abreast of new technology. Those respondents who considered themselves relatively up-to-date also reported that their management placed strong emphasis on being current. In fact, 77% of those who said management stressed currency reported that they were up-to-date against 45% whose superiors did not make a point about staying abreast of new developments.

CONCLUSIONS

From the two sets of findings described we arrived at a set of conclusions which have far-reaching implications for the human resource management of technical employees.

Most fundamentally, we confirmed that technical obsolescence is not an inevitable result of aging, but stems rather from the assignments generally given to older engineers. These are so unchallenging that there is no necessity, and little incentive, for them to renew their knowledge. Ironically, it is the very same mid-career engineers who say that what really matters to them is the degree of interest or challenge that they can obtain in their project assignments.

Management has fallen into a self-defeating policy of denying these engineers the type of work that would challenge them, satisfy them, and force them to keep current. Operating from a false set of assumptions, management has developed a set of policies, often informal, which not only seriously damage their own organizational performance but result in untold harm to the careers of the engineers whom they manage.

Note

1. Further details on the survey as well as more complete statistical findings are reported in Allen and Katz (1986).

Chapter 11

Managing Technological Innovation in Large Complex Firms: The Contribution of Human Resource Management

Yves Doz

Large firms have frequently been criticized for their lack of innovativeness, while smaller entrepreneurial firms have been hailed as paragons of innovativeness in such sectors as electronics, biotechnology, software, and services. One should not, however, jump to the conclusion that encouraging small firms (via venture capital, tax exemptions, increased mobility of managers and researchers, and more supportive networks) is the only answer to the lagging innovativeness of European industry. It would be a mistake to conclude that small firms have the edge on larger firms when it comes to innovation.[1]

Large firms are here to stay. In fact they contribute more than their share of new discoveries, product introductions, and expenditure on research and development when compared to smaller companies. Furthermore, larger firms have opportunities not available to smaller enterprises. They can draw on a whole range of internally available technologies, combine them, and exploit them in multiple application areas. The compact disk innovation at Philips is a case in point. It draws on laser technology, film technology, digital coding, recording technologies, and precision machinery. The compact disk technology can be exploited in multiple applications, from the substitution of audio records and turntables to the mass storage of documents, from navigation systems to hearing aids (Prahalad, Doz and Angelmar, 1989). Such an innovation could hardly be produced or fully exploited by a small firm.

But turning their potential strength into reality is all too often not achieved in large companies. This failure has frequently been put down to technological problems, the solution being greater investment in research and development. But in fact the challenge for large companies is of a different nature: in order to foster innovation, large firms need a different concept of organization and different attitudes and behaviors in top management. In our research on innovation processes in large companies in industries such as pharmaceuticals, chemicals, offshore oil production engineering, semi-conductors, information technology, and nuclear engineering, we have observed that innovation itself is not the problem. The problems are organization and management.

PROCESSES OF INNOVATION

The tradition research process is sequential. In separate laboratories and departments, new products and new technologies go through stages from basic research to applied research to the development of new products, then to manufacturing and marketing, and on to sales and service. This approach works as a relay race where the baton is transferred from one specialist to another.

The sequential process is best adapted to innovations where interdependencies are sequential and structured, and for which speed is not paramount. This is the case in the pharmaceutical industry, where serendipity in research, well-defined and sequential clinical tests, and the steps involved in registering a product create a series of interdependencies and provide time for the orderly transfer of new products from one set of specialists to the next. Yet in most other industries the interdependencies in the innovation process are much more complex and less sequential because of shorter product life cycles, technology-based competition, and greater interdependency between marketing, research, and production (e.g., the need to take "market pull" into account in research, or the principle of "design to cost"). Specialized roles are still needed, but in a much more interdependent fashion. Companies no longer run relay races but play rugby games.[2]

The typical answer has been to locate innovative activities in separate units. These were originally dubbed as "skunkworks" in the United States, now typically known as corporate ventures, independent business units, or entrepreneurial subsidiaries (Roberts, 1985). No matter what the unit's title is, the common idea is to create small, highly motivated, and self-contained research and development teams, each with their own marketing and manufacturing functions, and which act as autonomous business units.

This approach, much touted in the United States (see for example Pinchot's *Intrapreneuring*, 1985), has its own drawbacks. First, it is difficult to direct and control a number of small and divergent units. It may take the company into marginal and undesired directions, as seen in the rapid diversification of major oil and chemical companies using this approach (e.g., Exxon, Elf Aquitaine, and British Petroleum). When top management becomes aware of the strategic divergence created by such ventures, they are usually sold off or divested. Sometimes this may be profitable, but it does not serve the long-term interest of the corporation. Second, these ventures seldom draw on the core skills of the company. They are not supported by central research, they may not use established channels for market access, and so they do not exploit the existing skills and infrastructure of the large company (Burgelman, 1983; Burgelman and Sayles, 1986). Indeed, they implicitly negate the value of the large company.

The internal venture approach to managing innovation has the further drawback of not addressing what seems to be the most taxing problem for major European and American corporations: the technological and strategic rejuvenation of existing businesses. Unless the experience and learning gained in these ventures can be successfully transferred to existing businesses, they are of little use. New ventures starting with a clean slate can be quite useful, *provided* that a company's established divisions can then borrow and apply practices from the new venture. Successful learning from new ventures, though, seems to be difficult, as is the development of new core businesses from such ventures.

To overcome both the problems of size and the limitations of autonomous ventures, large firms need to create and actively manage a process of simultaneous differentiation and integration in the innovation process (Burgelman and Sayles, 1986). To be innovative, they need to differentiate new activities from existing businesses, to manage them with more flexibility and freedom. Yet to exploit such innovations, they also need to make them interdependent with the existing activities so that the new activities can rely on the existing skills and infrastructure of the firm. Furthermore, the balance between differentiation and interdependence may have to shift over time (Doz, Angelmar and Prahalad, 1986). Early in the development of a new technology or a new activity, it may be necessary to differentiate it from existing activities; later on, as the business grows and matures, it may be advisable to make it more interdependent of existing activities.

The example of the IBM personal computer (PC) illustrates this well. When IBM first entered the market for personal computers, it had to depart from a number of its usual business practices in order to succeed, and was obliged to emulate its smaller entrepreneurial competitors such as Apple, Tandy, Atari and Commodore. However, IBM was not only interested in the PC as a stand-alone consumer product. It saw in it an opportunity to increase overall demand for computing power in the professional and corporate markets, with PCs substituting for conventional work stations. As the market moved away from home computers – a short lived fad – to professional network applications, and from individual to corporate customers, IBM had to make its PC business more interdependent with other product lines. This business became part of the overall IBM computer strategy, increasingly managed like any other IBM product line rather than as an autonomous business unit.

CHALLENGES FOR INNOVATION: TOP MANAGEMENT TASKS

Our research suggests that in major corporations there are three critical top management tasks for ensuring successful innovation:[3]

- developing an understanding of the needs for differentiation and interdependence and their evolution over time;
- providing multiple channels for resource allocation;
- creating flexibility in the organization in order to encourage both differentiation and interdependence.

The Need for Differentiation and Interdependence

The first problem here is *recognizing* the need. To do that, a firm needs a culture of multiple perspectives, rich information sharing, excellent communications, and active internal debate. In a large company, the scope of an innova-tion, both with regard to technologies it can draw upon and to its applications, may not be clear from the outset. To define the scope of applications, and to ensure that relevant technologies are brought to bear on the innovation, active internal debate is needed. Managers from different units and functions are likely to have different *a priori* perspectives on an innovation. Some will see certain applications clearly, but not notice others; some will have one possible business concept in mind, others another. Provided that these different perspectives are anchored in data and analysis and are not vague or poorly defined, internal debate can be a valuable learning process.

Good analysis is based on high-quality data and richness of information. Gathering and processing information is another key to successful innovation. This applies externally, through information and intelligence systems (Ghoshal and Westney, 1988). Venture capital as a window to observe technology, gatekeepers with extensive networks, good scientific intelligence, and the mobility of people may all contribute to the richness of information available to the firm. European firms are at a disadvantage here *vis-à-vis* their American and Japanese competitors, who usually have a richer network for gathering and interpreting data as a result of greater professional mobility, better gatekeeping, strong high-tech venture capital intelligence, and actively managed information networks. Furthermore, reliable and multiple sources of information force the confrontation of perspectives, creating the tensions that generate stronger debate within the company.

Gathering information is not sufficient, however. Information must also be circulated and put to use within the company, and for this the company needs good internal mechanisms. These mechanisms are committees which cut across operating and strategic business units, technology programs common to many units, and incentives to share information across organizational boundaries. Nippon Electric, for example, makes extensive use of information sharing committees as a way of bringing multiple perspectives to bear on technology and strategy choices (see the Nippon Electric case study by Porter and Wells, 1982).

For these creative networks and tensions to be sustained, top management must actively encourage debate and even dissent. It must create conditions which allow employees to challenge conventional wisdom, and even the boss. Contrary to conventional views of planning, the role of top management in fostering and exploiting innovation is to *create* opportunities for tension and divergent thinking, rather than to reduce them (Nonaka and Takeuchi, 1986).

Multiple Channels for Funding Projects

Creative debate between multiple perspectives is not going to lead anywhere unless it is supported by multiple channels for resource allocation. A single channel for resource allocation (for example, a standard corporate-wide capital appropriation and budgeting process) may be too conservative and too constraining for innovation. Different perspectives are hard to sustain unless they can be supported by resource commitments in line with those perspectives. If resources can be allocated from only one perspective, for example via business units, then only that perspective will be strong. Yet, technological innovation cannot be delegated to the business unit alone, lest the core technologies be neglected. Matsushita, for example, decided in 1984 to take the responsibility for the development of microelectronics components away from its divisions, making it a corporate task. None of the divisions saw components as sufficiently important to warrant large investment, and Matsushita was lagging behind its competitors in microelectronic technologies. Resource allocation channels for technological innovation must work both at corporate and divisional (or business unit) levels. Some companies, such as GTE, have developed special processes to establish technological priorities and to allocate corporate resources to them, independently of investment programs run by individual business units (Mitchell, 1985).

Furthermore, projects need to be categorized (e.g., technical support projects, "blue sky" research) in order to prevent basic research from being shortchanged in favour of innovations with quicker development horizons. In some companies, new ideas rejected by the hierarchy may find a court of appeal in specific funding programs established independently of the usual approval line. 3M, for instance, has a "second chance" system which allows innovations to seek funding after having been rejected once. Texas Instruments has a process whereby any of forty corporate officers can provide up to $25,000 of seed money to fund interesting new ideas to a developmental stage at which a case can be made for funding through the regular resource allocation process.

Organizational Flexibility

However, our research suggests that many innovations fail not because they were narrowly conceived, not because of inadequate funding, but because the organization of the company was not sufficiently flexible to adjust to their requirements for success. The development of innovations was hampered by having to conform to organizational procedures that were probably quite adequate to run a maturing business, but not to foster new business or the exploitation of new technology. The third critical task of top management is to ensure that promising innovation does not become trapped in conventional organization. IBM, for example, departed from many standard practices which had almost become dogma within the organization in order to meet the need for differentiation in its PC business. Rather than rely on internally made components, as was customary, the PC business unit went for "outsourcing" of key components; instead of proprietary software they chose "open" software (allowing anybody to produce applications software for the PC); they ignored IBM's salesforce in favor of independent retail channels, and the staid institutional advertising was replaced by the famous "Charlie Chaplin" campaigns. With respect to management, the PC venture was exempted from planning, from reviews by corporate staffs, and from several other control systems. A management "board" was substituted, composed of senior executives from the corporation. IBM's top management was aware that such a dramatic departure from usual practices was needed if its entry into the PC business was to succeed. Once IBM's PC division was established, the usual control mechanisms were reintroduced step-by-step, and some of the earlier differentiation was diminished (for instance, the PC division lost its separate marketing function in 1985).

The flexibility in management and organization is not required for its own sake, but rather to relax possible constraints on competitive and strategic innovation. To a large extent, the PC was a competitive and strategic innovation for IBM, rather than a technological innovation (the only new technology, a 16-bit microprocessor, was provided by INTEL, not developed by IBM). It is unlikely that the development of the PC would have succeeded within the existing organizational context of IBM's mainline business.

The ability to recognize the need for temporary organizational differentiation, and to manage its fluctuation over time, is another critical task in managing innovation in large complex firms. Unfortunately large firms tend to develop well-defined "ideologies" regarding organization. These inhibit the ability of top managers to create organizational flexibility.

In the 70s, Hewlett–Packard devised a system of decentralized divisional and entrepreneurial management which was highly suited to the needs of the instrumentation industry. But this "small is beautiful" approach is less suited to the computer business. Following its subsequent entry into computers, Hewlett–Packard reorganized itself in several phases in the mid–80s in order to provide more interdependence between the units involved in the computer businesses. Similarly, with its move into office and factory automation, Matsushita reduced the autonomy enjoyed by its product divisions and gave more weight to central resource allocation. Yet, in Matsushita and Hewlett–Packard, as in most other firms, the need for flexibility emerged only as a result of less than successful entries into new businesses. This can be an expensive way to learn a lesson. Organizational flexibility is a source of competitive advantage, and as such has to be built into company strategy.

THE ROLE OF HUMAN RESOURCE MANAGEMENT

The human resource management practices of the firm facilitate or hinder the ability of middle level executives and technical specialists to sustain multiple perspectives and appropriate channels for resource allocation, as well the flexibility of organization.

Promoting and Maintaining Multiple Perspectives

As observed earlier, intense internal debate between units and managers with widely different interests and priorities is an essential aspect of establishing successful innovation in large companies. However, organizational and individual processes often tend to suppress rather than encourage debate, making creative disagreement and information sharing difficult (see Argyris and Schön, 1974; Argyris, 1985).

A healthy dialogue requires freedom for managers to voice dissent, including dissent from their boss's views. Legitimacy of dissent is made easier by a set of stable values and beliefs that transcend current business circumstances (Prahalad, 1983). No matter how such values and beliefs are stated, it is how they are applied that gives them credibility. IBM, for instance, may state "respect for the individual" as a principle, but it is only by showing this in its treatment of its own employees that this principle gains credibility.

Business issues need to be debated actively, in the general context of such common beliefs and values. This is what is called "push-back" at DEC, where an active advocacy process is created (see p. 180 for a more detailed discussion). Although building conflicting priorities into the organization is useful to facilitate debate between peers, vertical dissent between top managers and subordinates must also be possible, and the success of this depends on how a company manages people. Top management must act as a model, engaging in analytic rather than political debate. They should not limit themselves to managing procedures such as planning, budgeting, and control, but also get involved in the substantive dialogue with operating managers on critical strategic issues.

Competition within the organization also helps. The use of competing project teams for new products is widespread and well-known. Teams can also be used to develop alternative strategic concepts. A creative mix of skills and personalities can also generate debate and make learning easier (see Chapter 12).

A commitment from top management towards a broad vision, providing a sense of direction while leaving the specific means and strategies purposefully vague and ambiguous, can facilitate innovation. There are a number of reasons for this. First, innovation cannot be planned. The initiative for the development and exploitation of innovation lies with entrepreneurial middle managers. Top management then screens developments and recasts them in a strategic context (Burgelman, 1984), in a process not very different from resource allocation in diversified decentralized companies (Bower, 1970). The quality of that process is influenced by the quality of communications within the company and the strategic focus of internal organization (Doz and Lehmann, 1986). Second, it is easier to get the commitment of individual managers to a broad corporate vision that they can help make concrete when they have the latitude to define and interpret the vision in a way that suits them and is worthy of their personal commitment (Hamel and Prahalad, 1986). A vision that is too precise would not leave room for innovation, and would compromise the commitment of the whole organization to the concept of innovation. Third, success in innovation is far more than technological; success also depends on "competitive innovation" – that is, developing new business concepts to exploit an innovation in ways that competitors find difficult to counter (Hamel and Prahalad, 1986). A corporate strategy that is too well defined may not leave room for this creative business development. On the other hand, a broad vision may be reinterpreted and adapted constantly to foster competitive as well as technological innovation. Finally, multiplicity of perspectives, flexibility of organizational differentiation, and interdependencies make patterns of co-operation in the firm ambiguous: they cannot be specified ahead of time. In fact, ambiguity may be even more of a condition for co-operation in innovative circumstances than in others, permitting interdependencies to be identified and managed. Again, this differs from the widespread management practice, derived from quality management, of providing for specified "quasi-contracts" and creating customer–supplier relations within the firm. While the supplier–customer contract approach is useful in providing marketlike discipline for established activities, it may be too constraining to foster innovation.

Internal debate can create opportunities for "problems" and "solutions" to come together – and in turn create a new dynamic that sustains the debate itself. In many organizations, business units or individuals may have problems with no immediate solutions available. Conversely, solutions may exist (e.g., unused technical capabilities) that are not focused on particular problems (March and Olsen, 1976). The checkered evolution of 3M's now famous "Post-It" innovation (the yellow notes that stick on paper) provides a good illustration of this type of organizational process (Nayak and Ketteringham, 1986). Indeed, many of the innovation processes we observed in our own research evolved through coincidences of problems meeting solutions. The success of innovation processes in these cases depended on creating opportunities for unstructured, unprescribed communication (Kanter, 1983)[4].

Mobility is an obvious tool to facilitate communication. The movement of managers from research to operations, marketing or strategy development can stimulate creative debate within the firm. Mobility between business units within the same function can also be useful, provided that the technological content and the strategic logics of these units are sufficiently similar to allow a useful transfer of experience and viewpoints.

There are other ways to create networks, such as the use of matrix organizations. The matrix forces an active debate between overlapping perspectives which differ by design (e.g., country, product, and function in the multinational matrix; or core technology, product application, and contract in large system development in electronics). Networks can be extended to collaborative activities between firms, further differentiating perspectives and bringing together problems and solutions. To a large extent, such network development may well be the most significant contribution of government-sponsored collaborative research programs, whether in Europe or Japan (Westney, 1987). At the local level, within individual facilities, paying careful attention to the physical layout of offices and laboratories is also a well known way of encouraging communication (Allen, 1977). Similarly, the physical proximity of research, development, and manufacturing functions may also be critical (Fruin, 1987; Ferdows, forthcoming).

An intense, healthy debate between multiple perspectives, however, can be maintained only if the participants can draw not only on intellectual resources, but also on the financial resources which typically are a major basis for power in the organization.

Building Multiple Resource Allocation Channels

Resource allocation plays a key role in fostering successful innovation. Some approaches to triggering innovative activities, such as allowing slack time for researchers to initiate and "bootleg" their dearest projects, are well known. So is providing intervals between projects, "floating" periods where individuals can discover further opportunities for innovation. Beyond these approaches, the way in which resources are subsequently allocated to projects has a major impact on their outcome.

Tentative findings from our research suggest that multiple channels for funding, multiple logics for evaluating projects, and clear management expectations are important in order to nourish innovation.

Multiple channels

The companies we observed fell into two categories with respect to how they obtained resources. In some instances, resource allocation channels and processes were pre-set, and project managers merely followed the rules. In others, project leaders and their managers had to take unspecified routes to obtain resources rather than follow standard practices. The process of having to think through how to obtain resources forced the project leaders to adopt and debate multiple perspectives as they negotiated with potential sponsors or funders in the network. This process of mustering support also forced the innovators to clarify their projects, and tested the strength of their commitment. In this way, resource allocation was used as a means of managing projects, and paradoxical situations were often created to elicit more creative solutions.

For instance, in some companies resources were actually abundant, but all project managers were under great pressure to perform on a shoestring – not knowing how abundant the resources were. This acted both as a test of commitment on their part, and as a spur to creativity in the mustering and using of resources.[5] By extension, all team members were under great pressure to maximize performance, encouraging all-round high achievement. But although resources were allocated to each project only sparingly, top management was funding multiple parallel projects, and was providing a strong sense of support to the various managers involved. For the corporation as a whole, this multiplied the chances of success.

From a human resource management standpoint, these "engineered" shortages of resources, together with high pressures for achievement, could have detrimental consequences. While they can be effective with new young people who have little to lose and who know no other work environment (as suggested both in Kidder's study of Data General, Kidder, 1981, and our own research on the IBM PC business unit), the credibility of these pressures decreases with experience. Furthermore, the problems of loss of morale and motivation caused by killing projects with which teams are closely identified are well known, and have no simple solution. Creating a high commitment culture may help – that is, one of commitment to a transcending corporate vision – though commitment still comes more easily from the individual projects.

Multiple logics

Different categories of funds and of channels to access fund also help project managers develop a sense of the risks involved in their projects. A clear distinction between the logic of researchers and that of business developers is important, as well as different resource allocation channels appropriate to each logic. This distinction allows for explicit adjustments to the different risks and resource commitments of projects.

In the internal debate between research and the rest of the organization, clarifying the assumptions of each logic may be useful, facilitating choices about which logic should predominate on a particular innovation as well as timely shifts of logic. For instance, in the pharmaceutical industry, new areas such as biotechnology and immunology may for years remain scientific domains in which the logic of researchers predominates. Yet at the time when applications become feasible, a change to a business development logic is needed. By changing too early, a few major companies have wasted significant resources on biotechnology; by changing too late, others may be missing major opportunities. While the ideal timing obviously cannot always be found, it is helpful if the coexistence of multiple resource allocation logics and their respective assumptions within the firm are made clear.

The critical issue here is to maintain clear differences between the logics of the researchers and the business developers, and yet at the same time facilitate a shared understanding of both logics. From a professional development standpoint, moving individuals along with their projects from research to development may help sensitize them to these differences and better prepare them for managerial responsibilities. These moves sometimes speed up the pace of scientific development in research when the individual moves back to the research department. For example, it is useful to move people back and forth and in offshore oil-production engineering, where experience of application is important in developing new know-how. However, such moves would make no sense in pharmaceutical research, where experience in development roles contributes little to research, and where the pace of scientific evolution makes the return to research from downstream activities difficult.

Clear expectations

Individuals need fixed poles around which their activites and priorities can be oriented, providing a stable base for active internal debate and competition for resources. A clear vision of overall purpose, communicated through the company and expressed not as business objectives but as a set of values to which everyone can adhere, is critical in order to focus creative energies. This vision must not only be credible but also challenging, providing a goal without prescriptive plans and paths to reach it. It must motivate creative and entrepreneurial individuals to commit their efforts to it, but leave enough ambiguity for it to be constantly reinterpreted.

It is essential that performance expectations for innovative activities reflect the nature of the project. Innovative activities need to be sheltered from the short-term performance pressures of the traditional businesses which fund their development. Innovative activities and new business development, no matter how risky, should not fall prey to short-term fluctuations in other businesses, lest such fluctuations undermine the logic of the project. The usual criteria for business performance cannot be applied to the development of new businesses (Biggadike, 1976). Nor are simple criteria, such as growth targets, sufficient (Burgelman, 1984). New, entrepreneurial activities are typically intrinsically less predictable than established ones, and one thus cannot apply usual criteria, nor be bound by just one target number.

One of the key roles of top management in setting expectations is therefore to act as a buffer in the innovation process, and to measure innovations and new businesses with different yardsticks from those used in more mature businesses. While top managers may readily acknowledge this need intellectually, its translation into reality is more problematic. Based on our observation of several companies, it seems important to differentiate the role of corporate staff according to the innovativeness of the business. New and risky businesses may be kept totally independent, as was the case for the PC unit at IBM; corporate staff may have a support role for emerging businesses, and a central role for traditional established areas.

Top management itself must also live up to expectations, in particular by tolerating failure. Examples from 3M and General Electric are well-known but not widely emulated. A willingness to tolerate failure is necessary if the firm is to undertake risky projects, while encouraging thorough analysis of the risks involved and their possible consequences. An analytic approach, informed risk-taking, protects against uncontrolled laxity where excessive risks are taken without being properly understood.

Building Organizational Flexibility

Innovative activities and emerging businesses need to be managed differently from established business areas. This necessity for organizational flexibility was discussed earlier. How can that flexibility be built into the structure of a large corporation, and what are its implications for human resource management?

An evolving and carefully controlled balance must be found between differentiation and integration in the organizational context guiding the innovative effort. A whole range of management tools may be used for that purpose (Doz, Angelmar and Prahalad, 1986), and human resource management seems to be a determinant factor in managing that balance. We can take two contrasting examples to illustrate this. In the late 60s, Memorex established a system of "entrepreneurial subsidiaries". The objective was rapid growth through attracting innovative talent from other companies, offering high financial incentives to successful innovators and entrepreneurs (Hamermesh, 1986). Each of these entrepreneurial subsidiaries was supposed to contribute products to a central computer system division, some providing peripherals and others processors. Once the products were established, the division took over responsibility for them, and managers, engineers, and personnel from the entrepreneurial subsidiaries were mostly integrated into the division as well. However, neither the integration of the products nor that of the personnel proceeded easily. Corners had been cut in product development. The "integrated" personnel had more loyalty to their ex-subsidiary than to the Memorex company, and more incentive for the success of their "own" products than those of the computer division.

On the other hand, one domain where the management of the "independent" IBM PC unit was not autonomous was that of personnel management policy and practice. In fact, employment conditions and financial incentives in the PC unit in Florida were not extensively different from those in any other IBM division. This facilitated the re-entry (or entry for the large number of new hires) of PC personnel into IBM, both when the managers were moved to other units and when the PC unit lost its independence.

Blending mechanisms allows firms to achieve differentiation in the aspects where it is most required, maintaining integration where needed. Figure 11.1 summarizes the mechanisms which a major oil company employed in order flexibly to manage the development of new technology for its oil exploration business.

Degree of Integration

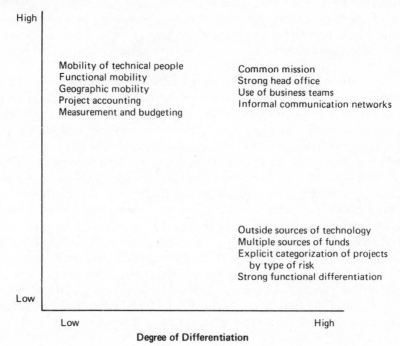

FIGURE 11–1
An Example of Mechanisms Employed by a Major Oil Company to Achieve Simultaneous Differentiation and Integration of Innovative Activities

Such flexibility is also made easier by fluid, informal matrix power structures rather than by clear hierarchies. The challenge here is for managers to perceive the flexibility of these loose matrix organizations as an opportunity rather than as a threat. In our research, we observed matrix organizations in which entrepreneurial behavior was actively encouraged; for example, managers were encouraged to exploit many avenues to push innovative projects. But we also observed matrix organizations where the interdependence and fragmentation of responsibilites became an excuse for inaction and a cover for blaming others.

The functioning of such flexible organizations is made easier by long-term employment, and by a motivation and reward system that puts the emphasis on achieving results, not on the way in which the process is managed. Top management thereby signals that the needs of an innovation may take the existing organization in new directions, but the organization is not sacred as an end in itself. An emphasis on socializing (creating opportunities for managers to meet and know each other), and an open-staffing procedure also allows the identification and the mobilization of resources and the differentiation of the management of innovative activities. A longer-term result-based orientation to rewards facilitates organizational differentiation and reduces immediate pressures. If the longer-terms motives and interests of managers are clear, their loyalty is not questioned when they depart from standard practice.

Mobility, with engineers moving with their projects from research and development laboratories to product development in divisions, also facilitates organizational flexibility: these engineers come with a concern for the success of their project and may be willing to challenge the conventional wisdom of existing operations, requiring divisions to differentiate the way in which new projects are treated. Conversely, the temporary assignment of divisional product development engineers, or even those from operations and manufacturing, to central laboratories may build interdependence between the innovative activities and the existing operations. Japanese computer companies, for example, seem to avoid many of the internal technology transfer problems by transferring product development engineers (Westney and Sakakibara, 1985). Elf Aquitaine facilitated the adoption of new technologies by conservative operational managers through temporary assignments to central research: their own engineers became advocates of the new technologies that they had contributed to develop, having developed a firsthand appreciation of their merit and feasibility.

CONTROLLED VARIETY

To sum up, the main issue of innovation in large complex firms can be captured in the metaphor of "controlled variety". The "variety" in the organization must be sufficient to foster experimentation, learning, adaptation, pursuing new roads and generating opportunities. Yet, at the same time this variety must constantly be controlled to allow for focused and efficient use of resources and to maintain a common identity in the organization, to provide stable poles for members of the organization so that the dynamic of creative ambiguity leads to commercial results rather than to anarchy.

Notes

1. The arguments developed in this chapter draw on research done jointly with Professor R. Angelmar at INSEAD and Professor C. K. Prahalad at the University of Michigan. They both contributed significantly to the concepts and ideas presented here.
2. The relationship between the type of interdependencies between tasks and the

required capabilities of organizations was first systematically analyzed in James D. Thompson's classic book *Organizations in Action* (1967).
3. Professor Doz, in collaboration with Professor Reinhard Angelmar at INSEAD and colleagues in the United States and Japan, is currently carrying out a research program on the management of innovation in large complex firms. It analyzes and compares the processes used to manage innovation in various firms and their relative success. Among the participating companies are Ciba–Geigy, Elf Aquitaine, British Petroleum, GTE, IBM, Mitsubishi, NEC, Philips and SGS. Two articles have been published so far and a book is in preparation, co-authored by Professors Doz and Angelmar, and C. K. Prahalad from the University of Michigan. This research is sponsored by selected companies: Ciba-Geigy, Elf Aquitaine, GTE and General Electric. The researchers are grateful for such support.
4. In many ways these innovations followed the process described by March and Olsen (1976) as "garbage can", but one in which the implicit market for innovation was very active, with many actors offering solutions and many bringing problems, with both sets communicating actively.
5. A good detailed account of such behavior is provided in Tracy Kidder's description of Tom West's inception of a new computer development program in Tracy Kidder's *The Soul of a New Machine* (1981).

Part V

Conclusions

Chapter 12

The Dualistic Organization

Paul Evans and Yves Doz

One underlying theme in most discussion of the challenges facing complex organizations is that of dualities. The proverbial organizational pendulum, once swinging leisurely over a generation from one desirable quality to its opposite, now gyrates from arc to arc. Organizations are besieged by the paradoxes that these dualities create. This book is full of examples, summarized in Figure 12.1.

We are experiencing unprecedented competition between business corporations, and at the same time we are witnessing a wave of partnerships and

Competition–Partnership
Differentiation–Integration
Loose–Tight
Control–Entrepreneurship
Planned–Opportunistic
Formal–Informal
Vision–Reality
Decentralization–Centralization
Business logic–Technical logic
Analysis–Intuition
Delegation–Control
Individuality–Teamwork
Action–Reflection
Change–Continuity
Formal–Informal
Top-down–Bottom-up
Tolerance–Forthrightness
Flexibility–Focus

FIGURE 12–1
Some Common Dualities in Today's Complex Organizations

joint ventures between direct competitors. Marriage and archrivalry go hand in hand. Balancing the dual forces of centralization and decentralization is a theme that runs throughout this book. "Globalization" turns out to be a simplification – the duality of "thinking global but acting local" is a better guide. Individualism and teamwork have long been acknowledged by football coaches as the formula for a winning team.

The field of innovation is fertile ground for dualities, as we saw in Part IV. Entrepreneurship must be moderated by control, control must be loosened to allow for entrepreneurship. Planning has to allow for opportunism. While creativity is facilitated by informality, disorder and adhocracy, making money out of creative ideas is the product of formality, organization, tightness. Thus organizations need strong formal and informal systems, the properties of both looseness and tightness. If entrepreneurship is the obsession in the overly formalized culture of the North American corporation, it is its complementary opposite – the design of formal systems – that is the concern in the more indigenously entrepreneurial culture of Italy.

One of the basic tenets of the theory of complex organizations is that they need to be both highly differentiated and tightly integrated. There is a need for specialization and generalism, for balancing business logic with technical logic. Top-down management processes must be combined with bottom-up processes.

The top managers of those diversified multinational enterprises confront an overwhelming degree of complexity. What top management needs is the ability to understand an organization in terms of these dualistic processes, in terms of inherent conflicts and tensions, oscillations from one side of the duality to the other. More particularly, the need is for road maps and mechanisms to build dualistic properties into their firms, to harness the tensions constructively, to play on the chords of opposing polarities.

In this concluding chapter, we discuss briefly dualities in social organization from a conceptual perspective, and in particular the guiding notion of "dynamic balance". Then we turn to outline how top management can build dualistic capabilities into the organization.

Dynamic Balance Between Dualities

Long-term survival depends on dynamically balanced management processes, argue Hedberg, Nystrom, and Starbuck (1976). They are among the few researchers to have recognized these paradoxes. They argue that maximization is an inappropriate concept for organizations. Instead of trying to *maximize* anything (decentralization, teamwork, formality, generalism . . .) an organization should seek to ensure that it maintains at least a *minimal threshold* of desirable attributes. It requires a minimal degree of consensus, but not so much as to stifle the dissension that is the life blood of innovation. And a minimal degree of contentment and satisfaction – sufficient to ensure that key actors wish to remain with the firm, but not so much as to allow arrogance or complacency. Minimal faith in plans is required, sufficient to ensure that the planning exercise leads its members to actually think through the future, but not so much that plans become road maps that blind attention to opportunity. Minimal attention should also be paid to rationality, though not to the extent of blinding us to the virtues of imperfection.

The notion of duality is not new. It can be traced back in philosophy (though it differs from similar concepts of opposition such as dialectic, dilemma, or tradeoff).[1] It is also the cornerstone of modern personality theory, where the dominant school views personality disorders as the product of an absence of balance in personal qualities.[2]

The normative idea behind a duality is the *complementarity* of opposites. The growth, prosperity, and survival of any social organism, from the human personality studied by Carl Jung to the entire civilizations analyzed by the historian Arnold Toynbee, depend on striking a dynamic balance between complementary dualities.

A social system is in a state of balance only if there is an equal proportion of the two complementary qualities. However, this balance is dynamic, and not a stationary equilibrium. Dynamic balance is analogous to a seesaw on a fulcrum. With delicately complementary weights on either side of the fulcrum, the seesaw is never still. There is a gentle oscillation from side to side, delicately maintained.

Organizational Degeneration

Sometimes the seesaw tilts so that one end touches the ground and stays there. This situation, if uncorrected, may ultimately lead to the degeneration of the organization. Toynbee's thesis in his monumental *Study of History*, for example, was that the decline of civilizations occurs when a society goes to excesses in its success formula. Kets de Vries and Miller (1984) show how the success formula of the entrepreneur becomes neurotic when there are no counterbalancing forces in the organization. Bateson points out that without the tension that exists between simultaneous opposites in organization, a cycle of "schismogenesis" occurs, a degenerative syndrome where an attribute in the organization perpetuates itself until it becomes extreme and thereby dysfunctional (Bateson, 1936; Cameron, 1986). Greiner (1972) has argued that organizations go through successive stages of evolution and revolution, where the properties that first lead to success eventually engender crisis and a rebalancing that facilitates further evolution.

THREE MANAGEMENT PARADIGMS

The concepts of duality and dynamic balance are new to the field of management and organization. Their relevance reflects the complexity of today's international organizations and the turbulence of their environments. We can trace the evolution of modern management in terms of three postwar periods, characterized by successively more turbulent and complex environments, illustrated in Figure 12.2.

Until the early 70s, the market, competitive, social and legislative environment of most firms was relatively static. Products had such long lives that the notion of product lifecycle had yet to be conceived. The larger companies dominated their national oligopolies, sellers' markets with little foreign competition. Labor was in plentiful supply.

The prevailing management paradigm was that of *structure*, and in a static environment it indeed makes sense to search for the most effective structure to guide action. The underlying value was the rational value of order.

What is an appropriate supervisory span of control? Are there limits to size and economy of scale? Is a product organization superior to a functional organization? Where there was a concern for management processes, it was with orderly, rational models that today seem mechanical: management as the process of planning, organizing, deciding, and controlling; the rational steps in the process of decision-making. Job evaluation systems placed the emphasis on orderly structure. The prevailing metaphor in applied organiza-

	50s–60s	70s–early 80s	mid-80s–90s
Management metaphor	**Structuring (providing order)**	**Fit, matching, consistency**	**Dynamic balance between dualities**
Nature of the environment	Relatively orderly and stable	Incrementally changing with increasing competition	Turbulent, complex, highly competitive
Focus of management attention	Structure and systems	Strategy and management processes	Innovation, flexibility, and organizational capabilities
	Planning systems	Strategic manegement: *matching* environmental threats and opportunities to internal strengths and weaknesses	Channeling entrepreneurship
	Budgeting systems		Focusing diversity
	Organizational structure		Integrating decentralized subsidiaries/business units
	Information systems		
	Job evaluation	Organization: ensuring *consistency* between the 7Ss	Creating teamwork among strong individuals
		Human resource management: *fitting* jobs to people	Planning opportunism
		Job design: *matching* technical and task specifications to social needs	Partnerships between competitors

FIGURE 12–2
Three Paradigms of Management in the Period After 1950

tional theory was "organizational design", as if an organization could be rationalized architecturally, while problems of change focused on resistance to the rational. Even so, awareness of dualities was surfacing in more complex firms in the shape of a structural metaphor, that of matrix organization.

The theory and practice of management began to change slowly in the late 60s, gathering momentum in the 70s. The outside environment became more competitive. Protected national markets were now open to international competition. The labor and legislative scenes were more active. Gone was the era of order and stability – change was now becoming a regular feature of organizational life, though largely incremental in nature.

Superimposed upon the concern for structure came a new paradigm, that of *fit* or matching (the initial insight is often ascribed to Hal Leavitt, 1965). The "one-best-way" search for the effective structure gave way to Contingency Theory, reflecting the notion that particular structures are appropriate only in particular environments, and this led in turn to a heightened concern for management processes to match coherently different aspects of the organization and its environment.

The historical studies of Chandler (1962) and Andrews's concept of strategy (Andrews, 1971) supported the contingency view that structure should fit with strategy. Strategic planning thus came into being, generally defined as a management process to "match" environmental opportunities and threats with organizational resources and capabilities. Within the organization, job design became the socio–technical task of "matching" task imperatives and technological capacities with human and social needs. Performance motivation became the "matching" of people, with their distinct skills and needs, with tasks – the human resource task of getting the right people into the right place at the right time. The underlying value shifted from that of order to short-term performance or effectiveness.

There are many firms where these notions of strategic management, job design, and performance motivation are still poorly rooted. Meanwhile, we' may be shifting to a third management paradigm, building on the two previous phases.

In a turbulent, competitive, and complex environment, the metaphor of "fit" breaks down. While a tight degree of fit, coherence, matching, or consistency has hitherto been the normative ideal, the fact is that tight fit or consistency results in rigidity. Competitive demands outrun the slow pace of organizational change and adjustment (Doz, 1978; Prahalad and Doz, 1987). Top management starts to feel that the organization is constantly behind, that the organization itself is the biggest barrier to competitive and strategic development.

Scholars of management have also sensed this breakdown, though they too are trapped by the absence of an alternative paradigm. They are increasingly questioning the definition of strategic management as the matching of corporate resources with opportunities and threats, however plausible this may be with yesterday's logic. This conception may have unduly constrained the ambitions of companies by driving out goals where the means of achieving them are not obvious. Hamel and Prahalad (1986) show that the phenomenal rise of Japanese and Korean multinationals (Honda in automobiles, Komatsu in earthmoving equipment, Canon in photocopiers, NEC in telecommunications) cannot be explained by now-conventional notions of strategic management. The strategic goals that fueled their early development appear ludicrous when assessed by such canons. They cannot explain, for example, Honda's goals of becoming a second Henry Ford, at a time when the company was a local manufacturer of ingenious but third rate motorbikes!

The overriding lesson of the experience of most of the sixty companies studied in this book, and of its nine scholarly contributors, is that in such a turbulent and competitive environment the key top management task becomes one of maintaining a dynamic balance between key oppositions. Dualities should be viewed not as threats to consistency and coherence, but as opportunities for creative organization development, for gaining competitive advantage, for organizational learning and renewal.

A frontier concern is with building responsiveness, adaptation, and learning into the organization. These imply maintaining a state of *constructive tension* within the firm. In fact, one of the classic "laws" of organizational change and development is that such processes involve tension (see Figure 12.3). There is an inverted U-shaped relationship between tension and change. Where there is no felt tension (in other words, where feelings of satisfaction, contentment, arrogance or apathy prevail), there will be no learning, development, or change in the social system. On the other hand, extreme tension (in the shape of threat, stress, crisis) typically leads to defensive or dysfunctional responses that are incompatible with learning and adaptation. To facilitate evolutionary change in the organization, an optimal degree of tension needs to be built into its culture – neither too much nor too little. Playing on the chords of dualities allows top management to build this tension into the organization in constructive and pragmatic ways: sufficient tension to ensure learning, adaptation and development, but not so much as to interfere with the operational demands of performance.

An example of this third paradigm is provided by a recent study of a "high velocity" industry, where the rate of technological and competitive change is so extreme that market information is typically unavailable or obsolete, where strategic windows open and shut quickly, and where the cost of error is exit. Such industries embody our paradigm three environment, and we would expect them to show dualistic capabilities. Two Stanford researchers studied the strategic decision-making process in four microcomputer firms, an industry with only thirty-odd survivors out of two hundred entrants

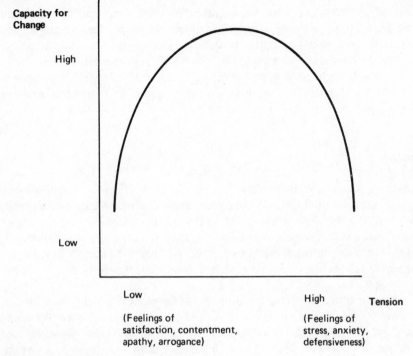

FIGURE 12–3
The Relationship Between Change and Tension

(Bourgeois and Eisenhardt, 1988). They found that the distinguishing characteristic of the more successful enterprises was that three dualities were balanced in their strategic decision-making processes. These firms made strategic decisions quickly but carefully, following breathlessly paced and intensely focused analysis. They had a powerful, decisive chief executive officer; but they also had a powerful management team, where functional vice presidents had more influence on decisions in their own areas than the CEO. And while seeking risk in decision-making, they executed safe and incremental implementation.

There is nothing virtuous about strong leaders unless they have strong teams. Risk-taking is foolhardy unless it is combined with complementary analysis and with implementation norms of "getting it right first time". It is norms such as these that must be inculcated into the complex organization, motoring development of the capabilities of the firm.

DEVELOPING DUALISTIC CAPABILITIES IN THE ORGANIZATION

How can a complex multinational develop the capabilities to balance opposites? How can top management develop and maintain dynamic balance? How can one exploit dualities so as to fuel strategic and organizational development? The dualistic paradigm raises new questions for researchers and executives, questions that are pragmatic "hows".

From our studies of such enterprises, we can identify three generic mechanisms for developing dualistic capabilities. We call these *layering, sequencing,* and *decision architecture*.

Layering

Layering focuses on the cultural facet of the firm. It involves building new capabilities and qualities into the organization's culture while reinforcing its past cultural strengths. New and complementary capabilities are *layered* on top of the existing capabilities. The enterprise thus becomes progressively more multi-dimensional, and more capable of handling complexity. Layering leads to a richer structure of shared meanings, mindsets, relationships, and networks.

A major tool of layering is management development – the recruitment, socialization, development, and career management of key position holders. Through changes in recruitment profiles, new qualities are introduced into the firm. Through management development, key individuals broaden their perspectives. An analogy can be drawn here to personality development. Each individual enters adulthood with a basic personality, and adult development involves the refinement and extension of that personality. Skills, qualities, and attitudes are acquired and layered on top of that basic personality, leading to greater complexity of the individual. However, the outer veneers of personality or organizational culture – those most recently learnt or layered – are stripped away under conditions of stress, as the person or organization falls back to more deeply ingrained behavioral and attitudinal responses.

An example of layering: the integration–responsiveness duality

An important application of layering is in balancing the dual forces of centralization and decentralization in the MNC (see the earlier discussion in Part III of this volume). The first step is to recognize that international integration and local responsiveness is an "and/and" duality. This then leads to the "how" question: how can we integrate companies that need their own local autonomy? How can we "layer" integration on top of local responsiveness? As we saw in Chapter 8, the field studies of Prahalad and Doz (1987) show that this requires subtle rather than crude management mechanisms – careful attention to the management of managers, as well as to what we call decision architecture.

For example, the basic principle behind Shell's organization is that its two hundred operating companies are autonomous, with group management acting as a shareholder. Nevertheless, it functions as an integrated organization: according to one of its board members the cohesion is provided by three elements – the common logo, some common business and financial principles, and above all the mobility of its managers. At Shell, as at other multinationals, the higher the potential of the manager, the more likely he or she is to change job (and for that matter location and function) every two to four years. The job itself forces the manager to take a local perspective; but personal career interests oblige the person also to take a wider group perspective, reinforced by the network of relationships and experiences that the person has acquired over the years.

Layering means that the managerial career culture is changing in international firms. As the firm internationalizes, so it becomes impossible to pursue a mother-company career unless one has successfully held a significant responsibility abroad. For local general manager positions, Philips favors third-country nationals as the most "layered" individuals, while other firms insist that local nationals must have successfully managed a headquarter position.

Some firms are going further, layering dualities into key appointments in order to bridge the headquarter–subsidiary gap. Thus at Digital Equipment Corporation (DEC), with its European headquarters in Geneva, the responsibility for serving financial institutions in Europe has been attributed to the general manager of its British subsidiary. Responsibility for international personnel at the Swedish group Alfa-Laval has been assigned to the British personnel manager, located in London.

Layering as a means of maintaining focus on core competencies

For non-diversified firms whose strength lies in a key strategic competence, layering can be used to provide key people with experience in other areas while maintaining a focus on the basics. The core competencies are developed in the early part of the career before other qualities are developed. Thus merchandising is the basic business of Marks & Spencer, the successful British retailing company. The career norm at Marks & Spencer is that all executives, including those who will land up in staff roles at headquarters, must have proved that they can run a store successfully before moving into career tracks that reflect their particular interests and competences. Even the senior personnel executive should thus have run a store earlier in his career. Similarly, the accounting business of the "Big Eight" audit firms is based on exacting technical and professional skills. No individual will be promoted into the partnership until he or she has shown strong capabilities in audit work; thereafter they may develop their professional skills along one of a number of competency tracks.

Layering in managing strategic development

Layering may be a successful tool for managing progressive strategic development. Davis (1984) has shown that reorientations or major culture changes will be rejected unless they are compatible with (or at least not incompatible with) the existing culture of the firm. In our terms, this means that they must be layered on its existing orientation.

DEC faces a development problem that is typical of many firms. Its culture is strongly dominated by engineering values, but the need is to complement that strength with a marketing orientation. Task forces and training serve only to sensitize employees to the problem, not to bring about change. Injecting strong marketeers, recruited from the outside, was largely unsuccessful. Sometimes a conflictual, dialectic balance was created, as the marketeers fought with the engineers; or the marketing people wrestled to obtain power, which would have created a pendulum process; and sometimes the two worked separately and independently, avoiding contact.

The strategy today is one of layering – that is, finding within the ranks of the mainstream engineers those who have a nose for marketing, and developing marketeers out of these individuals. DEC believes that it may be easier to develop such engineers into marketing people (that is, layer new competencies on them) than to socialize outside marketing recruits into the mainstream engineering culture.

The French food concern, BSN, came to a similar conclusion. Top management felt that organizational development skills were needed to manage social, technological, and operational changes in their plants, leading to the creation of an organization and development department. Behavioral scientists and organizational development professionals recruited for this function failed to make much mark on the organization. The ultimately successful strategy was to identify production engineers who appeared to have a sense for people and social dynamics, and to train them in behavioral science technology.

Marks & Spencer is also approaching strategic development through layering. The duality that they are striving to build is balancing a traditional culture of merchandising experimentation with new needs for analytic marketing skills (Evans and Wittenberg, 1986; see also p. 40). How should these new capabilities be developed? Although MBAs and marketeers from other firms had the desirable skills, it was felt that their recruitment would lead to a destructive clash with the old culture, the strengths of which were still invaluable. The solution adopted was a careful graduate recruit program, taking people with the right skills and then socializing them through fast-tracking up the traditional entry path into store management, a process to be monitored by a new management development function with board level attention. Over a generation, Marks & Spencer thus expects to layer a new business culture on its former strengths.

The subtlety of the layered organization

As noted earlier, the notion of subtlety is essential to the process of layering. Organizations that are deeply layered, with dualities built into their matrixed cultures, are far from simple. There are rules, but these are often guidelines where managers have a delicate sense of their freedoms and their constraints. There is a hierarchy, but much significant behavior cuts across the hierarchical lines. There are management processes, but underlying these management processes are complex attitudes and values. It is often difficult for the outsider, who has not been socialized into the nuances of the firm, to understand its culture, let alone operate within it.

Such organizations have the properties of the clan-type cultures of recent economic theory, in contrast with the clear-cut norms of market-type firms or the structural-authority values of bureaucratic-type enterprises. Recruitment is likely to be for longer-term careers, permitting the careful career development that leads to layering. Yet on the other hand, this involves another complex balancing act since one needs sufficient new blood and outside contact to avoid cloning and inbreeding. This new blood can be provided in a number of ways: hiring consultants into senior positions on temporary assignments; rehiring people who left the firm to join another company; management training consortia with clubs of other enterprises; building medium-term relationships with guest lecturers on management seminars who know enough about the "system" to challenge it realistically.

Indeed, in the process of organization development, it appears that mastering one duality creates in turn other developmental dualities. Further problems for the layered organization, notably excessive politics and paralyzing complexity, will be discussed later. Meanwhile, we shift our focus from the cultural aspects of developing dualistic capabilities to the strategic aspects.

Sequencing

Sequencing is a future-oriented strategic posture, explicitly recognizing that tomorrow's focus of strategic attention is likely to be very different from and yet complementary to today's. A strategy thus involves a sequence of focused stages, where top management consciously anticipates that the capability that is in the foreground today will be in the background tomorrow.

We can identify two types of strategic sequencing. The first could be called *strategic layering*, and it involves achieving a long-range goal by sequentially building and layering strategic capabilities. The second involves anticipating the next stage in strategic development and deliberately *building the future into the present*.

Sequencing as strategic layering

Until recently, most guiding theories of strategic advantage were one-dimensional. They suggested that firms should build their strength on a particular organizational capability – for example, either low cost economies of scale *or* market differentiated value-added, either global products *or* niche products. Yet the demands of competition today are such that strategies in many industries must be multidimensional (Ghoshal, 1987; Prahalad and Doz, 1987). Through sequencing, the firm may progressively build layers of strategic and competitive capability.

The growth of Japanese multinationals is a good illustration – whether it is Honda taking on the General Motors in the contest for the worldwide auto industry, Komatsu taking on the Caterpillar that ruled over the construction equipment business, or Matsushita faced with the RCAs and General Electrics of consumer electronics (Hamel and Prahalad, 1986).

Each of these Japanese firms were minor league players in their world industries back in the 60s, with the sole competitive advantage over their Western competitors of low labor costs. The initial sequence in strategic growth was to use their cost advantage to gain volume in Western markets. Having secured that, the next sequence was to invest heavily in product and process technology, which in turn led to complementary scale and quality advantages. The third step in the sequence was investment in order to create strong brand images in global markets and strength in distribution, adding another layer of competitive advantage. The products of these Japanese firms thus have the advantage of low cost, high quality, technological sophistication, and global marketing and distribution (Hamel and Prahalad, 1986).

What drives such strategic sequencing? It is rarely the result of calculated strategic and tactical planning. The motor is the *strategic intent* of the firm. Strategic intent differs from the current notion of heroic vision. It is a more down-to-earth goal that constitutes a stable, long-range competitive target. As Hamel and Prahalad (1986) point out, it focuses the firm's attention on winning, energizing the employees to achievement while encouraging personal initiative.

Honda set the goal of becoming a global company back in the 50s when it was still a small repair shop with fifty employees. Komatsu's vision was "Maru-C", or to "encircle Caterpillar", the world's largest manufacturer of earthmoving equipment, at a time when Komatsu was a weak player with inferior technology and no exports. Matsushita and other Japanese electronics firms set goals of global dominance, while RCA's implicit goal was merely to defend its US market, and that of Philips to defend and expand its established presence in multiple local markets. Such long-range intent leads a firm to marshall and exploit the competitive resources that it currently has, turning sequentially to invest in new and complementary competitive capabilities as the opportunities present themselves. In a similar way, some companies use strategic alliances and partnerships to access, expropriate and leverage the resources of their partners (Hamel, Doz and Prahalad, 1989). Sequencing is also illustrated in the annual improvement campaigns that are characteristic of Japanese factory management (Turner, 1988).

At this operational level, strategic sequencing occurs explicitly or implicitly through changing appointments to key positions, notably general manager appointments to divisions or subsidiaries. In selecting an appointee with a strong marketing background in contrast to his or her engineering predecessors, top management is obviously signalling its desire for a shift in strategic focus. Yet such a shift, involving layering marketing upon the technical culture of the subsidiary, takes time.

Here we confront another serious duality in international management development – that of *mobility versus continuity*. Numerous considerations lead MNCs to rotate key managers once every two to four years (see Chapter 7). New executives are more likely to take strategic initiatives, and mobility develops managerial potential, as well as the lateral relationships and layering that are important to the firm. Yet on the other hand, frequent mobility leads to superficial implementation of new strategic programs. The working through of such an initiative may take years to achieve. A critical mass of managers need to be committed, and the change process must often be extended to workers throughout the organization. This is compromised by frequent mobility, since successors have little vested interest in continuing the paths of their predecessors if they are to earn the visibility that is seen as necessary for a successful career.

Too frequent mobility leads to zig-zag management, and the development of organizations that are long on change initiatives but short on implementation and follow through. New capabilities never become embedded, or layered into the organization. It is often easy, gratifying, and rewarding to initiate a strategic shift, but difficult and time consuming to stay the course.

Many multinationals have norms and widely publicized averages for tenure in jobs. Yet no norm can apply universally to all positions. Under some circumstances, two years in a job may be sufficient, whereas in others a ten-year period may be required to see fruition. Regrettably, the prevailing managerial culture in most firms emphasizes rapid mobility. If others are moving faster than you are, this is interpreted as a sign of career failure by the individual and by colleagues.

Thus in some firms, the interests of personal career achievement are undermining the potential for successful sequencing of capability development. Mobility is important, as many chapters of this book have emphasized. However Pehr Gyllenhammar, Volvo's president, believes that many multinationals have been carried away by excessive mobility, that the key challenge is that of implementation (speech at INSEAD, 1987). When a former European head of DEC was asked about the relative lack of mobility of their European country managers, he replied, "just staying in the job was already a great achievement, given the pace of growth of the business!"

Building the future into the present

Sequencing also involves recognizing the likely patterns of change and evolution in the future – and building the future into the present. The management team and management processes of today are designed not only with the needs of this year's operating plan in mind, but also with an eye to the inevitability of a future transition. In this way, the transition becomes a smooth process rather than a disruptive, painful, and costly crisis.

One illustrative example is that of the management of large scale projects. It is now well-known that the leadership and structure of a project that is appropriate at one stage is not necessarily effective at its next stage. The requirements at the research stage of a project to develop a new aircraft, for example, differ from those at the prototype engineering phase, which differ in turn from those at the production phase (Galbraith, 1973). Top management, as well as the project leaders and their teams, must recognize this. To facilitate a smooth transition, the engineer who will assume leadership in the prototype development phase should be part of the initial design team, probably led by a more entrepreneurial individual. Indeed, in-company research in a major oil corporation showed the importance of this in large ten-year projects such as designing and building a billion dollar refinery. Such a project goes through some six recognizable and differentiated stages, each requiring a different project team, the final team being those persons who would actually run the refinery. It was found to be profitable to include key members of the ultimate operating team in the initial design group, even though their role did not become operational until more than a decade later!

The necessity for sequencing is particularly apparent in project management, since the concept of sequenced evolution is part of the notion of a project. But we are in fact suggesting that businesses themselves should be seen as projects, leading to another example – that of the development of the IBM personal computer (also discussed in Chapter 11). It was only when the PC project was spun off as a separate business unit, with relaxed checks and controls and a certain autonomy over hiring and procedures, that the project succeeded. But if the PC was successful, it was predictable that IBM would one day need to market this as part of a network for electronic data processing. If such a venture unit is allowed *total* freedom over budgets, salaries, and personnel practices, the problems of integration may be horrendous – key technical and managerial individuals, hired from the outside or accustomed to high autonomy and bonuses, may simply choose to quit the firm. In the IBM case, the policies and controls of the mother firm were relaxed at the venture stage, rather than abandoned – a measure of autonomy was allowed but with controls still in the background. The reintegration, while far from smooth, was accomplished over a four-year period without major crisis. Sequencing in cases such as this implies that top management is carefully manipulating the complementary qualities of autonomy or entrepreneurship and integration or control (Doz, Angelmar and Prahalad, 1985).

Anticipatory sequencing may involve taking probable but uncertain environmental or competitive scenarios for the future, and using these to power current development in the knowledge that one's competitive position can only be improved – even if the scenario does not come true. For example, when the dollar was at its strongest in the early 80s, priced at over 200 Yen, some Japanese firms were using exchange rates of 120–170 Yen to the dollar to drive cost reduction and remain competitive in case of strong Yen appreciation. The prospect of European integration in 1992 seems to be serving the function of motivating internationalization and competitive development in many European firms. Even if 1992 aborts for political reasons, these firms will find themselves in a stronger competitive and organizational position.

The concept of sequencing emphasizes the importance of a growing area of organizational theory, namely the understanding of organizational evolution (Kimberley, Miles *et al.*, 1980). Longitudinal research is needed into the dynamics of organizational growth and development, facilitating the ability of top management to build the future into the present. Yet while building the future into the present is intuitively appealing, we must also recognize that anticipating the future is fraught with difficulties (Makridakis, forthcoming). Developing decision capabilities that decrease the response time in the face of unfolding events is another complementary approach.

Decision Architecture

This brings us to the cognitive facet of building dualistic capabilities which underlies both layering and sequencing. The way in which information is processed and decisions are reached has to reflect the complexities of a dualistic world. In large, complex multinationals, where decision-making is necessarily decentralized, the organization has to learn to exploit dualities rather than be engulfed in sterile conflicts between irreconcilable priorities, or falling prey to poor compromises. Compromise, paralysis, anarchy, and open conflict are the symptoms of poor decision architecture.

Until recently, research has tended to focus on the individual as the decision-maker. However, decisions in complex international organizations are necessarily the result of a collective process of information gathering and decision-making. Theory has long established that organizations in complex and changing environments – "organic" as opposed to "mechanistic" firms – take decisions collectively through participative processess. Empirical research has also shown that firms with track records of successful adjustment and innovation have more participative decision-making cultures (Denison, 1984). Yet participation has long remained either a normative generalization, or the domain of study of individual decision styles.

In a complex environment where one is forced to manage dualities, information processing and collective decision processes need to be governed by structures and norms that ensure the reconciliation of multiple perspectives. Our research suggests that four complementary capabilities are critical:

- Selective asymmetry in the matrix structure.
- Multifocalism in information processing (problem identification and analysis) and decision making.
- Complementarity in judgemental norms.
- Reconciliation of different perceptions and analysis.

Selective asymmetry in the matrix structure

The formal structure of the organization provides the basic context for decision-making. Since the environment of the complex MNC is multi-faceted, that structure is necessarily matrixed. The matrix allows the firm to balance dualities: product logic versus market logic, technical or functional logic versus business logic.

However, dynamic balance does not imply perfect equilibrium on all salient dualities. It results from *selective asymmetries*, not from full symmetry. Some companies have viewed matrix organization as providing full balance, issue by issue, between executives representing different interests. These organizations have usually failed (Davis and Lawrence, 1977). The organization is maintained in a state of constant tension for no useful purpose; too much energy is devoted internally, rather than externally. In fact, although the organizational chart of the matrix organization may appear as one of straightforward reporting lines, this masks the dotted-line relationships, the buy-in and consultation obligations, that are the hallmark of a matrix firm.

It is through selective asymmetry that top management steers the matrix organization, with changing reinforcement of dimensions of the matrix (see George van Houten's description in Chapter 6 of the way in which the matrix of Philips has developed). This asymmetric matrix is essential to decision architecture lest dualities degenerate into single orientations. While single orientations (for example, cost effectiveness or differentiation or focus) are more simple to manage, they no longer allow companies to confront their competitive environments (Prahalad and Doz, 1987; Ghoshal, 1987).

Altering the asymmetry, reinforcing one dimension of the matrix at the expense of others, becomes a decision architecture tool of top management. For example, the Royal Dutch Shell group has a complex matrix structure of shareholder, regional, and product interests, which together with business and technical functions lead to the regulation of geographic operating companies. Recently, group management felt it necessary to reinforce the regional side of the matrix. It was decided that all contacts with operating companies by product and functional departments would proceed via the region co-ordinators and their small staffs. Group managers could no longer contact subsidiaries directly. The overloaded regional co-ordinators acted as a funnel, since they would screen out unimportant proposals and contacts, focusing only on what was essential to regional and group interests. Yet in the future, it is possible to relax this norm, allowing more intervention on the part of other functions, and thereby boosting their influence.

Multifocalism

The matrix structure allows for the multifocalism, asymmetric though this may be, that was emphasized in Chapter 11. Adjustment to the changing environment, as well as anticipatory layering and sequencing of new capabilities, requires that the organization be in a state of constant readiness, sensitive even to weak signals from that environment.

As Edgar Schein pointed out in Chapter 4, organizations tend to institutionalize dominant and simple logics, based upon their explanations for their past successes and failures. In several MNCs that we analyzed, technological leadership was seen as the key to worldwide success, even though success factors were clearly shifting to customer service, political negotiation with host countries, project management skills, and cost control. Since technologists dominated the hierarchy with few countervailing matrix forces, management looked for "solutions" to current problems by reinforcing the quest for technological leadership. This led to a few commercial successes, sufficient to reinforce the dominant technological drive. The opportunity cost of not responding to other competitive demands was ignored.

The early identification and review of new environmental conditions is facilitated by maintaining the organization in a state of tension between dualities. This means that asymmetry should never suppress other dimensions of the matrix. A simple example is provided by the MNC duality of local responsiveness – integration. Local subsidiary managers, concerned with serving their customers, are more sensitive to the need for differentiated responses to local conditions. Conversely, the product executives, concerned with the efficiency of product development and manufacturing, are more sensitive to the opportunities to standardize and rationalize. Managers need to be focused on different facets of the environment, trying to stretch the organization in the direction to which they are most sensitive.

Encouraging different perspectives may also lead to self-regulating adjustments in the matrix. Influence in the organization will flow to the managers who are most sensitive and best informed about the most critical sources of dependency and uncertainty affecting the organization (Crozier, 1964).

1. *Top management tools* need to be designed or adjusted so as to foster multifocalism (Doz and Prahalad, 1981; Prahalad and Doz, 1987). Information systems, measurement systems, and planning and budgeting processes must allow for different but complementary perspectives. In the planning process, for instance, local managers develop plans for key accounts and customer segments, while product managers develop worldwide product plans. Neither product nor country executives develop complete plans, but each develops elements of a plan from their different perspectives.

2. *Networking* becomes important. At senior management levels, multifocalism is facilitated by the interwoven network of contacts created by career mobility and project groups. At lower levels, networking means ensuring the existence of "weak ties" (person X knows someone who knows someone who knows person Y, Granovetter, 1973), and working through these chains of contacts. Many important environmental alarm bells have been ignored simply because the whistle blower did not have the network, or lacked the influence skills to present his or her case.

3. The *interpersonal skills* of managers become more important. In management theory, such skills have traditionally been seen as essential at the supervisory stage of the careers, while conceptual and leadership skills are the hallmark of senior managers (Katz, 1955). However, multifocalism implies that managers must be skilled in lateral and upward influence, in arguing their case, and in building network relationships. Philips, IBM, and Shell have placed heightened emphasis on such interpersonal skills in the development and selection of middle and senior managers. Moreover, in decentralized, segmented organizations, even top managers have to sell their decisions downwards rather than impose them, and their skills in communication become more important.

4. In the area of interpersonal skills, we have observed a particular problem in many complex matrix firms. Managers avoid open confrontation with superiors and other units to the point of avoidance, however strongly held their views. Multifocalism is blocked by a culture of playing it safe, of not rocking the boat. This is in part understandable. Research has shown that cultures capable of adjusting to uncertainty rather than avoiding it tend to be those where opinions are expressed with caution and reserve (Hofstede, 1980a). The naked

expression of conflicting views would split a complex society, and norms of tolerance and respect are indeed essential. Yet deference and tolerance must be balanced with norms of forthright expression of views, and of open debate and dissent. Sensitivity is needed to the subtle ways in which some cultures, such as Japan, express dissent.

Complementarity in judgemental norms

Decision architecture also means that the underlying norms for evaluating people, their behavior, and management processes should be dualistic in nature.

Our judgemental processes, especially with respect to people, tend to be binary rather than dualistic. We evaluate people as "good" or "bad". Some personal qualities are desirable, others are not. Yet from the dualistic perspective, few human qualities are bad or undesirable *per se*. They are undesirable only if taken to the extreme, if they are not balanced by the complementary quality. Similarly, no quality is good unless it is simultaneously balanced by its opposite.

A practical starting point for introducing dualistic thinking into organizations is necessary change in our systems for performance appraisal, potential assessment, and recruitment or selection decision-making. The frameworks to guide such judgements are typically based on lists or categories of desirable qualities – leadership, analytic ability, sensitivity, courage, decisiveness, planning ability . . . "He's decisive, and that's what we need in this job and this company!"

We cannot build and manage complex organizations with such simplistic reasoning. We need to build dualistic reasoning into evaluation scales, as the examples in Figure 12.4 illustrate. The observation that a person is decisive is not sufficient for a judgement. Is that person decisive to the negative point of impulsiveness, or is that decisiveness combined with complementary qualities of reflectiveness? In Figure 12.4, the shaded zone is that of desirable behavior, though where the person lies within that zone will have implications for the specific job assignment.

In complex organizations, it is essential that the judgemental mode underlying these personnel systems be dualistic rather than binary. These systems reflect and embody what for most employees are the most essential aspects of organizational life: the open and secret judgements that others make of them, which in turn lead to the assignment and promotion decisions that structure their lives. The way in which these judgements are made conditions the basic judgemental or cognitive architecture of the enterprise. If the firm wishes to inculcate a dualistic mindset into its culture, there can be few more useful levers of change than in this domain.

Dualistic reasoning also conditions people to manage their personal and

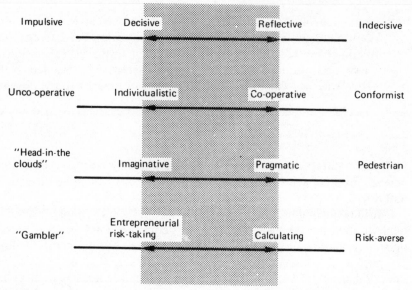

FIGURE 12–4
Four Examples of Dualistic Scales for Personnel Evaluation

professional development in constructive ways. People are encouraged to consolidate their strengths by paying attention to the complementary opposite, and to avoid the risk of excessive exercise of that strength.

Complementarity in behavioral norms is also illustrated in research on group decision-making processes. A Cambridge University professor, Meredith Belbin, spent a decade studying the composition of high-performing management teams, using performance on a business game as an indicator (Belbin, 1981). Using psychometric testing, he identified eight "team roles" that individuals can play, and he gave these popular labels such as "shaper", "chairman", "company worker", and "critical thinker". Most individuals are only comfortable playing one to four of these eight roles. Belbin discovered that if team members could collectively only play a few of the roles, then the performance of the group would be poor. High-performing teams were those where there was both strong diversity of roles within the team and strong complementarity between the roles of group members. His concepts are particularly relevant to the management of collective decision-making processes in complex firms, where the information processing capability of project teams, executive committees, and departments must be capable of handling that complexity.

Reconciliation

Multifocalism without reconciliation only fragments the organization.

Multifocalism in information processing and reconciliation in decision-making themselves constitute a basic decision architecture duality.

In several of the companies studied, unreconciled multifocalism resulted in a breakdown of communication. Affiliate companies no longer received support from the central product management groups. Product managers no longer received essential market information from the affiliates. A vicious circle started. Product executives, cut off from the markets, developed products ill-suited to the needs of the international customers. In turn, foreign affiliates started buying products from competitors, and the competitive strength of the companies declined quickly.

The legitimacy of resource commitments hinges on the reconciliation process. Unless a strong logic for focus emerges from the reconciliation process, resource allocation may become akin to sharing the spoils: each one gets his share, but the individual shares become so small that no successful competitive action can be undertaken. Recurrent problems here may provide top management with the signals and legitimacy to carry out power realignments, asymmetric adjustments to the matrix (Doz and Prahalad, 1987).

The mutual recognition of interdependencies facilitates, indeed forces, reconciliation. Asymmetry may and does exist, but not to the point in which one side is silenced. Neither side has a monopoly on the decision inputs.

While some companies manage interdependencies with a *formal process*, others employ *informal cultural norms* to reconcile interdependencies. IBM's contention procedure is an example of the former approach. The plans of interdependent business units are circulated to each other, and these units and corporate staff have formally to concur. Conflicts and synergies are worked through laterally, and there is an onus to reach reconciliation. More informally, Digital has developed a culture of "buy-in". Managers develop an informal understanding of how to work the network – who are the key managers for a particular decision, and the need to consult with them for support and commitment. At Shell, divergent matrix perspectives are also reconciled through buy-in norms. When a proposal is presented to the boss or to top management, the first question typically concerns whether one has consulted with key stakeholders. Prevailing matrix asymmetries mean that some stakeholders are more key than others.

Regardless of the formalism or informality of reconciliation norms, the process may however lead to opportunistic or expedient decisions. The reconciliation process may degenerate into a series of coalitions and side-deals which satisfy the various stakeholders, but which are unlikely to provide for consistent strategic direction.

To minimize this risk, the companies we analyzed provided both a strategic and an organizational frame for the reconciliation process. Clear strategic intent provided the former, a criterion for arbitrating different views that transcends individual positions and specific business conditions.

The organizational frame is provided by norms or procedures which also transcend business conditions – principles like IBM's "respect for the individual", DEC's "push back" (see Chapter 9), and the assurance that one will never lose one's job for arguing one's case. These provide a minimal level of personal security to managers engaging in complex interdependent decision processes. Once again, norms of reasoned analysis are essential to prevent political behavior. And explicit channels for conflict resolution may be provided. If interdependent IBM business units are unable to agree, the contention procedure ensures that the dispute will move up in the hierarchy.

Maybe the greatest merit of multifocalism combined with reconciliation is the *creation* of new information from conflicting data (Nonaka, 1988). Most of us have experienced the way in which conflict, when appropriately managed, leads to the generation of genuinely new meanings, insights, and information. In this sense, decision architecture is a mechanism to foster organizational learning, an attribute that many believe to be an increasingly important facet of the competitive firm.

PROBLEMS CONFRONTING THE DUALISTIC ORGANIZATION

The dualistic organization, with its cultural layers, its shifting focus of strategic attention, and its decision processes, is complex and subtle. Such organizations are difficult for outsiders either to penetrate or to understand.

This complexity and subtlety in turn creates its own problems – the resolution of certain dualities leads in turn to new dualities. In this final section, we wish to comment on two requirements in such organizations:

1. the need to avoid politicization of the decision-making process;
2. the need to streamline decision-making so that matrix buy-in processes do not lead to costly or paralyzing pseudo-bureaucracy.

We view these as the frontier problems of the complex international corporation, and they are recurrent themes in the above discussion.

Avoiding Politicization

The danger of subtlety and complexity is that decision processes risk becoming subverted by the vested interests of individuals or coalitions – leading to the blocking of decisions, negotiations for personal advantage, and various forms of subterfuge that can be camouflaged in the complexity of the firm.

Norms of hard analysis are vital, as are respect for facts and well-argued views regardless of the position and status of the advocate. To avoid political behavior and the misuse of position power or of coalitions, formal contention management systems need to be built into the structure: open door policies, ombudsmen, opinion surveys, committees of appeal, arbitration processes, management-by-walking-around. Such contention systems are not to be used regularly. Frequent recourse to arbitration is a signal to top management of the failure of dualism, and a call for attention to decision architecture. The existence of such contention systems serves to stimulate the climate of debate and subtle confrontation that is desired.

Clarity as to goals, targets, and visions also minimizes politicization. Where organizational ends or goals are confused, blurred or unstated, this may consciously or unconsciously foster behaviors where individuals project their own political agenda. In contrast, focused targets (the "Maru-C" of Komatsu, the "Beat Coca-Cola" of Pepsi) subordinate politics to the overarching interests, stimulating a climate of analytic debate.

Minimizing the Complexity of Organizational Processes

The complexity of dualistic organizations reflects the complexity of their environments. But this may lead to expensive and paralyzing pseudo-bureaucracy, and large amounts of time devoted to management processes.

In order to minimize bureaucracy, clear and understood strategic intent is once again of paramount importance. Values of lean organization, limiting staff and headquarter headcount, are also a tool. This is not just for cost reasons. The lean organization can afford to focus only on what is essential. It must focus on the facts and well-prepared analysis, rather than on efforts to justify positions or vested interests. A strong attachment to the quality of management development, to getting the right people into the right places, is a corresponding corollary.

Structure is also a tool. Some businesses are highly interdependent, while others manifest weaker relationships with other units. In an effort to reduce monolithic bureaucracy, IBM has reorganized its formerly integrated businesses. Some are integrated, governed by the disciplines of common reviews and shared planning. Other business units are quasi-independent, while still others are run as stand-alone business units. Conversely, Hewlett–Packard and Philips have recognized the need to integrate hitherto decentralized business units (Prahalad and Doz, 1987).

Finally, top management introspection becomes a mechanism for attacking complex bureaucracy. This occurred recently in one of the world's largest and most successful multinationals. While the catalyst was a bureaucratic cost reduction program, the underlying motive was that senior management felt that no-one really understood how the organization functioned. Following a series of top management meetings, it was decided to engage in a challenge exercise into the actual functioning of the firm, leading to actions that will take many years to work through.

A CONCLUDING OBSERVATION

The dualistic perspective on complex organization is both a product of the study of human resource management in multinational enterprises, as reported in this book, and an input into their future development. Perhaps it is fitting to conclude with a quotation from F. Scott Fitzgerald that epitomizes our argument:

> The test of a first rate intelligence is the ability to hold two simultaneous ideas in mind and still keep the ability to function.

As individuals, this thought merits our reflection. This insight seems to hold true for organizations as well as individuals.

Notes

1. While the notion of complementary duality can be found in the ideas of Pascal and the seventeenth century French moralists, it differs from other concerns with opposition in classical philosophy – from the Kantian philosophy of synthesis that underlies today's concept of synergy, or the Hegelian dialectic underlying Marxist economic theory. It is best described by the German philosopher Helweg (1951) and elaborated by the Dutch psychologist David van Lennep in an empirical study of what constitutes managerial potential, undertaken by Shell (Muller, 1970; see Chapter 7 for details on this "helicopter quality" study).
2. The foundations of modern personality theory were established by Carl Jung, who viewed dualities and oppositions as the core of human existence. The tension between opposites is what gives life its meaning.

    Jung's conception of psychic processes is based on the fundamental notion that all forms of life represent a struggle between contending opposites. All energy is the result of the see-sawing tension between dualities. This basic tenet was derived from the observation of mythology and religion, philosophy and individual experience. The tension between opposites is such a pervasive underlying theme of ancient and modern human existence, observed Jung, that it must be a basic process guiding the human psyche itself (Jung, 1933).

    Jung saw the psyche as having four functions in a compass of oppositions: thinking and feeling, sensation and intuition (popularized in the widely known Myers–Briggs Personality Inventory). Because of these oppositions, each individual tends to specialize in one dominant function, while another function from the other duality becomes the inferior function. Primitive societies where the pressures of life are less severe may permit a modest differentiation in all four functions, though in complex modern times an individual is obliged to specialize in one function at the expense of the others. While it is this "specialization" that gives rise to psychological types, Jung viewed the mid-life period as one of coming to grips with the opposite, "shadow" side of that personality.

Select Bibliography

Adler, N. J. (1981), "Reentry: Managing Cross-cultural Transition", *Group and Organization Studies*, 6 (3) 341–56.

Allen, T. J. (1977), *Managing the Flow of Technology: Technology Transfer and the Dissemination of Technological Information Within the R&D Organization* (Cambridge, Mass.: MIT Press).

Allen, T. J. and Katz, R. (1986)., "The Dual Ladder: Motivational Solution or Managerial Delusion?", *R & D Management*, 16, 2.

Amado, G. and Laurent, A. (1983), "Organization Development and Change: A Comparison Between USA and Latin Countries", INSEAD working paper.

Andrews, K. R. (1971), *The Concept of Corporate Strategy* (Homeward, Ill.: Dow Jones).

Argyris, C. and Schön, D. A. (1974), *Theory in Practice: Increasing Professional Effectiveness* (San Francisco: Jossey Bass).

Argyris, C. and Schön D. A. (1978), *Organizational Learning* (Reading, Ma.: Addison-Wesley).

Argyris, C. (1985), *Strategy, Change and Defensive Routines* (Marshfield, Mass.: Pitman).

Bartlett, C. A. and Ghoshal, S. (1987), "Managing Across Borders: New Strategic Requirements", *Sloan Management Review*, 28 (4) 7–18.

Bartolomé, F. and Evans, P. A. L. (1980) "Must Success Cost so Much?" *Harvard Business Review* (March–April) 137–48.

Bartolomé, F. and Laurent, A. (1986), "The Manager: Master and Servant of Power", *Harvard Business Review*, 64 (6) 77–81.

Bateson, G. (1936), *Naven* (Cambridge: Cambridge University Press).

Beckhard, R. and Harris, R. T. (1977), *Organizational Transitions: Managing Complex Change* (Reading, Ma.: Addison-Wesley).

Belbin, R. M. (191), *Management Team: Why They Succeed or Fail* (London: Heinemann).

Bettis, R. A. and Prahalad C. K. (1983), "The Visible and the Invisible Hand:

Resource Allocation in the Industrial Sector", *Strategic Management Journal*, 4, 27–14.

Berger, P. L. and Luckmann, T. (1966), *The Social Construction of Reality* (New York: Doubleday).

Biggadike, E. R. (1976), *Corporate Diversification: Entry, Strategy, and Performance* (Cambridge, Mass.: Harvard University Press).

Blake, R. R. and Mouton, J. S. (1964, *The Managerial Grid* (Houston: Gulf).

Blanchard, K. and Johnson, S. (1982), *The One Minute Manager* (New York: William Morrow).

Bourgeois, L.J. and Eisenhardt, K. M. (1988), "Strategic Decision Processes in High Velocity Environments: Four Cases in the Microcomputer Industry", *Management Science*, 34 (7) 816–35.

Bower, J. L. (1970), *Managing the Resource Allocation Process: A Study of Corporate Planning and Investment* (Boston, Mass.: Division of Research, Harvard Business School).

Brossard, M. and Maurice, M. (1976), "Is there a Universal Model of Organization Structure?", *International Studies of Management and Organization*, 6 (3) 11–45.

Burgelman, R. A. (1984), "Managing the Internal Corporate Venturing Process", *Sloan Management Review*, 25 (2) 33–48.

Burgelman, R. A. (1983), "A Process Model of Internal Corporate Venturing in the Diversified Major Firm", *Administrative Science Quarterly*, 28, 224–44.

Burgelman, R. A. and Sayles R. (1986), *Inside Corporate Innovation Strategy, Structure and Managerial Skills* (New York: Free Press).

Business Week (1988), "The productivity paradox" (June 6).

Cameron, K. S. (1986), "Effectiveness as Paradox: Consensus and Conflict in Conceptions of Organizational Effectiveness", *Management Science*, 32 (5) 539–53.

Chandler, A. (1962), *Strategy and Structure* (Cambridge, Mass.: MIT Press.)

Chandler, A. (1977), *The Visible Hand* (Cambridge, Mass.: Harvard University Press).

Cooper, C. L. and Jones, A. N. (1980), *Combatting Managerial Obsolescence* (Deddington: Philip Allan).

Cooper, J. and Croyle, R. T. (1984), "Attitudes and Attitude Change", *Annual Review of Psychology*, 35, 395–426.

Crozier, M. (1964), *The Bureaucratic Phenomenon* Chicago: Chicago University Press).

Dalton, G. W. and Thompson, P. H. (1971), "Accelerating Obsolescence of Older Engineers", *Harvard Business Review*, 36, 5.

Davis, S. M. (1987), *Future Perfect* (Reading; Mass.: Addison-Wesley).

Davis, S. M. (1984), *Managing Corporate Culture* (Cambridge, Ma.: Ballinger).

Davis, S. M. (1982), "Transforming Organizations: The Key to Strategy is Context", *Organizational Dynamics* (Winter) 64–80.

Davis, S. M. and Lawrence, P. R. (1977), *Matrix*, (Reading, Mass.: Addison-Wesley).

Deal, T. E. and Kennedy, A. A. (1982), *Corporate Cultures* (Reading, Mass.: Addison-Wesley).

Denison, D. (1984), "Bringing Corporate Culture to the Bottom Line", *Organizational Dynamics* (Autumn).

Derr, C. B. (1987), "Managing High Potentials in Europe: Some Cross-cultural Findings", *European Management Journal*, 5 (2) 72–9.

Donaldson, G. and Lorsch, J. W. (1983), *Decision Making at the Top* (New York: Basic Books).

Dore, W. R. (1973), *British Factory-Japanese Factory: The Origins of National Diversity in Industrial Relations*, (Berkeley, Ca.: University of California Press).

Doz, Y. (1986), *Strategic Management in Multinational Companies* (Oxford: Pergamon Press).

Doz, Y. (1978), "Managing Manufacturing Rationalization within Multinational Companies" *Columbia Journal of World Business*, 13 (3) 82–94.

Doz, Y., Angelmar, R. and Prahalad, C. K. (1986), "Technological Innovation and Interdependence: A Challenge for the Large, Complex Firm", *Technology in Society*, 7 (2 and 3).

Doz, Y. and Lehmann, J. P. (1986), "The Strategic Management Process: The Japanese Example", in E. Pauer (ed.), *Silkworms, Oil and Chips* (Bonn: Bonner Zeitschrift für Japanologie) 8.

Doz, Y. and Prahalad, C. K. (1987), "A Process Model of Strategic Redirection in Large Complex Firms: The Case of Multinational Corporations", in A. Pettigrew (ed.) *The management of strategic change* (Oxford: Basil Blackwell).

Doz, Y. and Prahalad, C. K. (1981), "Headquarters Influence and Strategic Control in MNCs", *Sloan Management Review*, 23 (1) 15–29.

Drucker, P. F. (1985), *Innovation and Entrepreneurship* (London: Heinemann).

Dyer, W. G. Jr. (1984)., "The Cycle of Cultural Evolution in Organizations", unpublished paper, Sloan School of Management (MIT).

Edstrom, A. and Galbraith, J. (1977), "Transfer of Managers as a Coordination and Control Strategy in Multinational Organizations", *Administrative Science Quarterly* (June).

Evans. P. A. L. (1984), "On the Importance of a Generalist Conception of Human Resource Management", *Human Resource Management*, 23 (4) 347–64.

Evans, P. A. L. (1983), "Gestion des réssources humaines: Evolution et tendences internationales", *Enseignement et Gestion*, 27 (Autumn).

Evans, P. A. L. (1975), "Orientational Conflict in Work and the Process of Managerial Career Development", INSEAD research paper 166.

Evans, P. A. L. (1974), "The Price of Success: Accommodation to Conflicting Needs in Managerial Careers", unpublished doctoral dissertation, Sloan School of Management (MIT).

Evans, P. A. L. and Bartolomé, F. (1979), *Must Success Cost so Much?* (London: Grant McIntyre; New York: Basic Books).

Evans, P. A. L. and Farquhar, A. (1986), "Marks & Spencer (A) & (B)" (Fontainebleau: INSEAD Case Series).

Evans, P. A. L. and Wittenberg, A. (1986), "Apple Computer Europe" (Fontainebleau: INSEAD Case Series).

Faucheux, C., Amado, G. and Laurent, A. (1982), "Organization Development and Change", *Annual Review of Psychology*, 33, 343–70.

Ferdows, K. (forthcoming), *Managing international manufacuturing* (New York: North Holland).

Festinger, L. (1957), *A Theory of Cognitive Dissonance* (New York: Harper).

Fombrun, C., Tichy, N. and Devanna, M. A. (1984), *Strategic Human Resource Management* (New York: Wiley).

Frost, P. J., Moore L. F., Louis, M. R., Lundberg, C. C. Martin, J. (1985), *Organizational culture* (Beverley Hills, Cal.: Sage).

Fruin, M. (1987), "Cooperation and Competition: Supplier Networks in the Japanese Electronics Industry", paper presented at The Center for Japanese Studies, University of California, Berkeley, (November 4 1987).

Galbraith, J. (1973), *Designing Complex Organizations* (Reading, Mass.: Addison-Wesley).

Geertz, C. (1973), *The Interpretation of Cultures: Selected Essays* (New York: Basic Books).

Ghoshal, S. (1987), "Global Strategy: An Organizing Framework", *Strategic Management Journal*, 8, 425–40.

Ghoshal, S. and Westney, E. (1988), "Building Effective Competitor Intelligence Systems in Large Corporations", INSEAD working paper.

Golden, K. A. and Ramaniyam, V. (1985), "Between a Dream and a Nightmare: On the Integration of the Human Resource Management and Strategic Business Planning Processes", *Human Resource Management*, 24 (5) 429–54.

Granick, D. (1972), *Managerial Comparisons of Four Developed Countries: France, Britain, United States and Russia* (Cambridge: Mass.: MIT Press).

Granovetter, M. (1973), "The Strength of Weak Ties", *American Journal of Sociology*, 78, 1360–80.

Greenfield, T. B. (1973), "Organizations as Social Inventions: Rethinking Assumptions About Change", *Journal of Applied Behavioral Science*, 9 (5) 551–74.

Greiner, L. E. (1972), "Evolution and Revolution as Organizations Grow", *Harvard Business Review* (July–August).

Gupta, A. K. (1986), "Matching Managers to Strategies: Point and Counterpoint", *Human Resource Management*, 25 (2).

Hall, E. T. (1983), *The Dance of Life: The Other Dimension of Time* (Garden City, New York: Anchor Press/Doubleday).

Hamel, G. and Prahalad, C. K. (1986). "Unexplored Routes to Competitive Revitalization", London Business School working paper.

Hamel, G., Doz, Y. and Prahalad, C. K. (1989), "Collaborate With Your Competitors and Win!", *Harvard Business Review* (January–February).

Hamermesh, R. G. (1986), *Making Strategy Work: How Senior Managers Produce Results* (New York: John Wiley).

Haspeslagh, P. (1983), "Portfolio Planning Approaches and the Strategic Management Process in Diversified Industrial Companies", unpublished doctoral dissertation (Harvard Business School, Boston).

Hedberg, B. L. T., Nystrom, P. C. and Starbuck, W. H. (1976), "Camping on Seesaws: Prescriptions for a Self-designing Organization", *Administrative Science Quarterly*, 21, 41–64.

Hedlund, G. (1986), "The Hypermodern MNC: A Heterarchy?" *Human Resource Management*, 25 (1) 9–35.

Heenan, D. A. and Perlmutter, H. V. (1979), *Multinational Organization Development: A Social Architectural Perspective* (Reading, Mass.: Addison-Wesley).

Helweg, P. (1951), *Charakterologie* (Stuttgart: Ernst Klett Verlag).

Hofstede, G. (1980a), *Culture's Consequences* (Beverly Hills, Cal.: Sage).

Hofstede, G. (1980b) "Motivation, Leadership and Organization: Do American Theories Apply Abroad?" *Organizational Dynamics* (Summer) 42–63.

Hofstede, G. (1985), "The Interaction Between National and Organizational Value Systems", *Journal of Management Studies*, 22 (4) 347–57.

Hunt, J. (1984), *Management Resources* (London: London Business School and Egon Zehnder International).

Inzerilli, G. and Laurent, A. (1983), "Managerial Views of Organizational Structure in France and the USA", *International Studies of Management and Organization*. 8 (1/2) 97–118.

Jung, C. G. (1933) *Personality Types* (New York: Harcourt, Brace).

Kanter, R. M. (1977), *Men and Women of the Corporation* (New York: Basic Books).

Kanter, R. M. (1983), *The Change Masters: Innovation for Productivity in the American Corporation* (New York: Simon & Schuster).

Katz, R. L. (1955) "Skills of an Effective Administrator", *Harvard Business Review* (January–February).

Kets de Vries, M. F. and Miller, D. (1984), *The Neurotic Organization* (San Francisco: Jossey Bass).

Kidder, T. (1981), *The Soul of a New Machine* (Boston, Mass.: Little Brown).

Killmann, R. H., Saxton, M. J., Serra, R. *et. al.* (eds). (1985), *Gaining Control of the Corporate Culture* (San Francisco: Jossey Bass).

Kimberley, J. R., Miles, R. H., and Associates (1980),*The Organizational Life Cycle* (San Francisco: Jossey Bass).

Kreacic, V. and Marsh, P. (1986), "Organization Development and National Culture in Four Countries", *Public Enterprise* 6 (2) 131–4.

Lammers, C. T. (1974), "The State of Organizational Sociology in the United States: Travel Impressions by a Dutch Cousin", *Administrative Science Quarterly*, 19 (3) 422–430.

Laurent, A. (1986), "The Cross-cultural Puzzle of International Human Resource Management", *Human Resource Management*, 25 (1) 91–102.

Laurent, A. (1983), "The Cultural Diversity of Western Conceptions of Management", *International Studies of Management and Organization*, 13 (1/2) 75–96.

Laurent, A. (1981), "Matrix Organizations and Latin Cultures: A Note on the Use of Comparative Data in Management Education", *International Studies of Management and Organization*, 10 (4) 101–14.

Lawrence, P. R. and Lorsch, J. W. (1967), *Organization and Environment* (Boston: Harvard Graduate School of Business Administration).

Lehman, H. (1953), *Age and Scientific Achievement* (Princeton: Princeton University Press).

Leavitt, H. J. (1965), "Applied Organizational Change in Industry", in J. G. March (ed.) *Handbook of organizations* (New York: Rand McNally).

Levitt, T. (1983), "The Globalization of Markets", *Harvard Business Review*, 3.

Lorange, P., (1980), *Corporate Planning: An Executive Viewpoint* (Englewood Cliffs: Prentice Hall).

Lorange, P. and Murphy, D. C. (1983), "Strategy and Human Resources: Concepts and Practice", *Human Resource Management*, 22 (6) 1–2.

Makridakis, S. (forthcoming), *Facing up to the Future: Attaining Pragmatism in Management* (New York: Free Press).

March, J. G. and Olsen, J. P. (1976). *Ambiguity and Choice in Organization* (Bergen: Universitätforlagen).

Maurice, M., Sorge, A. and Warner, M. (1980), "Societal Differences in Organizing Manufacturing Units: A Comparison of France, West Germany and Great Britain", *Organization Studies*, 1 (1) 59–86.

McKelvey, W. (1982), *Organizational Systematics* (Berkeley: University of California Press).

Mitchell, G. R. (1985) "New Approaches to the Strategic Management of Technology", *Technology in Society*. 7 (2 and 3) 227–39.

Muller, H. (1970), *The Search for the Qualities Essential to Advancement in a Large Industrial Group* (The Hague: Shell Publications).

Nayak, P. R. and Ketteringham, J. M. (1986), *Breakthroughs* (New York: Ramson Associates).

Nonaka, I. (1988). "Toward Middle-up-down Management: Accelerating Information Creation", *Sloan Management Review*, 29 (3) 9–18.

Nonaka, I. and Takeuchi, H. (1986), "The New New Product Development Game", *Harvard Business Review*, *64* (1) 137–146.

Ouchi, W. G. (1981), *Theory Z: How American Management can Meet the Japanese Challenge* (Reading, Mass.: Addison-Wesley).

Pascale, R. T. and Athos, A. G. (1981), *The Art of Japanese Management* (New York: Simon & Schuster).

Penrose, E. T. (1959), *The Theory of the Growth of the Firm* (Oxford: Basil Blackwell) 1980 edn.

Peters, T. J. and Waterman, R. H. Jr (1982), *In Search of Excellence* (New York: Harper & Row).

Peters, T. J. and Austin, N. K. (1985), *A Passion for Excellence* (London: Collins).

Pettigrew, A. M. (1983). *The Awakening Giant: Continuity and Change in Imperial Chemical Industries* (Oxford: Basil Blackwell).

Pinchot III, G. (1985), *Intrapreneuring: Why You Don't Have to Leave the Corporation to Become an Entrepreneur* (New York: Harper & Row).

Porter, M. E. and Wells, J. R. (1982), "Nippon Electric Co., Ltd.", Harvard Business School Case 0–383–098.

Prahalad, C. K. (1983), "Developing Strategic Capability: An Agenda for Top Management", *Human Resource Management*. 22 (3) 237–54.

Prahalad, C. K. and Doz, Y. (1987), *The multinational mission* (New York: Free Press).

Prahalad, C. K., Doz, Y. and Angelmar, R. (1989), "Assessing the Scope of Innovations: A Dilemma for Top Management", in R. Rosenbloom and R. Burgelman, *Research in Technological Innovation* (New York: JAI Press).

Pucik, V. (1984), White-collar Human Resource Management in Large Japanese Manufacturing Firms", *Human Resource Management*, 23 (3).

Quinn J. B. (1978), "Strategic Change: Logical Incrementalism", *Sloan Management Review*, 20, 7–21.

Roberts, E. B. (1985), "Entering New Businesses: Selecting Strategies for Success", *Sloan Management Review*, 26 (3) 3–17.

Roethlisberger, F. J. and Dickson, W. J. (1939), *Management and the Worker* (Cambridge, Mass.: Harvard University Press).

Rush, H. (1984), *Managerial Career Development in a Multinational Giant* (Fontainebleau: INSEAD Case series).

Sahlins, M. and Service, E. R. (eds) (1960), *Evolution and Culture* (Ann Arbor: University of Michigan Press).

Sainsaulieu, R. (1977), *L'Identité au Travail* (Paris: Presse de la Fondation Nationale des Sciences Politiques).

Sathé V. (1985), *Managerial Action and Corporate Culture* (Homewood, Ill.: Irwin).

Shaeffer, R. (1985), *Developing New Leadership in a Multinational Environment* (New York: The Conference Board).

Schein, E. H. (1985), *Organization Culture and Leadership* (San Francisco: Jossey Bass).

Schein, E. H. (1984), Coming to a New Awareness of Organizational Culture", *Sloan Management Review*, 25, 3–16.

Schein, E. H. (1983), "The Role of the Founder in Creating Organizational Culture", *Organizational Dynamics* (Summer) 13–28.

Schein, E. H. (1981), "Does Japanese Management Style Have a Message for American Managers?" *Sloan Management Review*, 23, 55–68.

Schein, E. H. (1980), *Organizational Psychology* (Englewood Cliffs: Prentice Hall) 3rd edn.

Schein, E. H. (1969), *Process Consultation* (Reading, Ma.: Addison-Wesley).

Schein, E. H. (1961), *Coercive Persuasion* (New York: Norton).

Schein, E. H. and Bennis, W. G. (1965), *Personal and Organizational Change Through Group Methods* (New York: Wiley).

Sofer, C. (1961), *The Organization From Within* (New York: Quadrangle).

Steward, J. H. (1977), *Evolution and Ecology* (Urbana: University of Illinois Press).

Taylor, F. W. (1911), *The Principles of Scientific Management* (New York: Harper).

Thompson, J. E. (1967), *Organizations in Action: Social Science Bases of Administrative Theory* (New York: McGraw-Hill).

Tichy, N. M. (1983), *Managing Strategic Change* (New York: Wiley).

Toffler, A. (1971), *Future Shock* (London: Pan).

Toynbee, A. (1946), *A Study of History*, Volumes 1–6 (Oxford: Oxford University Press).

Tung, R. L. (1984), "Strategic Management of Human Resources in the Multinational Enterprise", *Human Resource Management*, 23, 129–44.

Turner, C. (1988), "Socializing for Development: Factory Campaigns and Organizational Integration, paper present at the Euro–Asian Centre symposium, INSEAD, (December).

Von Hippel, E. (1976), "The Dominant Role of Users in the Scientific Instrument Innovation Process", *Research Policy*, 5, 212–39.

Weber, M. (1947), *The Theory of Social and Economic Organization*, ed. T. Parsons, New York: Free Press).

Westney, E. and Sakakibara K. (1985), "Comparative Study of the Training, Careers and Organization of Engineers in the Computer Industry in Japan and the United States", Working Paper, MIT Japan Science and Technology Program.

Westney, E. (1987), "Managing Innovation in the Information Age: The Case of the

Building Industry in Japan", working paper, Sloan School of Management (MIT).

Williamson, O. E. (1975), *Markets and Hierarchies: Analysis and Antitrust Implications. A Study in the Economics of Internal Organization* (New York: Free Press).

Index

accounting practices, 165, 170
action learning, 110, 182
adaptation
  to cultural differences, 152–6
  see also flexibility
Adler, N. J., 142
Aga, 152
age
  performance, effect on, 196–9
  work motivation, effect on, 194–6
Alfa-Laval, 227
Allen, T. J., 191–9, 209
Amado, G., 92
ambiguity, in organizations, 208
American Express Co., 152
Andrews, K. R., 223
Angelmar, R., 201, 202, 212, 233
Apple Computer, 54
appraisal, 237–8
  see also performance appraisal
Argyris, C., 75, 206
assessment centres, 129
assumptions, 4
  challenges to management
    orthodoxies, 164
  cultural differences in, 91, 94
  about organizational culture, 58–68,
    84–8
  about R&D staff, 192, 196–7
Athos, A. G., 88
attitude surveys, *see* opinion surveys
Austin, N., 185
automation, 171

balance in organizations, *see* dualities
Bartlett, C. A., 147
Bartolomé, F. P., 87, 140
Bateson, G., 221

Baxendell, Sir Peter, 123, 137
Beckhard, R., 59
Belbin, R. M., 238
Bennis, W. G., 68
Berger, P. L., 88
Biggadike, E. R., 211
Blake, R. R., 73
Blanchard, K., 2
Bonfield, Peter, 49
Bonsignore, Michael, 119, 175–6, 187
Borgeaud, Pierre, 150
Bourgeois, L. J., 225
Bower, J. L., 207
BP (British Petroleum), 122, 131
Brossard, M., 86
BSN, 171, 228
bureaucracy, 10, 182, 241–2
Burgelman, R. A., 202, 207, 211

Cameron, K. S., 221
career development, 130–43
  engineers and scientists, 191–9
  expatriates, 137–42
  models of, 123–8
  non-high potentials, 136
  international, 139–42
  see also dual career ladders,
    management development,
    mobility, potential
    development, potential
    identification
Carlzon, Jan, 34, 43
CEDEP, 120
centralization, *see* control,
  decentralization, dualities,
  integration
Chandler, A., 223

change in organizations, 3, 30–2, 33–55,
  65–80, 83–94, 169
  by crisis, 34–40, 63, 77–80
  cultural differences in, 93
  evolution, 37–9, 67–70, 224
  incrementalism, 76–7
  leadership of, 42–5, 50–1, 80
  mobility as a facilitor of, 231
  rationalization, 46–7, 50, 51–2
  resistance to, 85–6, 89
  strategic development, 228
  transformation, 42–51, 84
  triggers of, 34–42
  turnaround management, 42–7, 79
  see also corporate culture,
    flexibility, organization
    development
Ciba-Geigy, 143, 158–9
cloning in organizations, 135, 229
communications in organization, 9, 43
  cross-fertilization, 146
  innovation, effect on, 179–80,
    188–9, 203–4, 206–9
  single status, 179–80
  skills, 171
  Volvo's "Dialog" program, 188
comparative management, *see* cultural
  differences
compensation
  benefit systems, 27
  expatriate, 139
  see also reward systems
computers
  impact of, 170–1, 175–6
  industry environment, 224–5
contingency theory, 223
control
  normative or cultural, 118, 123
  "subtle", 123, 155–6, 158, 186, 226
Cooper, C. L., 197
Cooper, J., 76
Corbett, Graham, 122
corporate culture, 8, 11, 31–2, 88–90
  change in, 31–2, 36, 45–53, 65–80,
    90–1, 228
  culture change, mechanisms for,
    65–80, 120–1, 228
  definition of, 56–62, 89
  development of, 62–4, 226–9
  of multinational companies, 117–21,
    152–60
  need for culture audit, 90–1

"strong", 56, 64, 89, 135, 152
  subcultures, 67–8, 71–2
Credit Lyonnais, 172
Creusot-Loire, 47
crisis management, *see* change in
  organizations
Croyle, R. T., 76
Crozier, M., 125, 236
cultural differences
  in change management, 93
  in concepts of management, 91–3,
    114–15, 145
  in management development, 123–8
  management of, 99, 116, 153
culture of corporations, *see* corporate
  culture
customer service, 24

Dalton, G. W., 196
Davis, S. M., 5, 18–28, 65, 88, 188,
  228, 234
de Benedetti, Carlo, 51, 53
Deal, T. E., 88
decentralization, 8, 175–6, 178, 187
  centralization–decentralization
    duality, 15, 105–7, 111, 116–17,
    177, 226–7, 235–6
  in multinational corporations,
    116–17, 152–60
  see also integration
decision-making processes
  in complex organizations, 233–40
  innovation, effect on, 180–1
  "push back" at Digital Equipment,
    180, 207
Denison, D., 234
Derr, CB., 123–4
Devanna, M. A., 144
differentiation, 68, 72, 202–4, 212–13
Digital Equipment Corporation, 180–
  1, 207, 227, 228, 231–2, 239
diversification
  and innovation, 184–5
  dangers, 202
Donaldson, G., 77
Dore, R., 11
Doz, Y., 123, 155–6, 200–15, 219–42
Drucker, Peter, 185
dual career ladders, 192–6
dualities, 17, 26, 111, 177–8, 189,
  219–42
  autonomy–integration, 232–3

centralization–decentralization, 15, 105–7, 111, 116–17, 177, 226–7, 235–6
control–variety, 214
differentiation–integration, 202, 203–4, 212–13
entrepreneurship–control, 185–6
hard–soft, 6, 7, 12
individualism–teamwork, 13–14, 15–17, 50–1, 177–8, 186, 220, 224–5
instrumental–social, 91–2
leadership–subordinacy, 87
loose–tight, 178
mobility–continuity, 50, 231
partnership–competition, 16–17
technical–business, 210
top–down/bottom–up, 177–89
Durkheim, Emile, 8
Dyer, W. G., 69

economics, as field of study, 12
Edstrom, A., 123, 151
education, *see* training and education
effectiveness of organizations, 13
Eisenhardt, K. M., 225
Elf Acquitaine, 214
employment, by economic sector, 18–21
engineers and scientists, 191–9
entrepreneurship, 183–5
    channeling of, 185–9
    duality with control, 185–6
    business ventures, 201–2, 212
Ericsson, 119
Europe, '1992', 233
Evans, P., 33–55, 97–9, 113–43, 144–61, 169–90, 219–42
Evian, 171
"excellence" movement, 115
expatriate careers, 137–42
Exxon Corporation, 47, 128–30, 133, 139

Farquhar, A., 33–55, 97–8, 113–43, 169–90
Faucheux, C., 91, 92
Ferdows, K., 209
Festinger, L., 76
flexibility
    in organizations, 53–4, 151, 205–6, 224, 235–6

in new plants, 188–9
Fombrun, C., 144
France, concept of management, 92, 125
Frost, P. J., 88
Fruin, M., 209

Galbraith, J., 123, 128, 151, 232
Geertz, C., 89
General Motors, 19
Générale de Biscuits, 156
Germany, concept of management, 92, 114, 125–8
global approach to human resource management, 152–60
globalization, *see* internationalization
Granick, D., 125
Granovetter, M., 236
Great Britain, concept of management, 92
Greenfield, T. B., 84
Greiner, L. E., 221
Gyllenhammar, Pehr, 52–3, 172, 231

Hall, E. T., 84
Hamel, G., 207, 224, 230, 231
Hamermesh, R. G., 212
Hanada, Mitsuyo, 143
Harris, R. T., 59
Harvey Jones, Sir John, 44, 50–1, 187
Haspeslagh, P., 159
Hedberg, B. L. T., 220
Hedlund, G., 87
Heenan, D. A., 161
"helicopter quality", 132
Helweg, P., 242
Hewlett–Packard, 135, 152, 153, 158–9, 170, 171, 172, 173, 175, 176, 177, 206, 241
Hofstede, G., 86, 91, 114, 145, 153, 236
Holderbank, 152, 156
Honda, 124, 224, 230
Honeywell, 119, 173, 175–6, 187
human relations, 10, 12
human resource management
    corporate policy, 145–51, 152–60
    global *v.* polycentric approaches, 152–60
    meaning of, 2–3

in multinational companies, 98–9, 111, 144–61
origins of, 8–12
Hunt, J., 129

IBM, 19, 53, 119, 122, 128, 130, 134, 135, 138, 139–40, 141, 151, 152, 154, 158–9, 177–8, 179, 182–3 184, 187, 202–3, 205–6, 212, 232, 233, 239, 240, 241
ICI, 34, 36, 44, 50–1, 122, 128, 131, 187
ICL, 34, 45, 46, 47–9, 118, 120, 151
IMEDE, 119–20
IMI, 119
individualism, 13–14, 17, 177–8, 178–83
   see also dualities
information, value of, 23–4
information processing in organizations, 233–40
   innovation, effect on, 203–4, 206–8
information technology, 25, 170–4, 175–6
innovation, 4, 89, 164–7, 169–90
   in complex firms, 200–15
   experimentation, 184–5
   in small *v.* large firms, 200–1
   innovative organization, 177–89
   new technologies, 170–7
INSEAD, 120, 121
integration
   corporate, 71–2, 73, 90, 98–9
   of decentralized firms, 97–8, 105–6, 117–21, 147, 152–6, 158, 226–7
   innovation, effect on, 202, 212–14
   mechanisms to build, 118–21, 156, 212, 226–7
   see also corporate cultures, decentralization, dualities, interdependencies
interdependencies
   within corporate structures, 76, 206, 241
   innovation processes, effect on, 201–2, 203–4
   reconciliation of, 238–40
internationalization, 4, 96, 101–2, 113, 227
   competition, 101, 169, 230
   globalism, 101–2, 107, 220
   global markets, 26–7, 144–5

management development, 107–11
   strategy, 104–5
   trends, 160
interpersonal skills, in management, 132, 236
Inzerelli, G., 92
Italy, concept of management, 114–15

Japan
   competitive strategy, 230–1, 233
   Japanese challenge, 115, 116
   management development, 124–5
   R&D co-operation, 16–17
job challenge, 196–9
job rotation, *see* mobility
Johnson, S., 2
joint ventures, *see* partnerships and joint ventures
Jones, A. N., 197
Jönsson, Berth, 186
Jung, Carl, 221, 242

Kanter, R. M., 11, 130, 185, 208
Katz, R., 191–9
Katz, R. L., 236
Kennedy, A. A., 88
Kets de Vries, M. F., 221
Ketteringham, J. M., 208
Kidder, T., 210, 215
Kilmann, R. H., 88
Kimberley, J. R., 233
Komatsu, 230
Kone, 119
KPMG (formerly Peat, Marwick & Mitchell), 37, 122
Kreacic, V., 91

Landreth, O., 169–90
Lammers, C. T., 11
Laurent, A., 83–94, 114–15, 125, 135, 145, 153
Lawrence, P. R., 68, 72, 77
layering, 226–9
leadership, 43, 50, 80, 87–8, 119, 176–7, 225
   dependence on charismatic leaders, 50–1
   subordinacy, 87
   see also change in organizations, vision

learning
  in organizational culture, 62–4, 224
  in training, 173, 181–2
Leavitt, H., 223
Lehman, H., 196
Lehmann, J. P., 207
Likert, R., 10
Lorsch, J. W., 68, 72, 77

Makridakis, S., 233
management
  challenge for organizational
      innovation, 201, 203–6
  hard–soft duality, 6, 7, 12
  instrumental *v.* social conceptions,
      91–2
  middle management, 51
  new models of, 18–21, 221–4
management development, 121–42
  building corporate integration, 97–8
  developing managers, 52, 122
  management of, 98, 130–7, 149
  models of, 123–9
  for organization and strategic
      development, 52–3, 122–3, 146,
      147–51, 226–9
  at Philips, 107–11
  see also mobility, potential
      development, potential
      identification
manufacturing, 171
  new-style plants, 52, 174–5, 186–7
March, J. G., 208, 215
Marks & Spencer, 39–40, 128, 129,
      133, 158, 179, 182, 183–4, 184–5,
      189, 227, 228
Marsh, P., 91
Maslow's hierarchy of needs, 10
matrix organization, 87, 117, 234–7,
      238–40
  at Philips, 107–11
  organizational flexibility, 213
Matsushita, 124, 204, 206, 230
Maurice, M., 86, 92
MBAs, 129
McGregor, Douglas, 10, 187
McKelvey, W., 67
measurement systems, 138–9
Memorex, 212
mentoring, 182
Miles, R. H., 233
Mitchell, G. R., 205

mobility
  continuity–mobility duality, 50, 231
  to develop managers, 122–3, 124–8
  innovation, consequences for, 208,
      210–11, 214
  international, 133, 139–42
  management of, 137–42
  organizational change, consequences
      for, 50, 231–2
  at Philips, 110
motivation of engineers and scientists,
      192–6, 199
Mouton, J., 73
Muller, H., 132, 242
Murphy, D. C., 144
Myers–Briggs inventory, 242

National Health Service (Great
      Britain), 177–8, 186
National Westminster Bank, 129, 169
Nayak, P. R., 208
networks in organizations, 99, 123, 236
  creation of, 208–9
  innovation, effects on, 203–4
Nestlé, 113, 119–20, 152
Nippon Electric Co., 204
Nissan, 124
Nonaka, I., 204, 240
Nystrom, P. C., 220

obsolescence, professional, 192, 196–9
Olivetti, 43, 44–5, 46, 51, 53, 54, 119
Olsen, J. P., 208, 215
opinion surveys, 41–2, 154, 187
Ouchi, W. G., 2, 4–5, 7–17, 88
organization
  assumptions about, 84–7, 221–4
  concepts in different cultures, 91–3
  decision architecture, 233–40
  developmental stages in, 65–7
  evolution, 221, 233
  "fit" or consistency in, 153–4, 223
  innovation, consequences for, 201–6
  networks, 99
  new models of, 18–28, 221–4
  subtlety in, 229, 240–1
  see also communications in
      organization, control, dualities,
      integration, interdependencies,
      networks in organizations
organization development, 72–3, 92,
      224, 228

organizational capabilities
  dualistic capabilities, 225–40
  strategic management, 149–51
organizational design, *see*
  organizational structure
organizational structure
  business units, 48, 145–6, 182, 206,
    241
  centres of competence, 104–5, 116
  change in hierarchic organization,
    87, 175–6, 179, 221–2
  delayering, 176, 186
  flexibility, 212–14
  types of structure, 14–16
  see also matrix organization

participative management, 10, 234
partnerships and joint ventures, 16–17
  at Philips, 104
  strategic diversification, mechanisms
    for, 159
Pascale, R. T., 88
Peach, Len, 177–8
Peat, Marwick & Mitchell, *see* KPMG
Penrose, E. T., 160–1
performance
  managers, 136, 223
  management teams, 238
  new plants, 174–5
  relationships with age of staff, 196–9
  US–Japan comparisons, 164–5
performance appraisal, 53–4
  in Japan, 124
  at Philips, 109
Perlmutter, H. V., 161
personality
  assessment, 237
  theory, 221, 226, 242
'Peter principle', 131
Peters, T. J., 2, 11, 56, 88, 115, 152,
    185
Pettigrew, A., 35–6, 91
Philips, N. V., 96–7, 101–12, 115–16,
    122, 130, 132–3, 141–2, 143, 182,
    227, 230, 241
  centralization–decentralization,
    105–7
  global strategy, 103–5
  globalism, impact of, 101–2
  management development system,
    107–12
Pinchot, G., 202

Pineau-Valencienne, Didier, 35, 46–7
planning, strategic and business, 204,
    223, 229–33
polycentric approach to human
  resource management, 152–60
population ecology, 153, 160
Porter, M. E., 204
post-industrial society, 18–21
potential development, 134–7, 149
  in different companies, 123–9
  at Philips, 109
potential identification, 128–30, 130–5,
    137–9
  appraisal approaches, 237–8
  in different companies, 123–8
  at Philips, 109, 132–3, 137, 138
Prahalad, C. K., 123, 155–6, 202, 207,
    212, 223, 224, 226, 230, 231, 233,
    234, 236, 239, 241
productivity, *see* performance
project management, 232
Pucik, V., 143

quality management, 37–9
Quinn, J. B., 76

rationalization, 45–51, 233
  see also change in organizations
Raynor, Lord, 40
RCA, 230
recruitment
  in multinational companies, 153
  policy, 137, 173–4, 183, 228
reentry, expatriate, 140–2
research and development
  innovation processes, 201–3
  managing careers in, 191–9
  management of, 16–17
  project categorization, 205
  technical and business logics, 210–11
resource allocation
  innovation, effects on, 204, 209–10
  process of reconciliation, 238–40
retention management, 154
reward systems, 138
  for engineers and scientists, 191–9
  innovation, effects on, 187–8
  in multinational companies, 146
  see also compensation, dual career
    ladders
Roberts, E. B., 201

Roethlisberger, F. J., 9, 12
Rush, H., 143

Sahlins, M., 67
Sainsaulieu, R., 125
Sakakibara, K., 214
SAS, 25, 34, 42, 43, 50, 51–2, 53
Sathé, V. J., 88
Sayles, L., 202
Schaeffer, R., 148
Schein, E. H., 56–82, 88, 90, 92, 133
Schneider Group, 35, 46–7
Schön, D., 75, 206
Schumpeter, Josef, 164
science, lessons for business, 21–7
secondments, 183–4
sequencing in strategic management,
    229–33
Service, E., 67
service economy, 19–28
Shell (Royal Dutch/Shell), 113, 115,
    123, 128, 130–1, 132, 134, 137,
    141, 179–80, 227, 235, 239, 242
SKF, 35, 43–4, 49
skills, requirement of new
    technologies, 171–2
Siemens, 115
single status, 179–80
Smith, Adam, 8, 10, 12
Sofer, C., 77
Starbuck, W. H., 220
Steward, J. H., 67
strategic goals, 230–1
    see also vision
strategic management
    concept of, 223–4
    flexibility, 159, 225
    in multinational companies, 147–51
    'sequencing' in, 229–33
strategy
    focus on core competences, 227–8
    global, 104–5
    implementation, 22, 36–7, 57, 93,
        145, 225
    relation with structure and culture,
        90
    see also internationalization,
        organization, planning
stress, 53
structure, *see* organizational structure
suggestion schemes, 184
Sulzer, 150

Sweden, concept of management, 115
symbols in management, 89, 186–7

Takeuchi, H., 205
Tawadey, K., 33–55
Taylor, Frederick W., 9, 12
teamwork, 14
technical staff, *see* engineers and
    scientists
technology
    in change management, 73–4
    engineers and scientists, 191–9
    high technology stereotypes, 172
    interdependence between, 176,
        200–1
    keeping abreast of, 196–9
    new technologies, 170–7
Texas Instruments, 205
Thompson, J. D., 215
Thompson, P., 196
3M, 205, 208
Tichy, N. M., 76, 144
time
    linear concept of, 84
    real-time technology, 21–3
Toffler, A., 53
Toynbee, Arnold, 221
training and education
    to build a new culture, 48–9
    for innovation, 181–2, 188–9
    to build corporate cohesion, 119–20
    at Philips, 110
    for upgrading worker skills, 171–4
    Volvo 'Dialog', 188
Tung, R. L., 140
Turner, C., 231

Unilever, 113, 117–18, 122, 152
United States, 115
    concept of management, 92, 114

values
    creating shared values, 118–21,
        152–6, 207
    organizational culture, 60–1
Vancil, R. F., 148
Van Houten, G., 97, 101–12
Van Lennep, David, 132, 242
ventures, internal, 201–2, 212, 232
vision
    cultural differences, effect of, 93
    imprecise, 207

innovation, effect on, 207–8, 211
leadership, 80, 176–7
as strategic intent, 230–1
unifying force in MNCs, 118–19, 211
Volvo, 52–3, 172, 174–5, 181, 184,
    185, 186–7, 188–9, 231

Wärtsila, 173, 181–2
Waterman, R. H., 2, 11, 56, 88, 115,
    152
Weber, Max, 10, 12

Wells, J. R., 204
Westney, E., 203, 208, 214
Williamson, O., 13
Wilmott, Robb, 46–8
Wittenberg, A., 158
work groups, semi-autonomous,
    174–5, 176
World Bank, 37, 41

Xerox Corporation, 37–9